The World of Pressure Cooking

THE HEALTHY COOKER®

Text | Katrin Wittmann
Photography | Mathias Neubauer

The World of Pressure Cooking

Contents

Introduction — 06

    PREFACE — 06
    PREAMBLE — 08

Theory — 10

    THE PRINCIPLE – what is pressure cooking and how does it work? An overview of the key information — 13

    HISTORY – from the invention to the production of the Fissler pressure cooker — 20

    FUNCTION – how are Fissler pressure cookers structured? How do the current premium model ranges differ? What can be cooked in them? — 28

    DOS & DON'TS — 48

Practical information — 50

    HOW PRESSURE COOKING WORKS – from the choice of pot through the correct fill level, pre-heating and releasing the steam to maintenance — 52

    BASIC PREPARATION – information about pressure cooking everything from vegetables & legumes through meat & fish to rice & sweet dishes — 70

    TIPS & TRICKS – handy hints on perfecting stock and sauces as well as seasoning and flavoring — 98

    FAQS — 106

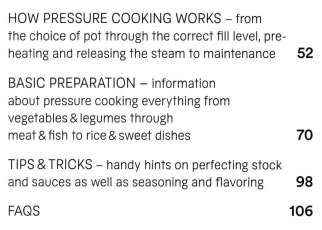

Recipes 108

QUICK & EASY Paella, pilaf & risotto, Bolognese & chili	110
SALADS, SNACKS & BOWLS With vegetables, rice, octopus & meat	134
SOUPS & ONE-POT DISHES Mediterranean & Asian, smooth & spicy	156
CLEVER COMBINATIONS Marinated, cooked until tender, then browned	198
CURRIES & BRAISED DISHES From Asia to the USA, tender and aromatic	218
SIDE DISHES & BABY FOOD Dumplings, vegetables & purées	244
SWEETS & DESSERTS From rice pudding to custard dishes & cakes	264
MULTILEVEL COOKING Stack things up	282
BASIC RECIPES Fish, veal, lamb & game stock	292

Appendix 294

COOKING TIME FINDER Meat & poultry, fish & seafood, legumes, vegetables, sides & sweets	294
INDEX	302
RECIPE INDEX	305
PUBLISHING INFORMATION	312

Pressure cooking with Fissler®

One pot – endless possibilities: Fissler Vita® pressure cookers embody appreciation, are surprisingly versatile and guarantee great taste and healthy meals. Their functions and features make them the perfect fit for modern-day living.

A Fissler pressure cooker – The Healthy Cooker® – is the answer to our needs in today's day and age, fitting perfectly with current dietary trends and modern lifestyles. It preserves vitamins, minerals and flavor, saves time and uses up to 50% less energy.

Here at Fissler, we regard cooking as far more than just meal preparation. It is about passion, creativity and appreciation – for the chef, the fabulous produce and the people we love. It is not just about the food but about the special experiences that we share.

This passion burns inside all of us and we have made it our mission to use our products to make cooking a unique experience. Since 1845, we have been using our craftsmanship skills and experience to create cookware that inspires and excites people, helping them lead a healthy lifestyle. This especially applies to pressure cooking, the benefits of which make it the perfect fit for today's day and age. Pressure cooking is healthy: pressure cookers use little water and preserve all the goodness of the ingredients – their natural colors, flavors, vitamins and nutrients. They also save time as the pressure reduces cooking times by up to 70%, plus they reduce energy consumption by up to 50% too.

70 YEARS OF SAFE PRESSURE COOKING WITH FISSLER

We do not just produce pressure cookers, we have tamed them. The invention of the multilevel cooking valve for the Fissler 'Comet' in 1953 made pressure cooking at home safe for the first time. Pressure cookers became part of our DNA. This has been proven by the over 50 patents and utility models that we have registered within the scope of optimizing our pressure cookers. As such, Fissler has played a major role in how advanced this cookware technology has now become.

MADE IN GERMANY

Here at Fissler in Idar-Oberstein, we have been passionately working to continuously improve our pressure cookers for over 70 years.

Sustainably made in Germany from durable, up-to-90% recycled stainless steel, the safety systems on each and every pressure cooker are carefully inspected by hand before the appliances leave our Rhineland-Palatinate plant. Fissler employees ensure that every Fissler Vita® pressure cooker works perfectly and meets the highest standards of quality 'Made in Germany'.

We have created this book to inspire people to turn to pressure cooking. This appliance offers a surprising range of possibilities, whether for starters, mains or desserts, or for regional, Mediterranean or Asian cuisine. Almost anything can be pressure cooked quickly, easily and with flavorsome results.

We hope you enjoy the culinary journey into the world of pressure cooking and find joy in both making and eating your many concoctions.

The world of pressure cooking in a book

Not only is pressure cooking highly efficient, saving time and energy, but it has also been shown to produce healthier and more flavorsome results than when boiling food. As such, the modern art of pressure cooking is well worth discovering.

With information about what exactly pressure cooking is, how it works and what dishes you can make, this book provides all the theoretical and practical knowledge you need to immerse yourself in the world of pressure cooking and creatively implement your own ideas.

Pressure cooking makes it possible to quickly whip up mouthwatering meals while also offering several additional benefits: it preserves vitamins and minerals, saves time and energy, and makes food more flavorsome. Achieving these results requires a special pot with an airtight lid and various safety features. Made in Germany, Fissler pressure cookers offer premium quality and are specially designed for precisely that. Equipped with sophisticated features and innovative details, they make pressure cooking safe and easy.

PRESSURE COOKING IN THEORY AND PRACTICE

When the pressure inside the pot rises, the water boils at higher temperatures than with conventional cooking. As a result, dishes cook up to 70% quicker. The 'Theory' chapter provides a detailed explanation of the principle of pressure cooking together with a range of technical information. Fissler has two model ranges: Vitavit® Premium makes it possible to discover the whole world of pressure cooking through the use of four cooking settings, including pressure-free steaming. These can be conveniently selected on the pressure regulator before you start cooking. The colored indicator uses the traffic-light principal to show whether the desired operating temperature has been reached or whether the heat needs to be reduced or increased. The Vitaquick® Premium models offer an introduction to the world of pressure cooking and come with two cooking settings for gentle and fast cooking. Descriptions and images of everything you need to know about how to use the pressure cookers can be found in the 'Practical information' chapter: from preparing the pot through preheating to releasing the steam. The considerations required in relation to different types of food are described in the 'Basic preparation' chapter. This also offers helpful information and preparation advice.

THE RECIPES – SUGGESTIONS AND INSPIRATION

The recipes in the 'Quick & easy' chapter provide the perfect introduction to pressure cooking. They will help you get used to your pressure cooker and teach you the two most important basic rules: always add the minimum amount of liquid to the pot and never exceed the maximum fill level. Once these have both been complied with, you are ready to start cooking! The remaining chapters offer suggestions and recommendations that can be varied in many ways. Gradually discover the world of pressure cooking and you will soon be using this technique for all of your favorite dishes – bon appétit!

The theory of pressure cooking

How do pressure cookers work and when were they first invented? How are they made and how do they differ from conventional pots or pans? What can they be used for and what food can be cooked in them? This chapter answers all of these questions and provides detailed explanations of what makes Fissler pressure cookers so special.

The principle of pressure cooking
with liquid and steam

Pressure cooking is classed as a 'moist' cooking method and works only if sufficient liquid has been added to a suitable, pressure-resistant piece of cookware – a pressure cooker.

When using pressure, food cooks up to 70% faster than with conventional methods. This has several benefits: pressure cooking is not only healthier as it preserves vitamins and minerals but also it saves time and energy and has been proven to create more flavorsome results!

The temperature at which water boils depends on the ambient air pressure. At sea level with normal pressure, the boiling point is 212°F (100°C). As the air pressure reduces with altitude, however (e.g., at over 3,280 feet/1,000 meters), the temperature at which water boils reduces. As a result, it takes far longer to fully cook food in mountainous regions. Conversely, as the pressure rises, so, too, does the boiling point. In other words, the higher the ambient pressure, the higher the temperature at which water starts to boil. This makes food cook far faster as it is subjected to higher temperatures. It is this principle that is used by pressure cookers.

RISING PRESSURE

When heated, the liquid inside the pressure cooker evaporates. More and more steam is produced, displacing the atmospheric oxygen in the pot. Once this process is complete, the venting valve (the Euromatic) closes. It is now no longer possible for any more steam to escape and the pressure inside the pot builds. In hermetically sealed pots, the pressure continues to rise in a controlled manner, causing the boiling point to rise above 212°F (100°C). Depending on the manufacturer, the liquid in the pot starts to boil at temperatures between 234°F and almost 248°F (112°C and 120°C). The higher temperatures in the pot shorten cooking times by up to 70% and reduce energy consumption by up to 50%.

GENTLE COOKING

The short cooking times with almost no atmospheric oxygen enable food to cook particularly gently in little liquid or in steam alone. This helps to preserve valuable water-soluble and fat-soluble vitamins, minerals and flavors, and thus the food's color and natural taste. When cooked using pressure, healthy meals can be easily whipped up in a matter of minutes.

PRESSURE AND BOILING TEMPERATURE

PRESSURE (OVER-PRESSURE)	BOILING POINT OF THE WATER	
(kPa)	(°F)	(°C)
0	212	100
40	228	109
45	230	110
60	235	113
75	241	116
80	243	117

The table shows the correlation between the rising pressure and the temperature in a pressure cooker. (Source: Fissler)

Steaming in the Vitavit® Premium without pressure

PRESSURE-FREE STEAMING

The pressure regulator is set to the steam symbol (pressure-free steaming)

The food to be cooked (e.g., broccoli) always sits in an insert on the tripod

The perforated insert is usually used when steaming vegetables

The liquid in the pot (water) boils at approx. 212°F (100°C)

Steaming differs from conventional boiling in that the food cooks particularly gently in the flowing steam without coming into direct contact with the liquid in the base of the pot. The food is always placed in an insert.

The Vitavit® Premium can be used to cook both with and without pressure, making it exceptionally versatile. A brief overview follows of the differences between the two cooking methods and the particular considerations.

PRESSURE-FREE STEAM COOKING

The pressure cooker contains liquid (water, stock) with food above it in an insert that sits on a tripod. When heated to the highest setting, the liquid boils at 212°F (100°C) (normal pressure). Steam forms, rises and envelops the food throughout the cooking process. It escapes through the opening in the cooking valve, preventing pressure from building up. Continuing to heat the pressure cooker does not increase the boiling point, it simply produces more steam.

KEY FEATURES

- Particularly gentle cooking (e.g., for fish, delicate vegetables or dumplings)
- More liquid required
- Food always placed in an insert
- Food takes slightly longer to cook than with pressure-free cooking in water
- The lid can be removed during the cooking process

Pressure cooking in the Vitavit® Premium **with pressure**

COOKING WITH PRESSURE

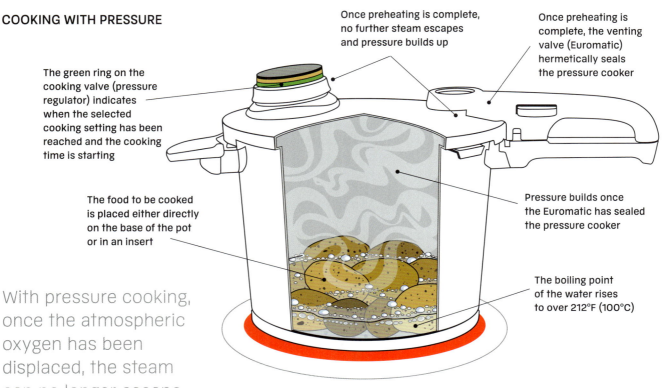

The green ring on the cooking valve (pressure regulator) indicates when the selected cooking setting has been reached and the cooking time is starting

Once preheating is complete, no further steam escapes and pressure builds up

Once preheating is complete, the venting valve (Euromatic) hermetically seals the pressure cooker

The food to be cooked is placed either directly on the base of the pot or in an insert

Pressure builds once the Euromatic has sealed the pressure cooker

The boiling point of the water rises to over 212°F (100°C)

With pressure cooking, once the atmospheric oxygen has been displaced, the steam can no longer escape from the hermetically sealed pressure cooker. Pressure builds and the temperature in the pot rises, cooking the food more quickly and more healthily.

COOKING WITH PRESSURE

When cooking with pressure, the liquid and food are often placed directly on the base of the pressure cooker. Heating this on the highest stovetop setting forms steam, which displaces the atmospheric oxygen (which can damage vitamins) in the pot. Once the Euromatic is closed, the sealing ring and lid with safety features seal the pressure cooker so that it is airtight. Pressure builds and the temperature in the pot rises to about 241°F (116°C) depending on the cooking setting. This makes it possible to cook food more quickly and efficiently. The yellow ring on the pressure regulator shows when the heat needs to be reduced. The green ring indicates the start of the cooking time.

KEY FEATURES

- As the pressure rises in a controlled manner, the boiling point of the water increases from 212°F to about 241°F (100°C to about 116°C). The cooking temperature in the pot is higher than with pressure-free steaming
- Food cooks more quickly and healthily when using pressure than without pressure
- Once preheating is complete, no further steam escapes
- Only the specified minimum amount of liquid is required for cooking
- The food to be cooked is placed directly on the base of the pot and/or in an insert
- The maximum fill level must always be observed, even when multilevel cooking
- The pot can be opened only once depressurized after the steam has been released

The benefits of pressure cooking

Pressure cooking offers multiple benefits: meals are ready faster, take less time and energy to prepare and are healthier and more flavorsome.

Pressure cooking is sustainable: every time this method is used in the kitchen, the amount of time and energy saved adds up, meaning that buying a modern pressure cooker pays off with every use.

Foods such as potatoes or rice can be fully cooked in a pressure cooker in a matter of minutes. This is an unbeatable benefit when cooking in a hurry. Even one-pot dishes can be quickly prepared and are very popular with many people. The shorter cooking times make pressure cooking particularly efficient. It also saves time and energy and is healthier than conventional cooking.

PRESSURE COOKING IS HEALTHY

Food cooks particularly gently when using pressure and retains more water-soluble and fat-soluble vitamins than with conventional cooking methods. Scientific studies (Justus Liebig University Giessen and the University of Koblenz, 2012; ipi Institute für Produkt-Markt-Forschung and the University of Hohenheim, 2022) prove that vegetables prepared in a pressure cooker score measurably better with regard to nutrient content: broccoli contains 63% vitamin C after being boiled and as much as 91% when cooked in a pressure cooker. Similar results were found when comparing potatoes (92% vitamin C when pressure cooked compared to just 71% when conventionally cooked) and carrots (88% vitamin C when pressure cooked compared to 49% when conventionally cooked). The differences recorded for thiamine and provitamin A in these three types of vegetables are also similar. The results can be attributed to the shorter cooking times, the displacement of atmospheric oxygen in the pot and the lower amount of liquid required for cooking. Vitamins and minerals have less time to break down or degrade. The nutrients remain in the food instead of transferring to the cooking water. Pressure cooking also preserves colors and flavors more successfully; vegetables come out of the pot with wonderfully fresh colors and a more intense natural taste.

PRESSURE COOKING SAVES TIME

Depending on the ingredients, huge amounts of time can be saved when pressure cooking, which is a major benefit for people for whom time is of the essence. Mixed vegetables or rice dishes such as paella and risotto are done in just 5 minutes – and without having to be stirred. As shown in the table on the right, cooking times are reduced by up to 70%.

This is particularly noticeable for foods that take a long time to cook, such as legumes (dried beans, lentils, chickpeas) or sinewy meat (beef brisket). Vegetables such as squash or cabbage also benefit from pressure cooking and are done far quicker than when steamed without pressure or boiled. Even more time can be saved by layering multiple dishes or meal components on top of each other and cooking them at the same time. What's more, cooking the main and sides in the same pot also saves on water for cleanup.

PRESSURE COOKING SAVES ENERGY

Efficient cooking uses less energy and helps to reduce costs. Cooking with pressure in a pressure cooker is far superior to conventional cooking in this regard as the shorter cooking times make it possible to reduce energy usage by up to 50%, sometimes even more.

Once the cooking valve indicates that the pressure for the desired cooking setting has been reached, the heat can be reduced to a minimum or the stove can be completely switched off to use the residual heat, which again saves a great deal of energy.

This is also made possible by the patented, energy-efficient, encapsulated base on the Fissler pressure cookers, which enable optimum, even heat distribution. Multilevel pressure cooking saves huge amounts of gas or electricity as only one heat source is needed rather than two or three rings.

The Healthy Cooker® is quicker than conventional cooking methods and excludes nearly all oxygen. This preserves vitamins and minerals as well as the color, texture and natural taste of the food more effectively.

PRESSURE COOKING PRESERVES VITAMINS AND MINERALS

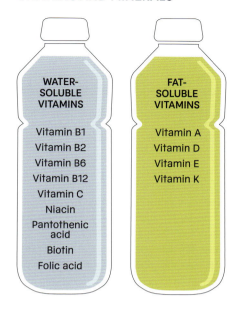

Vitamins are either water-soluble or fat-soluble. Some are also sensitive to oxygen and/or heat. When briefly cooking food in gentle steam with barely any oxygen, vitamins and water-soluble minerals are optimally preserved.

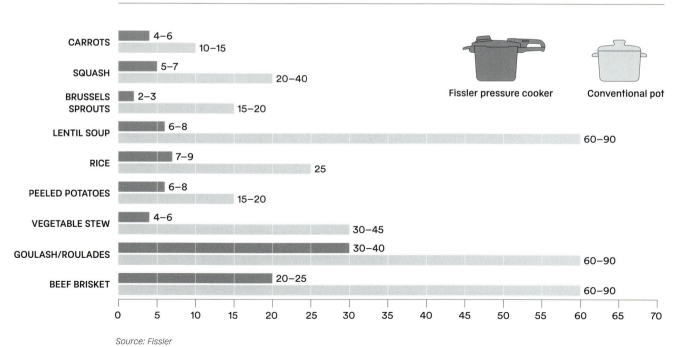

Source: Fissler

The working principle behind
Fissler pressure cookers

Modern, high-quality pressure cookers by Fissler are the result of decades of research and experience. Their functions and safety systems are continually developed and enhanced – as is evident from the premium models made in Germany.

Fissler pressure cookers are special types of pressure-resistant cookware that are made from high-quality stainless steel and meet the company's stringent standards in terms of function and safety. They make it possible to prepare food particularly efficiently, quickly and healthily through the use of pressure in an airtight pot. For this to work, the pot must contain a minimum amount of liquid, which is heated in the sealed pot on the highest setting on the stove. As the water temperature rises, the molecules absorb more and more energy and transform from a liquid to a gas. The steam pressure rises.

During the preheating stage at the start of the cooking process, the rising steam gradually displaces the atmospheric oxygen in the pot. Once there is no more atmospheric oxygen, the venting valve and sealing ring hermetically seal the pot and pressure builds up. With this, the boiling temperature of the water also rises from 212°F (100°C) to anything between about 228°F and 243°F (109°C and 117°C), depending on the selected cooking setting and pot model. As a result, the temperature in the pot rises and the food cooks quicker, saving time and energy. At the same time, the food's vitamins and taste are better preserved. Depending on the model, modern Fissler pressure cookers have two or three different pressure cooking settings, which each correspond to a certain cooking temperature and are visible on the cooking valve. The safety systems ensure that the internal pressure cannot get too high. And should this ever still happen, Fissler pressure cookers safely restrict the pressure: the valves and sealing ring allow a controlled release of steam. In such cases, the heat source must be immediately turned down. The aim is to regulate the heat in such a manner that the selected cooking setting can be maintained throughout the pressure cooking process (visible from the central position of the green ring on the pressure regulator [Vitavit®]). The right cooking setting depends on both the items being cooked and the cooking method. As a rule of thumb, it takes food about half the normal amount of time to cook when pressure cooking using setting 1 and about a third of the normal time when using the highest pressure setting. The tables at the end of the book provide guidance on cooking settings and times.

The innovative Vitavit® Premium and Vitaquick® Premium include highly refined technology that makes them easy to use.

THE PRESSURE COOKING PROCESSES

VITAVIT® PREMIUM HAS THREE PRESSURE COOKING SETTINGS

The pressure cookers in the Vitavit® range have three different pressure cooking settings that can be selected on the cooking valve (pressure regulator):
- Setting 3 (express cooking setting at approx. 241°F/116°C): suitable for meat, stews, potatoes and rice
- Setting 2 (quick cooking setting at approx. 235°F/113°C): ideal for robust vegetables
- Setting 1 (gentle cooking setting at approx. 230°F/110°C): suitable for sensitive foods such as fish or delicate vegetables

VITAQUICK® PREMIUM HAS TWO PRESSURE COOKING SETTINGS

The pressure cookers in the Vitaquick® range have two different pressure cooking settings that can be found on the cooking valve:
- Setting 2 (express cooking setting at approx. 243°F/117°C): suitable for meat, stews, potatoes, rice and more robust vegetables
- Setting 1 (gentle cooking setting at approx. 228°F/109°C): ideal for sensitive foods such as fish or delicate vegetables

At the end of the cooking process, the steam release function on the handle can be used to release the steam from the pressure cooker easily and safely. Steam can also be conveniently released from the Vitavit® Premium in several intervals by twisting the pressure regulator towards the steam cooking symbol.

Pour SUFFICIENT LIQUID into the pressure cooker – the minimum volume mark must be reached.

Heat is supplied, producing STEAM, which displaces the ATMOSPHERIC OXYGEN in the pot.

THE EUROMATIC VALVE hermetically seals the pressure cooker, preventing any further steam from escaping.

MORE AND MORE STEAM is produced, pressure builds and the traffic light indicator rises.

THE PRESSURE INSIDE the pot continues to rise until the temperature is regulated.

FOOD COOKS far more quickly and healthily AT TEMPERATURES OVER 212°F (100°C) (see pp. 16–17 + 71 onward).

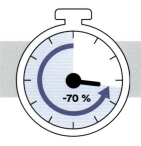
THE COOKING TIMES with pressure cooking are reduced by up to 70% and the energy consumption by up to 50%.

The history of pressure cooking ...

Strictly speaking, the story of efficient cooking began with the first pan lid. Since metal cookware was invented, simple covers have evolved into tightly closing lids. To cook meals, you not only need ingredients and something to cook them in but also time and energy. The longer the cooking process and the more energy used, the higher the food preparation costs.

THE AIM: TO MINIMIZE TIME AND ENERGY USAGE

In 1679, the French physicist, mathematician and inventor Denis Papin dedicated himself to the question of how to minimize the cost of food preparation.

The fact that pressure influences the boiling point of water led him to the ingenious idea of constructing a steam-pressure pot. This made history in its day and became known as the Papin's digester.

The design involved a boiler that could be hermetically sealed through the use of a clamp and a kind of weighted vice. This prevented steam from escaping, resulting in a buildup of pressure and the boiling point rising from 212°F to 248°F (100°C to 120°C). The higher cooking temperature accelerated the cooking process, measurably reducing the amount of energy needed to prepare meals. Cooking times and energy usage were actively influenced for the first time. Following from this innovation, a wide range of approaches were developed to improve energy-saving pressure cooking.

In the years of the global financial crisis and civil unrest around 1920, the subject of efficient cooking became essential

Drawing of the first Papin's digester with the corresponding fire pit (around 1679).

Denis Papin (1647–1713), a French physicist and mathematician, invented the first pressure cooker.

Ironically, when Papin revealed his invention to the London Royal Society, it did not withstand the pressure and exploded. Fortunately, no one was injured. Over time, however, his idea took off – and became a great success, especially after the pressure cooker was 'tamed' by safety features from Fissler.

and various pressure cooking technologies were developed in parallel during this decade. Some manufacturers opted for special cookware bases, others for pressure devices that tightened around the lid. Fissler also researched new ways to improve its existing cookware during this period. In 1928, the company patented its aluminum cookware for electric stoves. Thanks to its reinforced base, this was the first cookware to be able to sit flat on the burner without warping. In addition to such patents, Fissler continued to work on improving the concept of pressure cooking. At the time, pressure cookers were regarded as dangerous and unpredictable as they did not yet have effective safety features or valves. People were afraid of accidents and private households long avoided the large, unsafe pots, which also tended to be rather unsightly.

... and the pressure cooker

The invention of the cooking valve finally made pressure cooking safer. In 1952 to 1953, Fissler patented a particularly safe and user-friendly valve unit. Unlike the conventional pressure cooker lids and valves from the 1950s, Fissler pressure cookers now came with a multi-stage safety valve that displayed the internal pressure and enabled it to be custom controlled. In combination with its thick and energy-efficient base and its modern, plastic 'stay cool' handle, the first safe Fissler pressure cooker model, the Comet, set new standards. The successor Vitavit® was launched in 1953 with further patented functions and features – and has since become a pressure cooking icon.

For the first time, the valve unit could be detached from the lid after use, making it far easier to clean the pressure cooker. The enhanced safety features, such as the bayonet lock with a sealing ring, were also far more convenient and safer to use than models with complicated clamp or screw locks.

The integrated sealing ring hermetically sealed the pressurized pot and was pressed outwards in the event of excessive overpressure to allow the steam to escape quickly. The patents obtained for Fissler pressure cookers played a major role in the development of the modern-day pressure cooker. Safe pressure cookers by Fissler were launched on the market in 1953 and impressed with their clever functions.

In around 1962, Fissler invented a safety and venting valve for pressure cookers, known as the Euromatic. This is sometimes also referred to as the automatic preheating function. The patented valve system is connected to the handle and automatically seals the pot once the atmospheric oxygen has escaped. This preserves the oxygen-sensitive parts of ingredients extremely well. In the event of excessive overpressure, this valve unit is the first of its kind to prevent the unwanted leakage of the pot contents via the valve. Unlike the current Euromatic venting valve, the original version required the internal pressure to be manually regulated. Users could do this by controlling the pressure in the pot with the aid of a scale that protruded from the valve as a pin.

Pressure cooker with a laborious screw-on lid from around 1910.

Other manufacturers made conventional pressure cookers with a screw-on lid around 1920.

The Vitavit® – 70 years of pressure cooking at Fissler

An instant success, waypoints and milestones in the history of Fissler pressure cookers – The Healthy Cooker® – from the invention of the multi-stage cooking valve in the first Vitavit® in 1953 to the development of the latest innovations.

1953

Fissler invents and patents a multi-stage safety valve, which makes the pressure cooker safe for home use for the first time. In doing so, it revolutionizes cooking in kitchens all over the world.

1958

The first Fissler Vitavit® pressure cooker makes its market debut with an unmistakable red lid. Its safety valve is the first of its kind and still preserves flavors and vitamins to this day.

1962

Fissler patents the Euromatic – a safety and venting valve for pressure cookers. In addition to automatically venting excess pressure, the valve is the first of its kind to prevent the unwanted leakage of the pot contents via the valve.

1969

Sixteen years after the global success of the pressure cooker, Fissler responds to the needs of passionate cooks and launches its first pressure skillet.

1973

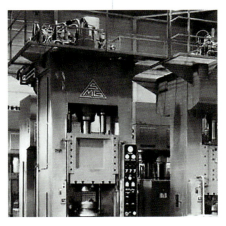

Leading technology: Fissler opens a new production facility in Hoppstädten-Weiersbach, 15 miles from Idar-Oberstein. This provides the foundations for the sustainable production of premium cookware 'Made in Germany.' To this day, Fissler pressure cookers are still produced in Hoppstädten-Weiersbach and manually inspected prior to their dispatch.

1976

Fissler launches its first pressure cooker with the iconic Solar design, which reflects the colors of the Hoppstädten-Weiersbach coat of arms. The design proudly references the origins of the Fissler brand – 'Made in Germany' – and is still very popular, especially in Asia. Even today, products with the tradition-steeped design are successfully marketed all over the world under the name Solaryme.

Fissler Vitavit® pressure cookers 'Made in Germany' always have been and remain icons of their time and have received multiple design awards – such as the Red Dot Design Award 2022 for the Vitavit® Premium.

At the start of the 1990s, Fissler sets new standards in function and design with the Magic range. The innovative look of the new Fissler pressure cooker raises the bar across an entire category.

1982

1989

1992

1995

Fissler unveils the Quattro pressure skillet. In combination with the additional lid, the pressure skillet becomes a true multi-talent that can cook, fry, steam and deep-fry at speed.

In the 1980s, Fissler and Annweiler Emaille- & Metallwerke, a German specialist for enameled cookware, capture the zeitgeist of a generation. The colorful, floral designs of the enameled pressure cookers are loved by passionate cooks around the world and create an industry trend.

Fissler launches the Vitaquick® pressure cookers. These impress with all the key functions of a safe pressure cooker and provide an easy introduction to the world of healthy and delicious pressure cooking 'Made in Germany.'

One hundred and seventy-five years of passion for cooking – the Fissler brand celebrates its 175th anniversary.

2009

The Vitavit® Premium and Vitaquick® pressure cookers come in an even better and safer design: cooking and locking indicators, the multi-stage safety system with patented technology and up to 90% recycled 18/10 stainless steel highlight the Fissler brand's leading position in the field of pressure cooking.

2020

2021

Leading technology and premium materials: the Vitavit® Premium pressure cooker now comes with a beautifully elegant satin finish and an additional cooking setting. Four cooking settings, including a pressure-free steaming setting as a health-conscious option for foods such as fish or vegetables, enable even gentler or extremely fast cooking.

2023

Seventy years of pressure cooking: Fissler celebrates the invention of the safe pressure cooker with two special anniversary editions. The design of the limited-edition Vitavit® and Vitaquick® range is inspired by the fashion and colors of 1950s modern art and features stunning color blocking, characteristic of this era.

26 THEORY ›› PRODUCTION

The production of a Fissler pressure cooker – The Healthy Cooker®

All production activities take place in the Fissler plant in Hoppstädten-Weiersbach, about 15 miles from Idar-Oberstein: from punching out the stainless steel blanks to producing the pressure cookers' bodies and bases to the finishing touches, final assembly and packaging, everything is 'Made in Germany.'

The high-quality Fissler pressure cookers are made from up to 90% recycled 18/10 stainless steel sheeting. At the start of production, blanks (disks) are punched out **(1)**. This is followed by deep drawing, a process that gives the pot its later shape **(2)**. Next, the edge has to be punched, embossed and folded to create the finished pot body with all the recesses into which the lid will then fit perfectly.

THE 'WEDDING'

The base of the pressure cooker is produced separately. To this end, an aluminum disk is placed in a stamped stainless steel capsule. The base and pot body are then spot-welded together in a second step **(3, 4)**. Before the final union of the pot body and base – the 'wedding' – the pot has to be burned-in in a continuous furnace and heated to a temperature of up to 1,022°F (550°C) **(5)** so that it optimally bonds with the base materials. The pot body and base are then joined in a screw press with 2,200 tons / 1K kilos of impact force – uniting them forevermore. The force of the impact evenly and seamlessly distributes the hot aluminum core in the stainless steel coating **(6)**. This creates a completely flat pot base for optimum heat distribution and storage capacity, enabling energy-saving and efficient pressure cooking. The pots then receive the finishing touches in several further steps.

FINISHING TOUCHES AND FINAL ASSEMBLY

The pots are now smoothed and polished inside and out **(7)** as well as satin-finished depending on the model before the bars for the handle joints are welded on. Each and every pot is also marked with the Fissler logo and laser-inscribed on the inside with a measuring and fill level indicator. Finally, the handles are attached to the pot and the lid. During the final assembly phase, the lid and handle have their screws fully tightened, the lid is placed on the pot and the pot is sealed. All components are then reinspected to check that they are safe and fully functional **(8)**.

9, 10 *Attachment of the decorative film (e.g., for the Fissler anniversary edition).*

11 *Final inspection: all lids are reinspected (100% inspection) and all safety valves are checked to ensure that they respond in the correct order and to the correct pressure.*

12 *From Hoppstädten-Weiersbach to locations all over the world: all Fissler pots and their accessories are carefully packaged and shipped.*

Structure and function
The Vitavit® Premium

The Fissler premium model 'Made in Germany' with a multi-stage safety system: three different pressure cooking settings can be conveniently selected on the cooking valve (pressure regulator), including a pressure-free steaming setting.

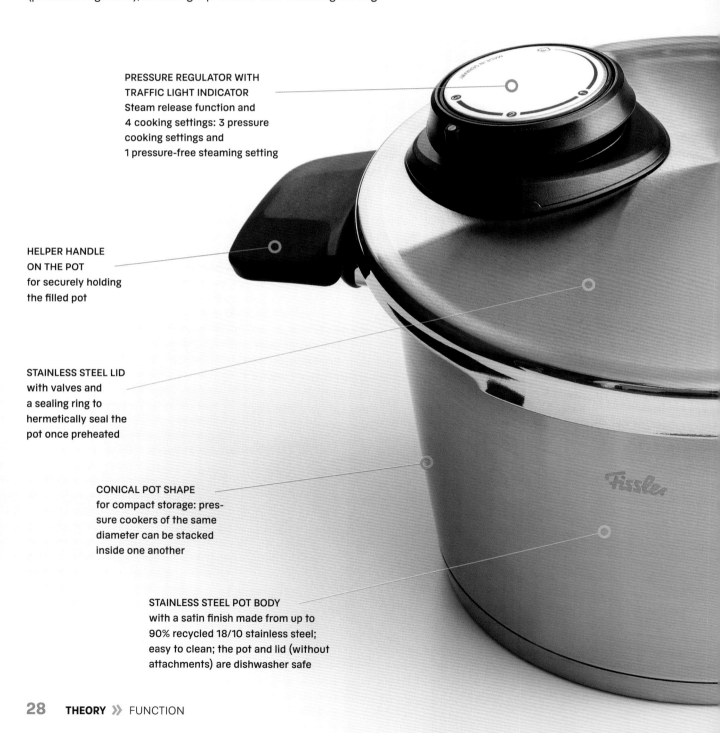

PRESSURE REGULATOR WITH TRAFFIC LIGHT INDICATOR
Steam release function and 4 cooking settings: 3 pressure cooking settings and 1 pressure-free steaming setting

HELPER HANDLE ON THE POT
for securely holding the filled pot

STAINLESS STEEL LID
with valves and a sealing ring to hermetically seal the pot once preheated

CONICAL POT SHAPE
for compact storage: pressure cookers of the same diameter can be stacked inside one another

STAINLESS STEEL POT BODY
with a satin finish made from up to 90% recycled 18/10 stainless steel; easy to clean; the pot and lid (without attachments) are dishwasher safe

STEAM RELEASE OPENING on both sides of the lid handle

LOCKING INDICATOR with acoustic signal (click) and optical indicator (switches from red to green)

SIDE CONTROL BUTTON for quickly releasing steam and opening the depressurized pressure cooker

REMOVABLE SAFETY LOOP HANDLE Ergonomically shaped for a secure hold

ANTI-SLIP STOP for a secure hold when closing the pot

POSITIONING AID The red marking makes it easier to position and put on the lid

ENCAPSULATED COOKSTAR® BASE for optimum heat distribution and all stove types, including induction

Highly intuitive: the traffic light indicator on the pressure regulator makes it possible to instantly identify and easily control the cooking process with any cooking setting. Discover the world of pressure cooking in a pot with the Vitavit® Premium.

THEORY » FUNCTION

Structure and function
The inside of the Vitavit® Premium

Even the insides of the high-end pressure cookers in the Fissler Vitavit® Premium range impress with a surprising array of sophisticated details that make pressure cooking easier and ensure safety.

NOVOGRILL® FRYING SURFACE with a waffle structure for frying with a grill effect – even when using little fat; ideal for the low-fat preparation of grilled vegetables or for searing meat

ENERGY-EFFICIENT ENCAPSULATED BASE with an aluminum core shown as a cross section, suitable for all stove types, including induction

LASER-ENGRAVED FILL LEVEL INDICATOR (minimum, maximum, ½ and ⅓ marks) inside the pot to enable filling without a measuring jug

Even the inside of the Vitavit® Premium impresses with its high-end workmanship and exclusive features such as the Novogrill® frying surface, which ensures optimum fat distribution.

PRESSURE REGULATOR AND TRAFFIC LIGHT INDICATOR shown as a cross section with a relaxed spring

SEALING RING on the inner edge of the lid

LASER-ENGRAVED MEASURING SCALE in ½ quart (0.5 L) increments inside the pot makes it easy to add the right amount of liquid without measuring

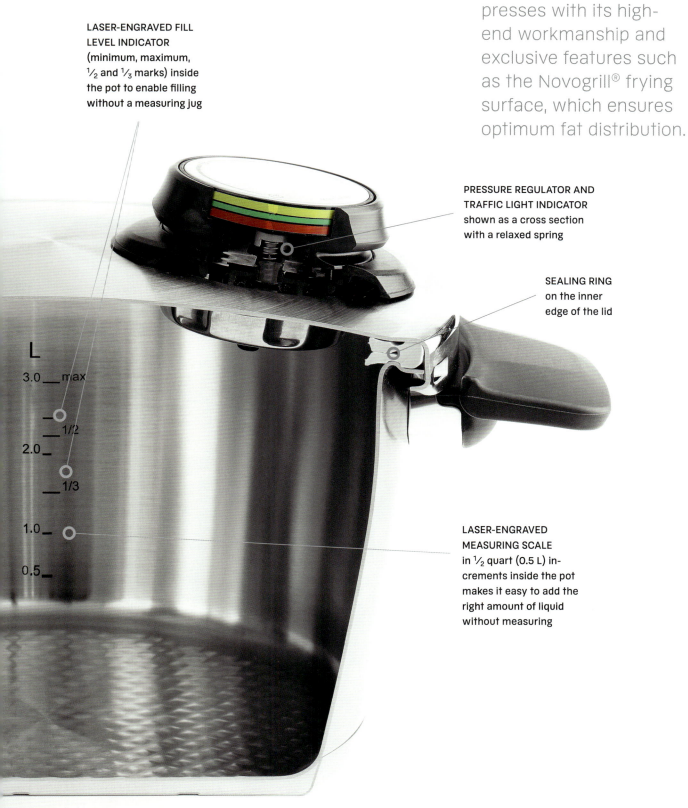

THEORY » FUNCTION

Structure and function
The Vitaquick® Premium

The entry-level Fissler model 'Made in Germany' with two easy-to-check cooking settings on the cooking indicator. The cooking valve on the Vitaquick® Premium offers the necessary flexibility for simple and quick pressure cooking.

COOKING VALVE with 2 cooking settings (white rings).

COOKING VALVE with 2 cooking settings (white rings); easy to check for gentle and quick cooking.

HELPER HANDLE ON THE POT for securely holding the filled pot

CONICAL SHAPE for compact storage: pressure cookers of the same diameter can be stacked inside one another

STAINLESS STEEL POT BODY with a satin finish made from up to 90% recycled 18/10 stainless steel; easy to clean; the pot and lid (without attachments) are dishwasher safe

Healthy, quick and simple – the Vitaquick® Premium provides the ideal introduction to the world of pressure cooking.

STAINLESS STEEL LID
with valves and a sealing ring to hermetically seal the pot once preheated

STEAM RELEASE OPENING
on both sides of the lid handle

LOCKING INDICATOR
with acoustic signal (click) and optical indicator (switches from red to green)

DETACHABLE HANDLE

SIDE CONTROL BUTTON
for quickly releasing steam and opening the depressurized pressure cooker

ANTI-SLIP STOP
for a secure hold when closing the pot

POSITIONING ORIENTATION
makes it easier to attach and position the lid

ENCAPSULATED SUPERTHERMIC BASE
for even heat distribution and all stove types, including induction

THEORY » FUNCTION

Which steps are necessary?

Pressure cooking
Pressure cooking requires suitable, specially developed cookware such as state-of-the-art Fissler pressure cookers with patented safety features. These automatically restrict the pressure in the pot. The following images illustrate what you need for pressure cooking and what happens inside the pot once preheating is complete.

Adding liquid
Pressure cooking is possible only with a certain amount of liquid, the minimum volume of which depends on the pot diameter. The perfect amount can be added at the start of the cooking process: simply pour in as much water, stock or wine as you need to reach the minimum volume mark. More liquid is not usually required unless making soup or one-pot dishes with pasta, etc.

Adding the food
Once the liquid is in place, it is time to add the food, in our example potatoes. Unpeeled potatoes can be placed directly on the base of the pot, whereas peeled potatoes are usually cooked in a suitable insert and placed in the pot on a tripod. Either way, the maximum volume mark must not be exceeded. When cooking food that swells or foams (e.g., legumes), the pot must be only half or a third filled.

Preheating
Once the food has been placed in the pot, check the safety features on the lid (valves, sealing ring) and correctly seal the pressure cooker. Select the desired setting on the pressure regulator and heat the pressure cooker on the stove on the highest heat setting (exception: induction and booster burners, see p. 61). The continuous heat supply causes the water in the pot to start evaporating.

What happens inside the pot?

Steam forms
As the heat builds up, so does an increasing amount of steam. The water starts to boil more and evaporate. As the temperature rises, even more steam is produced. At this point, the water still has a boiling point of 212°F (100°C) (under normal pressure).

The pressure increases with the heat
As the heat supply continues, more and more steam is produced in the pot, displacing the atmospheric oxygen, which escapes through the open venting valve (Euromatic) – visible here from the gap between the black O-ring and the metal lid.

Also visible from the outside
This process at the start of pressure cooking is also visible from the outside: oxygen and steam visibly and audibly escape through the openings on both sides of the circular end of the lid handle. This indicates that the Euromatic is still open.

Euromatic seals the pot
Once all of the atmospheric oxygen has escaped, the Euromatic hermetically seals the pot – the black O-ring now lies against the metal lid and no further steam can escape. The internal pressure increases as, too, does the boiling point. The traffic light indicator shows when the burner needs to be turned down: the yellow ring means that the heat should be reduced; the green ring indicates the start of the cooking time.

A video on this topic can be viewed here:

THEORY » FUNCTION

For maximum safety:
Fissler technology

1st safety level – the pressure regulator: the cooking valve on the Vitavit® Premium pressure cooker is characterized by an automatic pressure limitation function. The steam release pressure is tailored to the three different pressure cooking settings. The enclosed interior is sealed against dirt.

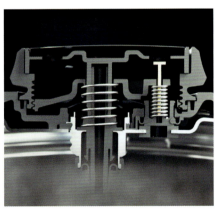

Relaxed without pressure (setting 3 has been selected): as more and more heat is supplied, the water in the pot starts to evaporate but the steam escapes with the atmospheric oxygen through the openings on the handle. The internal view on the left shows the springs at rest, in a relaxed state. The steam pressure is still too low to push the traffic light indicator up. The colored rings on the pressure regulator are not yet visible.

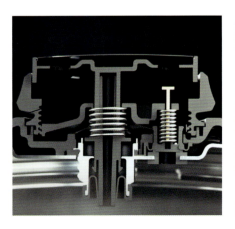

Tensioned with pressure (setting 3): once the atmospheric oxygen has been displaced, the venting valve (Euromatic) hermetically seals the pot and the internal pressure rises. The steam pressure pushes the traffic light indicator up. The springs become tensioned. If the yellow ring appears, this acts as a clear visual indication that it is time to reduce the heat. If the green ring is visible, the cooking time is starting.

To meet its self-imposed stringent safety requirements for pressure cookers, Fissler has developed a safety system comprising various components that automatically work together and ensure that the cookware is safe. This prevents overpressure while cooking or when opening and closing the pot.

AUTOMATIC SAFETY PRECAUTIONS

Pressure can build up only if the pressure cooker has been correctly sealed. If this is not the case, the small black nose on the handle (safety nub) pushes the sealing ring away, allowing the steam to escape and preventing pressure from building. Similarly, thanks to the Euromatic, the pressure cooker can only be opened once fully depressurized (zero pressure safety feature). The CE mark on the base of the pot also indicates that this complies with EU directives for pressure cookers.

THREE-LEVEL SAFETY SYSTEM

The first level, automatic pressure limitation, is provided by the cooking valve. If the pressure in the pot exceeds that for the selected cooking setting, the red ring on the traffic light indicator appears and steam automatically escapes. The heat source must be instantly turned down or briefly switched off. If the pressure does not reduce quickly enough, the second safety level, the Euromatic, kicks in, automatically controlling the device and releasing steam and pressure. Thanks to its special structure, the sealing ring automatically acts as the third safety level.

2ⁿᵈ safety level – the Euromatic valve: positioned away from the cooking valve, the venting valve prevents pressure from building up if the pot is not correctly sealed. It also prevents the pot from being opened while pressurized.

Euromatic components: the stainless steel valve body is 100% safety tested and does not age. When in use, the black O-ring seal must fully sit in the groove provided.

3ʳᵈ safety level – the sealing ring: the patented sealing ring is made of high-quality silicone and automatically limits the pressure if the pressure regulator and Euromatic fail.

Intentional thin areas: the inside of the sealing ring has been designed with 7 double safety pockets spaced out all around it. It must be replaced after 400 uses or every two years, whichever comes first.

Fissler has the highest safety and quality standards: the pressure cookers only ever leave production once they have been subjected to multiple inspections and 100% safety tested.

38 THEORY » FUNCTION

The surprising versatility of pressure cookers

In daily use in the kitchen, the pressure cooker proves to be a genuine multipurpose tool. It excels in its specialist discipline of pressure cooking but, depending on the version and the lid, this multi-talented utensil can also do so much more.

- Cooking with pressure
- Cooking without pressure
- Pressure-free steaming
- Cooking in a bain-marie
- Toasting
- Roasting
- Braising with pressure
- Braising without pressure
- Multilevel cooking
- Defrosting
- Reheating
- 'Baking'

With a twist of the cooking valve, the pressure cooker (Vitavit® Premium) becomes a steamer. This function is not directly available as a setting on the pressure cookers in the Vitaquick® range but is still possible through the use of optionally available, conventional glass or metal lids and inserts of a suitable size for the pot.

PRESSURE COOKING AND PRESSURE-FREE STEAMING

Cooking and braising with pressure can save a great deal of time (up to 70%), energy (up to 50%) and water. The best setting to use for this depends on the food to be cooked. The highest efficiency is achieved when simultaneously cooking various dishes with the use of pressure (multilevel or menu cooking). The pressure-free cooking setting on the pressure cookers in the Vitavit® range makes steaming with these appliances extremely easy. Food can be placed in a perforated or unperforated insert on a spacer (tripod) and cooked over boiling liquid particularly gently – and with great efficiency by using several levels at the same time. Frozen vegetables or meat can be easily defrosted in the perforated insert. Cooked dishes can be quickly reheated in the unperforated insert, which can also be used to cook crèmes and other custard desserts with particularly consistent results.

Even with pressure-free steaming, the maximum fill level must still be observed to prevent the food itself from pushing out the venting valve (Euromatic) and locking the pot. Ensure that the Euromatic remains free. The pot can be easily opened during the cooking process. Always ensure that there is enough liquid in the pot throughout the pressure-free steaming process, especially in the case of longer cooking times.

IN AN UNCOVERED POT

When used without a lid or with an additional lid, the pressure cooker can act like a normal large pot – for example, for toasting spices or nuts, cooking long pasta (spaghetti, bavette, macaroni), deep-frying doughnuts in hot oil or frying tempura vegetables, seafood or fries.

Pressure cooking
in the Vita® pressure cookers

Roasting, browning, frying and cooking in a bain-marie are all child's play for the Vitaquick® Premium. It can even be used to cook side dishes or multi-course meals on multiple levels.

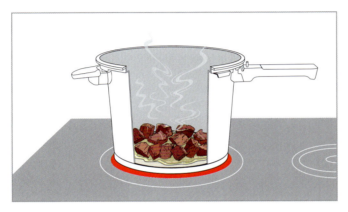

Searing
With its high-quality base, the pressure cooker is ideal for searing and browning meat and vegetables to enhance their flavor. The deep design also makes it possible to fry food in the uncovered pot. The (optionally available) glass lid can be placed on the pressure cooker in order to use it like a conventional pot (for example, to cook long pasta or make jam).

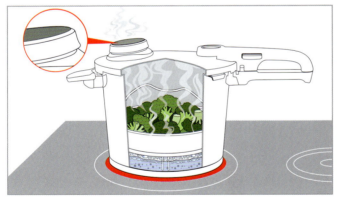

Pressure-free steaming in an insert
Thanks to the pressure-free steaming setting on the Vitavit® Premium, the pressure cooker transforms into a steamer with a simple twist of the pressure regulator. The ingredients in the (usually perforated) insert do not come into contact with the cooking water. Vitamins and minerals are preserved and sensitive foods such as broccoli or fish cook particularly gently.

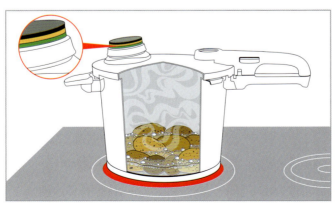

Pressure cooking in little liquid directly in the pot
Many foods, such as potatoes, robust vegetables, fish or meat, can be directly cooked in the pot. When stewing in little liquid using pressure (observe the minimum liquid volume), food largely cooks in the steam and does not lose anything (i.e., valuable nutrients but also the color and shape are preserved). More liquid is required only when making soup or sides that swell, such as rice and pasta.

Pressure cooking in an insert

Vegetables, in particular, benefit from the short cooking times. When using the perforated insert, these do not come into contact with the boiling liquid in the base of the pot, so nutrients are not washed away. The benefits are clear: carrots and other vegetables have a higher vitamin and mineral content when pressure cooked than when conventionally boiled. Their color, shape, texture and taste are all preserved.

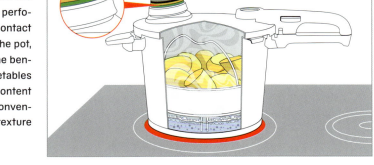

Multilevel cooking without pressure

Steaming several dishes on top of each other (observe the maximum fill level) saves time and energy. Foods like vegetables or dumplings are placed in an insert on a tripod in the pot with the pressure regulator turned to the pressure-free setting. Important: always add sufficient liquid as steam constantly escapes while cooking. In the case of longer cooking times, it is best to check the remaining liquid level in the pot at regular intervals.

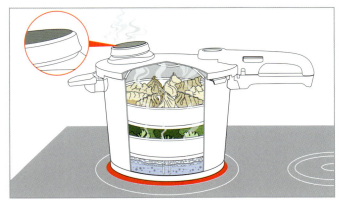

Multilevel cooking with pressure

Multilevel cooking with pressure can result in even greater savings. If items such as meat and rice take different lengths of time to cook, add and partially cook the ones that take longest first. Release the steam from the pot, add the items that take less time to cook and finish cooking everything together. Important: always observe the minimum liquid volume and maximum fill level and use a sufficiently large pot (minimum 4½ quarts/4.5 L, ideally 6 quarts/6 L or above.

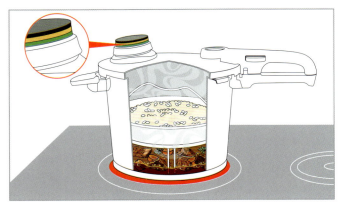

Which foods are suitable for pressure cooking?

The types of food that can be cooked in pressure cookers are as diverse as the cookware's uses and include everything from vegetables, poultry, fish and seafood through to dumplings and rice.

Carrots

Broccoli and cauliflower

Asparagus

Artichokes

Bell peppers and eggplant

Squash

Potatoes

Beet

The range of food that can be prepared in a pressure cooker is astounding. It even includes rice, pasta and cereals. Rice, in particular, can be made with exceptional results as pressure cooking produces the perfect consistency and flavor, making this one of the main reasons to purchase a pressure cooker in Asia.

Vegetables come out of the pressure cooker with bright colors and a higher vitamin and mineral content than when conventionally prepared (see p. 72 onward). Meat that takes hours to become tender when cooked at low temperatures in the oven, a slow cooker or a sous-vide bath cooks far quicker when using pressure. Beef shoulder, short ribs and pork belly become wonderfully succulent and tender with pressure. Duck or chicken

legs and breast fillets also cook beautifully. Whole chickens are not cooked as often but when they are, a large pressure cooker (minimum 6 quarts/6 L) is required, like when making stock. Octopus takes far less time to cook when using pressure than with conventional cooking. Prawns and fish fillets are ready in minutes on setting 1 or, like delicate vegetables, can be beautifully prepared using the pressure-free steaming setting (Vitavit®). Dim sum and dumplings can be cooked in an insert using little pressure or steamed without pressure. Legumes such as beans, lentils or chickpeas are done far quicker when using pressure. Pasta with a longer cooking time, such as orecchiette, can also be successfully cooked. For more information, see p. 71 onward.

Save by stacking: multilevel cooking

When using a pressure cooker, several items, such as mains and sides, can be simultaneously cooked on top of each other. This not only saves time and energy but also reduces the amount of cleanup.

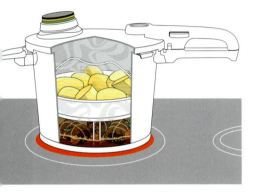

Roulades, goulash or tofu cubes braise on the base of the pot while potatoes, dumplings or rice cook in the insert above them. If the food in the insert takes less time to cook, it is simply added at a later stage.

Important: if repeatedly releasing the steam and opening the pot, check that it still contains enough liquid.

In principle, multilevel cooking is extremely easy. All you need is an insert and a tripod of a suitable size for the pot (included with the Vitavit®, otherwise optionally available), on which the second level can be placed. As a rule of thumb, start by adding the minimum amount of liquid (¾ cup + 2 tbsp to 1¼ cups/200 to 300 ml of water, stock or wine), then cook fish over vegetables or potatoes over meat. Even when multilevel cooking, the maximum fill level must not be exceeded. Large pressure cookers are therefore ideal.

FOOD WITH THE SAME COOKING TIME

Multilevel cooking is easiest when all food items take the same amount of time to cook. In such cases, meat, onions and/or other vegetables can be seared first to enhance their flavor and deglazed with the minimum amount of liquid. Place the insert on top, seal the pot and cook everything at the same time.

FOOD WITH DIFFERENT COOKING TIMES

If food items take different amounts of time to cook, start by adding and partially cooking the one that takes the longest. Release the steam from the pressure cooker, add the sides or other meal components, reseal the pot and finish cooking everything together.

Tip: when cooking mixed vegetables, different cooking times can be balanced out by chopping them into larger and smaller pieces.

Vegetables, potatoes and fish can be steamed in the perforated insert on the tripod with just the minimum amount of liquid in the pot.

Foods that swell, such as rice, or dishes cooked in a sauce are prepared in the unperforated insert with the necessary amount of liquid.

Original accessories and spare parts
for the pressure cooker

The right accessories make a Vitavit® Premium or Vitaquick® Premium even more universal: appropriate inserts enable gentle and efficient cooking; additional lids allow them to be used like conventional cookware.

Perforated insert with tripod: the special perforations in the base of the Fissler steamer insert allow the steam to circulate freely, making it ideal for vegetables and fish.

Unperforated insert with tripod: Idea for cooking foods that swell or stain. Makes it possible to cook succulent dishes and cakes on multiple levels.

Clever accessories like inserts and glass lids are available in an array of sizes tailored to the diameter of the Fissler pressure cooker ranges (7, 8¾ or 10½ inches/ 18, 22 or 26 cm).

INSERTS AND TRIPODS

Cooking in hot steam is a particularly gentle food preparation method that is ideal for vegetables and fish. When using a pressure cooker, this can also be combined with pressure. To this end, the ingredients are placed in the perforated insert and cook over the liquid. An insert support (tripod) provides sufficient clearance to prevent the food from coming into direct contact with the water, wine or stock. Depending on the pot size, several inserts with tripods can also be stacked on top of each other, making the cooking process even more efficient. Unperforated inserts are ideal for cooking succulent dishes, swelling foods (rice, pulses or pasta) or of foods that stain (beet) in several levels on top of each other. Made from high-quality stainless steel (18/10), the inserts and associated tripods are easy to clean and dishwasher safe.

MULTI-PURPOSE

A second lid, which can be purchased separately, can be used to instantaneously transform a Fissler pressure cooker into a normal pot for cooking food without pressure (e.g., by frying it). Just one pot is required instead of two, saving on cupboard space. Tightly fitting lids made from heat-resistant glass make it possible to see into the pot while cooking and are available for all pressure cooker sizes (7–10½ inches/18–26 cm). Metal lids (10½ inches/26 cm) are also available for large pots.

PRESSURE COOKERS ARE DURABLE

Fissler premium pressure cookers are made from high-quality materials, inspected multiple times during and after production and rigorously tested. When used properly, they will last for many years. Fissler provides a 10-year (Vitaquick®) or 15-year (Vitavit®) warranty on all stainless steel parts (body and lid). Attachments and wear parts are made from plastic or silicone. These materials are also of extremely high quality but have a shorter service life than stainless steel. Sealing rings, valve seals and elastomer parts must therefore be checked regularly. Cooking valves can be replaced if necessary. To ensure the pressure cooker is fully functional and safe, maintenance and repairs must be performed only using Fissler original spare parts. These are available from Fissler customer service or specialist retailers. Further information and the product numbers for the spare parts for each pressure cooker model can be found in the user instructions.

All wear parts made of elastomer and silicone must be replaced with Fissler original spare parts after 400 cooking processes or two years, whichever comes first, to ensure that the pressure cooker remains fully functional.

Additional pressure cooker lids: the tightly sealing, perfectly fitting lids made from heat-resistant glass or metal are optionally available as accessories and make it possible to use the pressure cooker like a conventional pot. Both lid types are made from high-quality materials and are dishwasher safe.

Handles and other spare parts: the pot handle and helper handle can be purchased separately, as can all necessary seals and valve components (Euromatic incl. O-ring).

Sealing rings: the latest Fissler models feature a sealing ring made from high-quality, gray silicone. This must be regularly replaced.

Vitavit® Premium cooking valve: with four cooking settings and a traffic light indicator (known as the pressure regulator), the convenient cooking valve for the Vitavit® range is also separately available.

Vitaquick® Premium cooking valve: the cooking valve for the Vitaquick® range has a two-stage ring indicator (known as the cooking indicator) and can also be ordered as a spare part.

Dos &

Add the minimum amount of liquid to the pressure cooker

If there is too little heat or liquid, no steam can be produced. As a result, pressure cooking is not possible and food will burn to the pot, which can damage the valves.

Preheat the pressure cooker on the highest heat

Supplying too little heat when preheating the pressure cooker delays the pressure buildup, uses more energy and distorts the specified cooking times. The pot should therefore be heated on the highest setting, but without using a burner booster.

Save energy by using residual heat

When the indicator appears (Vitavit®: yellow ring/Vitaquick®: 1st ring), reduce the heat or, depending on the stove and with very short cooking times, switch it off completely.

Take care when moving the pressure cooker before opening it

Always use the handles when moving the pressure cooker while pressurized and do not touch any hot surfaces. Briefly shake the pot before opening it to prevent steam bubbles from spraying out.

Maintain a safe distance when releasing the steam

When using the control button on the handle or the pressure regulator to release the steam at intervals, always keep your hands, head and body away from the hot steam that escapes.

Only heat empty pressure cookers briefly

When uncovered, empty or containing fat, pressure cookers should never be heated on the highest setting for more than 2 minutes as the base can otherwise be damaged by overheating.

Correctly store the sealing ring

To protect the sealing ring and prevent it from being crushed, after cleaning, place the lid upside down on the pot and store it in a dark place (protected against sunlight and UV radiation).

Regularly replace the sealing ring

The sealing ring in the pressure cooker's lid must be replaced with a new Fissler original sealing ring after 400 uses in the kitchen or every two years, whichever comes first.

Perform minor repairs yourself

Only perform repairs that are authorized in accordance with the manufacturer's specifications (e.g., tightening screws or replacing the sealing ring or valves with original spare parts).

Note the cooking time reference tables

Use the pressure cooker to bring your own ideas to life. The details about different foods and cooking settings provided in the Practical information chapter and the cooking time reference tables at the end of the book provide you with the necessary expertise to do this.

Don'ts

Open the pressure cooker by force

Fissler pressure cookers can be opened only when depressurized (zero pressure safety feature). Improperly opening them by force can destroy the locking system.

Leave the pressure cooker unattended when cooking

If too much heat has been supplied and too much internal pressure has built up (red ring on the traffic light indicator), the heat must be immediately reduced. The traffic light indicator must therefore be constantly monitored.

Add too much liquid to the pressure cooker

No liquid equals no pressure cooking. However, the more liquid you use, the longer it takes for the pressure to build up in the pot. To conserve vitamins, time and energy when cooking, add only the minimum amount.

Exceed the maximum fill level

So as not to impair its functionality and safety features, depending on the ingredients, the pressure cooker must be filled only by a third, half or to the maximum volume mark.

Use the pressure cooker in the oven

Pressure cookers are not intended for use in an oven and must never be placed in one, even without a lid.

Ignore the manufacturer's instructions

This book does not replace the relevant manufacturer's user instructions. Please read the use and care instructions carefully prior to using the pressure cooker.

The golden rules of pressure cooking

When using a pressure cooker, both the **minimum amount of liquid** and the **maximum fill level** must be observed. The maximum volume mark must be particularly heeded in the case of **food that expands when cooking**. Here, the **fill level should not exceed the halfway mark**.
The pressure cooker lid features several safety mechanisms that must not be blocked, touched, covered or clogged. As such, food in the pressure cooker should never be covered with tin foil or parchment paper as these could come loose during the cooking process. Some foods tend to foam or spatter and can potentially affect the safety features.

These are therefore not suitable for cooking in a pressure cooker. Any accessories used (e.g., baking tins), must be suitable for use in a pressure cooker. The relevant manufacturer's specifications must be observed.

The pressure cooker must be regularly serviced and maintained using the manufacturer's **original spare parts** only.

Always observe the manufacturer's user instructions. These contain further important information about the safe use of the pressure cooker.

Practical information
Pressure cooking

Who should use which pot? Do the model ranges differ from one another? What are the key considerations when pressure cooking, from filling the pot to adding liquid and from preheating to releasing the steam? And which methods are best for cooking which food? This chapter answers all of these questions and provides valuable tips and tricks on how to get perfect results every time.

Who should use which pressure cooker? Choosing the right size

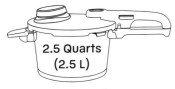

2.5 Quarts (2.5 L)

for 1–2 people
7 inches (18 cm)

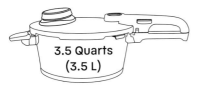

3.5 Quarts (3.5 L)

for 2–3 people
8¾ inches (22 cm)

4.5 Quarts (4.5 L)

for 2–4 people
8¾ inches (22 cm)

6 Quarts (6 L)

for 3–4 people
8¾ inches (22 cm)

8 Quarts (8 L)

for 4–5 people
10½ inches (26 cm)

Modern Fissler pressure cookers come in an array of different sizes. The best size depends on the number of people being cooked for as well as what is primarily cooked.

WHAT SIZES ARE AVAILABLE?

Fissler pressure cookers and pressure skillets in the Vitavit® Premium and Vitaquick® Premium ranges come in a number of different sizes (volumes) with diameters of 7 to 10½ inches (18 to 26 cm). An important criterion when choosing the right pot size is the number of people to be served: 2.5- to 3.5-liter pots generally suffice for households with one to two people. When pressure cooking for three to four people, the pot should be somewhat larger (with a volume of 4.5 to 6 liters). If five or more people regularly come together for meals, the largest Fissler pressure cookers, which hold 8 liters (Vitavit® Premium and Vitaquick® Premium) or 10 liters (Vitaquick® only), should be used. The images on the left provide an overview of the available pot sizes.

Smaller pots are particularly light and easy to handle. They are ideal for cooking rice and small amounts of meat or vegetables. Larger pots are a better choice when cooking larger amounts of potatoes. When cooking with pressure, the pots should be only about two-thirds filled as the maximum fill level must always be observed. As a general rule of thumb, it is better to opt for a bigger pressure cooker than a smaller one.

WHAT DIFFERENCE DOES THE DIAMETER MAKE?

It is not only the volume of a pressure cooker that affects the way dishes are cooked, but also the diameter. This determines the minimum amount of liquid required to produce the pressure needed for cooking. In the case of smaller pots with a diameter of 7 inches (18 cm), ¾ cup + 2 tbsp (200 ml) of liquid will suffice. The most commonly used medium-sized pressure cookers have a diameter of 8¾ inches (22 cm) and need a minimum of 1 cup (250 ml) of liquid. The largest pots in both model ranges have a diameter of 10½ inches (26 cm) and a minimum fill volume of 1¼ cups (300 ml). The minimum volume mark on the inside of the pot, which eliminates the need for measuring, is helpful in this regard.

MAKING THE MOST OF THE BENEFITS

Although it is possible to cook small amounts of food in a large pressure cooker, this is not recommended. In such cases, it takes an unnecessarily long time

The following rule of thumb applies when purchasing a new pressure cooker: it is better to opt for a bigger version than a smaller one.

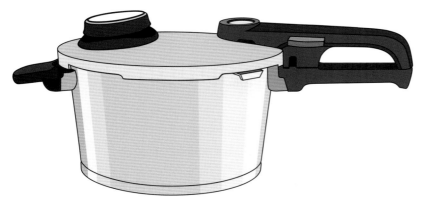

4.5-liter Vitavit® (4.5 qt) Premium pressure cooker: a single piece of cookware for (almost) anything! The medium-sized pot is highly versatile. It can even be used to simultaneously cook mains and sides through the use of inserts, as well as to make stock.

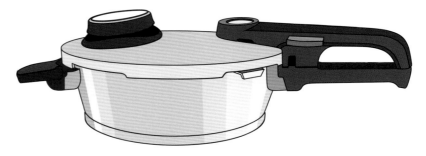

2.5-liter (2.5 qt) Vitavit® Premium pressure skillet: ideal for searing meat (goulash, roulades) and then braising it using pressure. The pressure builds up quickly due to the smaller volume.

for 1–2 people
7 inches (18 cm)

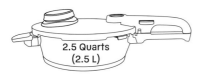

for 2–6 people
8¾ inches (22 cm)

to produce steam and build up pressure, more energy is used and food takes longer to cook.

It is therefore better to use a medium-sized pot. The 4.5-liter pressure cookers from both model ranges are versatile multitaskers suitable for many different dishes. On the other hand, those who want to frequently cook using multiple levels, steam without pressure, cook entire meals at once or batch-cook large amounts of stock for future use should preferably opt for one of the large pressure cookers with a volume of 6, 8 or 10 liters. These also offer plenty of room for cooking foods that swell (e.g., dried beans), although the pot must never be more than one-third full when doing so.

PRESSURE SKILLETS

The choice of pressure cooker also depends on the food to be cooked in it: when searing, braising and cooking foods that reach only a low fill level, such as diced meat for goulash and ragouts, meat rolls, roulades, sliced potatoes or chopped vegetables, the shallower pressure skillets are ideal.

Both Fissler ranges offer these in volumes of 2.5 and 3.5 liters, with the Vitavit® Premium range additionally including a 1.8-liter version. Fissler pressure skillets are often available in a set with a pressure cooker of the same diameter.

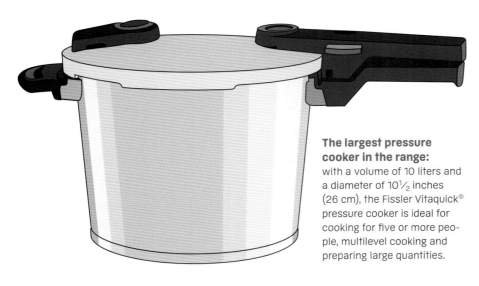

The largest pressure cooker in the range: with a volume of 10 liters and a diameter of 10½ inches (26 cm), the Fissler Vitaquick® pressure cooker is ideal for cooking for five or more people, multilevel cooking and preparing large quantities.

Model range: Vitavit® Premium

Pressure cooking and steaming in a single pot: the Fissler premium model 'Made in Germany,' has a four-stage cooking valve known as the pressure regulator. This makes it possible to preselect the cooking setting and conveniently control the cooking process.

Vitavit® Premium pressure regulator with 4 selectable settings and a traffic light indicator: 3 cooking settings with steam and 1 pressure-free steaming setting

The Vitavit® Premium enables precise, gentle and quick cooking. The adjustable four-stage cooking valve (pressure regulator) makes pressure cooking even simpler.

PRESSURE REGULATOR

The main difference from other pressure cooker models is the shallow pressure regulator (**1**), which displays three different colored rings (**2**) when the device is pressurized.

The pressure regulator can be turned clockwise to select four cooking settings: if the position with the small steam cloud (steam cooking symbol) is selected, no pressure builds up in the sealed pot during the cooking process. The rising steam envelops the food and escapes via the pot lid. This provides a particularly gentle means of cooking sensitive produce such as fish fillets or dishes with very short cooking times. The other three pressure cooking settings are numbered accordingly. Cooking setting 1 (gentle cooking – approx. 230°F/110°C) is ideal for delicate foods such as fish, cauliflower, broccoli or spinach. Cooking setting 2 (quick cooking – approx. 235°F/113°C) is suitable for most other types of vegetables. Cooking setting 3 (express cooking – approx. 241°F/116°C) is ideal for meat, rice and legumes.

TRAFFIC LIGHT INDICATOR

The yellow/green/red traffic light indicator shows when the desired operating temperature has been reached and when the heat needs to be reduced or increased (regardless of the pressure cooking setting 1–3).

- Yellow ring: it is time to turn down the burner and reduce (or in the case of very short cooking times completely switch off) the heat or to turn up the heat again during the cooking process.
- Green ring: indicates that the selected cooking setting/temperature has been reached. The cooking time now begins.
- Red ring: indicates that the pot interior is too hot and the heat needs to be reduced in order to reduce the pressure.

Model range: Vitaquick® Premium

Pressure cooking made easy. The Fissler entry-level model is also 'Made in Germany,' comes with a two-stage cooking valve for gentle and quick cooking and makes it possible to monitor the cooking process through the appearance of the white rings.

Vitaquick® Premium cooking indicator with 2 pressure cooking settings for gentle and quick cooking

Both Fissler ranges feature a multi-stage safety system with patented technology.

The Vitaquick® Premium comes with all the necessary functions for efficient pressure cooking, including high-quality materials and patented safety functions. The two-stage cooking valve (cooking indicator) makes using the cookware simple: on the pressure cookers in this range, the cooking setting is not selected but instead automatically displayed based on the progressive build-up of internal pressure.

COOKING INDICATOR

The cooking indicator on the Vitaquick® Premium (3) has two pressure cooking settings, which are indicated by two markings (white rings). These show when the respective cooking operating pressure has built up inside the pot. The appearance of the first white ring indicates that cooking setting 1 (gentle cooking – approx. 228°F/109°C) has been reached. If this should be used for cooking, the heat needs to be reduced before the first ring is visible. If the second white ring appears, cooking setting 2 (quick cooking – approx. 243°F/117°C) has been reached. To cook using this setting, the heat must be reduced as soon as the first white ring becomes visible.

TWO COOKING SETTINGS

Depending on the pressure in the pressure cooker, the markings on the cooking indicator clearly show when the relevant cooking operating pressure and cooking temperature have been reached and when it is time to reduce the heat again.

- 1st ring: if this ring is visible, cooking setting 1 has been reached. If meals should be cooked using higher pressure, the stove can be left on for longer.
- 2nd ring: if this ring is visible, cooking setting 2 has been reached and the heat source must be turned down. It should remain visible throughout the cooking process. If the cooking indicator rises further, steam is released in a controlled manner and the heat source must be turned down.

Preparation
before the initial use

Ready for use in a few simple steps: Fissler Vitavit® Premium and Vitaquick® Premium pressure cookers are easy to use and quick to set up but there are still a few things that should be noted.

Use a sponge and a little dishwashing detergent to wash the pot and lid (without the handle) prior to their initial use or place them in a dishwasher. The pressure regulator, valve, handle and sealing ring must be manually cleaned.

Once the new Fissler pressure cooker has been removed from the packaging, the pot, lid and sealing ring must be thoroughly cleaned to remove any residual polishing dust or other light dirt.

The pot and lid (without the handle and pressure regulator/cooking indicator) are made from stainless steel and dishwasher safe. None of the other attachments may be placed in a dishwasher. The sealing ring and lid handle must be washed by hand with water and mild dishwashing detergent while the pressure regulator and pressure cooking indicator can usually just be wiped with a damp cloth.

Following their initial clean, the pot and lid should ideally be treated with a stainless steel care product (available from

ATTACHING THE HANDLE, PRESSURE REGULATOR AND SEALING RING

1. Attach the handle: move the lid handle into position, turn the lid over and twist the wing nut clockwise until the handle is tightly secured.

2. Attach the pressure regulator: insert the pressure regulator (note the straight edge) and twist the bell nut clockwise to secure it in place.

3. Attach the sealing ring: insert the silicone ring so that it lies flat below the inward-tapering edge segments.

Important: check that the safety features are fully functional prior to every use of the pressure cooker in the kitchen. There are three parts that must always be checked to this end: the sealing ring, the cooking valve (pressure regulator or cooking indicator) and the Euromatic valve.

Fissler) to make their surfaces more resistant to acids and salts. Wash off any residues and thoroughly dry all parts with a towel – the pressure cooker is now ready for assembly.

ASSEMBLING THE LID

Attaching the lid components is easy but requires a little care (see steps 1–3 on the left): first, move the lid handle into position and tighten the wing nut until it is fully secured. The Vitavit® Premium's pressure regulator must also be correctly positioned and lie completely flat before it is secured with the bell nut. With Vitaquick® Premium pots, the cooking indicator can be tightened with a screwdriver or a small coin. Finally, the sealing ring must be inserted into place so that it lies flat and fits tightly (see figure 1 on the right).

CHECKING THE SEALING RING AND VALVES

Fissler pressure cookers are equipped with several safety features (valves and a sealing ring). However, these can function correctly only if all safety-related components are clean, correctly attached and movable. As a result, the traffic light indicator on the pressure regulator (indicator piston) should be checked for ease of movement by pressing on it from below prior to every use, for example (see figure 2 on the right). A safety check must therefore be performed before every use of the pressure cooker. Only when all of the questions on the right about the sealing ring, pressure regulator (Vitavit® Premium) and Euromatic can be clearly answered with a 'yes' is the pressure cooker ready for use.

It is also necessary to check whether the white ball on the Euromatic can be moved freely (see figure 3 on the right). The same stipulations apply to the pots in the Vitaquick® range – on these, the cooking indicator must move up and down freely and spring back when pressed.

CHECKING THE RING AND VALVES

1. Is the sealing ring properly in place? Is it clean and undamaged? Is it tightly positioned and in front of the safety nub?

2. Does the pressure regulator move freely up and down while set to setting 3 when a finger is pressed on the valve and does it spring back?

3. Can the Euromatic's ball be pushed in and does it spring back? Does the O-ring sit fully in the groove provided?

Filling the pot – adding the right amount of food and liquid

To work safely, pressure cookers must only ever be filled to the maximum fill level. In the case of food that swells or heavily foams, the fill level is lower.

CAUTION: always add the minimum amount of liquid to the food. Never(!) pressure cook food with too little or no liquid.

Cooking with a pressure cooker is easy. Despite this, there are a few basic things to bear in mind to successfully and safely cook with pressure. Two things are particularly important and generally apply: firstly, the maximum fill level marked in the pot must not be exceeded when pressure cooking, and secondly, the pot must always contain a minimum amount of liquid. This is because no liquid equals no steam, and no steam equals no pressure.

HOW MUCH FOOD CAN A PRESSURE COOKER HOLD?

The fill volume depends on the size of the pressure cooker. When cooking for multiple people, a large pressure cooker (minimum 4½ quarts/4.5 L, ideally 6 quarts/6 L or more) is useful as a large amount of food fits in the pot before the maximum fill level is reached.

The maximum level must be adhered to for safety reasons as this prevents the valves and safety features from becoming clogged and enables steam to circulate sufficiently. This particularly applies in relation to foaming foods (stock or soups) or foods that absorb water and expand when cooked, such as rice or pasta. In such cases, the pressure cooker must be filled only halfway.

When cooking legumes, the thin skin on beans or lentils can come off, rise up and block the valves. With such foods, the pot should therefore be filled only by a third.

Although pressure cooking is not possible without liquid, the minimum amount required should ideally not be exceeded (exception: stock, soups or one-pot pasta dishes). This ensures that valuable vitamins and minerals are largely preserved while cooking.

CAUTION:
only fill the pressure cooker to a maximum of two-thirds of its capacity!

DO NOT EXCEED THE MAXIMUM FILL LEVEL

- With food that does not expand, fill the pot with food (e.g., potatoes) and liquid to a maximum of two-thirds its height.
- When adding food to the pressure cooker, always observe the maximum fill level (maximum volume mark), even when multilevel cooking.
- Expanding or foaming foods, such as rice or soup, including the water, should be added only to halfway up the pot ($\frac{1}{2}$ mark).
- With dried legumes such as beans or lentils, the fill volume including the liquid must not exceed a third of the pot height ($\frac{1}{3}$ mark).

HOW MUCH LIQUID IS NEEDED WHEN?

When pressure cooking, a certain amount of water or another thin liquid (stock, wine) must always be added to the pot. This needs to be done at the start of the pressure cooking process, together with the food, prior to sealing the pot. The precise amount required primarily depends on the diameter of the pressure cooker and is the same for all Fissler model ranges. A mark inside the pot shows the necessary minimum amount of fluid (minimum volume mark). With smaller pots measuring 7 inches (18 cm) in diameter, $\frac{3}{4}$ cup + 2 tbsp (200 ml) suffices to build up the necessary pressure during the preheating stage. Medium-sized pressure cookers (up to 6 liters) have a diameter of $8\frac{3}{4}$ inches (22 cm) and require 3 tbsp + 1 tsp (50 ml) more to build up pressure. The largest Fissler pressure cookers have a diameter of $10\frac{1}{2}$ inches (26 cm). With these, at least $1\frac{1}{4}$ cups (300 ml) of liquid are required to displace the atmospheric oxygen in the pot and produce enough steam pressure for the venting valve (Euromatic) to hermetically seal the pot and the desired cooking setting to be reached. This basic rule also applies when pressure cooking multiple items on top of each other in (unperforated) inserts. The specified minimum amount of liquid also suffices here. A different situation applies when cooking heavily swelling foods like rice or noodles. Here, the necessary amount of liquid is added to the unperforated insert together with the food.

ADDING THE MINIMUM AMOUNT OF LIQUID

- Never pressure cook food without sufficient liquid.
- The minimum amount of water, stock and/or wine required depends on the pot diameter and is as follows:
  with Ø 7 inches: $\frac{3}{4}$ cup + 2 tbsp (18 cm: 200 ml)
  with Ø $8\frac{3}{4}$ inches: 1 cup (22 cm: 250 ml)
  with Ø $10\frac{1}{2}$ inches: $1\frac{1}{4}$ cups (26 cm: 300 ml)
- While pressure cooking, ensure that the liquid in the pot does not evaporate completely.
- When cooking sides that swell, such as rice or pasta, add enough liquid to the unperforated insert together with the food.
- When steaming without pressure (Vitavit® Premium), add slightly more water as steam continually escapes during the cooking process.
- In the case of lengthy pressure-free steaming processes, regularly check that the pot still contains enough water. If this is not the case, food can burn to the pot and damage it.

FILL LEVEL INDICATOR

Fill level indicator: the minimum/maximum marks for liquid and the fill level make it easy to determine how much to put in the pot. The scale also shows when the pot is half ($\frac{1}{2}$) and a third ($\frac{1}{3}$) full.

Fill level indicator and measuring scale: with the Vitavit® Premium, the amount of liquid and food can be conveniently determined as it not only features a fill level indicator but also a measuring scale in liters.

Starting to pressure cook: sealing the pot and building up pressure

Colored markings and a visual and acoustic signal are handy Fissler tools for correctly locking the pressure cooker before it starts its work when preheated on the highest burner setting.

CLOSING AND LOCKING THE VITAVIT® PREMIUM

1. Hold the lid at a slight angle and place the positioning aid (metal tab inscribed with the word 'Close') in the groove in the pot handle.

2. Twist the lid to the left as far as it will go until the pot locks with an audible click and the indicator turns green.

Once the food and minimum amount of liquid have been added and the safety features have been checked to ensure that they are fully functional (see p. 57), the pressure cooker must be correctly sealed. Thanks to the positioning aid on the lid and the locking indicator on the handle, this is a simple but important step. A Fissler pressure cooker will build up pressure only if the lid is correctly fitted.

PUTTING ON THE LID

A circle symbol on the top of the lid shows the position in which it should be placed

SELECTING A COOKING SETTING AND PREHEATING

1. Twist the adjusting ring on the pressure regulator (Vitavit® Premium) clockwise until the desired cooking setting is reached.

2. Place the correctly locked pressure cooker on the heat source (burner) and heat it on the highest setting.

3. The steam produced displaces the atmospheric oxygen, which escapes with a little steam from both sides of the lid handle near its end.

on the pot. This is also indicated by a red dot on the positioning aid and a red ring around the locking pin on the handle. If both points are positioned precisely opposite one another, the lid can be easily fitted and the pot correctly locked. A quick glance shows whether the pressure cooker is ready for use: if the locking indicator at the bottom of the oval recess in the lid handle is green, everything is in order. If it is red, the pot has not been properly sealed and pressure cannot build up.

BUILDING UP PRESSURE

Fissler pressure cookers are suitable for all burner types. They are preheated on the highest setting to generate the steam needed for pressure cooking. This process may take a few minutes. Once the venting valve (Euromatic) is closed, the pressure and temperature in the pot rise. The cooking valve (pressure regulator: yellow ring, cooking indicator: 1st ring) shows when it is time to reduce the heat again. Minor differences also exist depending on the burner type: with glass ceramic or electric burners, the heat should be turned right down when the yellow ring starts to appear; with induction/gas burners, the heat should be turned down only once the yellow ring is fully visible. In the case of very short cooking times, the heat source can often be completely switched off at this point to save energy.

EXCEPTIONS: INDUCTION AND BOOSTER BURNERS

Induction burners and burners with a booster function work at higher power than other heat sources on their highest setting. This closes the Euromatic faster, which can mean that not all of the atmospheric oxygen has time to escape and the cooking results are not the same as usual.

Recommendation: when preheating a pressure cooker using induction or booster burners, do not set these to the highest setting. The device should also be briefly vented once during the process.

Reducing the heat: the pressure starts to build up as soon as no more steam escapes. When the yellow ring on the cooking indicator appears, it is time to reduce the heat.

Additional venting: when preheating the pressure cooker on an induction or booster burner, release the steam once during the pressure-building stage by briefly pressing the control button on the side of the handle.

Monitoring the cooking time: for dishes to come out of the pot perfectly cooked, always use a timer to adhere to the precise times specified.

TIMER RECOMMENDED:

the cooking time begins as soon as the green ring appears on the pressure regulator (Vitavit® Premium) or the first or second ring (depending on the cooking setting selected) becomes visible on the cooking indicator (Vitaquick® Premium). Using a timer reminds you to remove the pot from the heat at the end of the cooking time and release the steam.

Monitoring the cooking process
and releasing pressure

Fissler pressure cookers are safe and prevent the internal pressure from becoming too high. Despite this, it is still advisable to monitor the cooking valve and subsequently release the appropriate amount of steam from the pot.

IMPORTANT: when pressure cooking, the heat should always be controlled in good time. If the temperature is too high, the safety features kick in and the pot starts to automatically release steam in a controlled manner. In doing so, it loses liquid, which can affect the cooking process.

Pressure cooking in itself is a highly efficient method of preparing almost all foods in a healthy, quick and energy-saving manner. If you also pay attention to a couple more things before and while cooking, you can further minimize energy usage and reduce costs.

TIPS FOR SAVING ENERGY WHEN PRESSURE COOKING

- Where possible, select an appropriate pot size for the amount of food to be cooked. Smaller amounts of rice or vegetables require less energy usage when made in smaller pots (7 cup–3.5 quart / 1.8–3.5 L) as the necessary pressure builds up quicker.
- The burner should not be larger than the pot diameter.
- When preheating the pressure cooker, reduce the heat in good time or, in the event of short cooking times, switch off the burner completely and use the residual heat.
- While cooking, adjust the burner so the red ring does not become visible on the pressure regulator or the cooking indicator does not rise past the second ring, so the cooking valve does not start to release steam.
- Switch off the burner before the end of the cooking time and use the heat stored in the base of the pot.
- When pressure-free steaming (Vitavit® Premium), adjust the heat so only a small amount of steam is released via the pressure regulator and handle.

Monitoring the cooking process: when pressure cooking, the heat source should be adjusted throughout the cooking time so the green ring (or selected cooking indicator mark) in the middle position remains permanently visible. If only the yellow ring is visible, the pressure and heat are too low. If the red ring appears (or the cooking indicator rises above the second white ring), the temperature in the pot is too high.

SAFELY RELEASING STEAM FROM THE PRESSURE COOKER

Depending on the model, there are three or four ways to safely reduce the pressure inside the pressure cooker. The chosen method primarily depends on the food. In the case of lightly foaming foods (legumes, soups or stews) or food with a sensitive skin (unpeeled potatoes), the steam should always be released slowly to prevent the food from escaping or the skin from bursting. In the case of less sensitive foods, the steam can be released more quickly. Only when the pot is completely depressurized does the Euromatic sink down and the control button on the side of the handle becomes fully compressible to open the pot. Always shake the pot briefly before removing the lid to avoid steam bubbles or spatter.

Method 1 – rapid steam release
Lightly press the control button on the side of the lid handle several times until no further steam escapes. If the pot is still pressurized, the button will not fully depress for safety reasons. This prevents the Fissler pressure cooker from being accidentally opened.

Method 2 – gradual steam release
The pressure regulator (Vitavit® Premium) can be used to gently release the steam in small or slightly larger bursts depending on the food. Complete the process by setting the ring to the steam symbol and waiting until the pressure has been fully released. Shake the pot gently before removing the lid.

Method 3 – slow steam release by allowing the pot to cool down
Remove the pressure cooker from the heat, allow it to cool down and then release the steam. This method is primarily suitable for dishes that take a long time to cook as they continue cooking somewhat while the pot cools.

Method 4 – rapid steam release under cold running water
To prevent steam from escaping, it can also be released from the pot while placing it under running water in the sink. To do this, allow the cold water to run over the lid (not the lid handle and cooking valve). Before opening the pot, press the control button on the side several times until all of the pressure has been released.

BEFORE OPENING THE POT

- Briefly press the control button on the side to release any residual pressure.
- Gently shake the pot to prevent spatter and steam bubbles.
- Remove the lid only when the cooking valve and Euromatic have sunk down. Fissler pressure cookers can be opened only once fully depressurized.

> IMPORTANT: never open the pressure cooker by force. It must be opened only once the cooking valve has fully lowered and no further steam escapes.

1. Quick steam release using the control button: gently press the control button on the lid handle several times (do not use force!). Steam escapes from both sides of the front end of the lid handle.

2. Gradual steam release using the pressure regulator: gradually (never instantly!) turn the adjusting ring towards the steam symbol. The steam escapes from under the pressure regulator.

3. Releasing the steam by cooling down the pot: use the handles to carefully remove the pot from the heat shortly before the end of the cooking time and allow it to slowly cool down.

Before opening: gently press the button on the side of the lid handle again to release any residual pressure. Lightly shake the pot before opening it.

Save even more time and energy
by pressure cooking in levels

Simultaneously pressure cooking two or more dishes on multiple levels has many benefits: it saves time, energy and therefore money, plus everything finishes cooking at the same time.

Entire meals can be easily pressure cooked in a single pot if all of their components take the same length of time to cook or have been cut up into larger or smaller pieces to balance out the cooking times (see tips). Meat, stews or other main dishes are often found at the lowest level – on the pot base itself. Side dishes or other meal components can be placed above them in inserts on a tripod. It is even possible to make sweet and savory dishes at the same time. Only very odorous stock (beef stock) should ideally be cooked separately.

USE LARGE POTS

Large pots with a capacity of at least 4.5 but ideally 6 liters or more can be used for multilevel cooking. The pot size restricts layering as the maximum fill level must be observed.

TIPS AND TRICKS

- Even with multilevel cooking, the minimum amount of liquid and maximum fill level must still be observed.
- In the case of foods that take different lengths of time to cook, put the ones that take the longest in the pot first, release the steam partway through the cooking process and use an insert to add the foods that cook quicker.
- Cook fish over vegetables, or vegetables and potatoes over meat.
- To enhance the flavor, sear meat or vegetables first and then deglaze them with the minimum amount of liquid.

WHICH INSERT FOR WHAT?

More sensitive foods, such as fish, vegetables, peeled potatoes or dumplings, can be beautifully steamed in the perforated insert. Puddings, custard dishes or meal components with juice are added to the unperforated insert. Side dishes that absorb liquid when cooking, such as rice, cereals or pasta, are also placed in the unperforated insert with the necessary amount of water or stock.

Sear meat: to enhance their flavor, sear meat and vegetables in a little fat before cooking.

Add the minimum amount of liquid: pour it in directly or use it to deglaze the food.

Space things out: spread the food out flat in the insert and place it on the tripod.

Observe the fill level: the food in the insert must not exceed the maximum volume mark.

Multilevel cooking without pressure

The pressure regulator on the Vitavit® Premium is equipped with a pressure-free steaming setting that enables entire dishes or individual meal components to be gently cooked in an insert.

Whereas the food on the lowest level when pressure cooking using multiple levels cooks directly on the pot base, with pressure-free steaming, it always sits in an insert and only comes into contact with the steam that envelops it, not with the cooking liquid (water or stock) in the base of the pot. When using this cooking method, slightly more liquid should be added to the pressure cooker than when pressure cooking as water evaporates and escapes via the cooking valve throughout the cooking process. However, care must be taken not to add too much liquid as this must not touch the food in the insert when it boils. Pressure-free multilevel cooking is also possible in the Vitaquick® Premium through the use of optionally available, conventional, additional lids made of metal or glass.

STEAMING WITHOUT PRESSURE

Start by preparing the food and placing items such as vegetables, potatoes and fish in a perforated insert. Add rice or other meal components that swell to the unperforated insert together with the necessary amount of liquid. Pour approx.

Cook entire meals in one go: depending on the pot size, different dishes with different cooking times, such as vegetables, potatoes and salmon, can be steamed one on top of the other in levels without pressure, including sweet dishes and desserts.

No contact between food and water: when pressure-free steaming, add a little more water and place a tripod in the pot.

¾ inch (2 cm) of water into the pot, insert a spacer (tripod) and place the food in the insert on top of it. Seal the pressure cooker with the lid, heat it on the highest burner setting and reduce the heat again as soon as steam starts to escape from the cooking valve.

DEFROSTING AND HEATING

Large pressure cookers are ideal for multi-level cooking without pressure. A 6-liter Vitavit® Premium can hold two inserts, one on top of the other, while deeper pots can hold up to three inserts. Alternatively, an additional lid (without valves and a lock) is available that enables the pot to be filled to the brim. Further benefits: frozen food can be quickly defrosted in the steam and dishes such as precooked pasta can be gently heated up.

TIPS AND TRICKS

- Even when multi-level cooking without pressure, food should still be placed in the inserts as flatly as possible.
- Do not fill the top insert with food that will expand and ensure that there is sufficient clearance from the venting valve (Euromatic) so that this cannot be pushed upwards by the food.
- Add plenty of liquid to the pot as water evaporates throughout the cooking process.
- In the case of foods that take different lengths of time to cook, place the ones that take the longest in the insert first. Further foods can then be added to the insert during the cooking process by simply removing the lid.
- In the case of longer cooking times, the remaining liquid level in the pot should be checked at regular intervals.

Using inserts: even when pressure-free steaming, ensure sufficient clearance from the lid (Euromatic).

Cleaning and care
Maintaining the pressure cooker

To ensure that they are always fully functional and ready for use, pressure cookers must be thoroughly cleaned after every use and require a little maintenance and care from time to time.

CLEANING THE VITAVIT® PREMIUM PRESSURE COOKER AFTER USE

1. Remove the gray sealing ring from the lid for pre-cleaning purposes and wipe it with a damp cloth.

2. Twist the bell nut counterclockwise on the inside of the lid, which secures the cooking valve (pressure regulator).

3. Remove the bell nut, then detach the pressure regulator from the lid and set it aside.

4. Dip a cloth in some hot water with a little household dish detergent and manually clean the pressure regulator and handle.

5. To loosen the lid handle, twist the wing nut counterclockwise, remove the handle and rinse it with water.

6. The pot body and lid (without attachments) are made from stainless steel and are dishwasher safe. Finally, thoroughly dry all parts.

Like any other pot, pressure cookers have to be cleaned after every use. Limescale marks and rainbowlike discoloration on the stainless steel surfaces can be removed with a stainless steel cleaner.

CAREFULLY CLEAN THE POT

Before cleaning the pot itself, the sealing ring, cooking valve and lid handle must be removed from the lid and washed by hand as described on the left. The pot body and lid (without attachments) can be manually washed with household dish detergent or simply placed in a dishwasher. In the event of heavier soiling, a biodegradable stainless steel cleaner (available from Fissler) gently removes any residues and encrustations on the stainless steel surfaces without scratching them.

STORAGE TIPS

Once all parts are clean and dry, the pressure cooker should be returned to a cupboard as the sealing ring needs to be stored in a dark place protected from sunlight and UV radiation. To protect the silicone ring and prevent it from being crushed, insert it back into the lid and place this upside down on the pot (with the pressure regulator or cooking valve pointing downward). Thanks to their conical shape, Fissler pressure cookers with the same diameter can be easily stacked and thus compactly stored.

CARE AND MAINTENANCE

To keep the pressure cooker looking great for many years or even decades, the metal surfaces on the pot and lid should be regularly treated with a stainless steel care product (available from Fissler). This makes it easy to remove white or rainbowlike discoloration.

In addition, pressure cookers require occasional maintenance (after 400 uses or two years, whichever comes first). This involves all silicone and elastomer parts (sealing ring, O-ring and valve covers) being replaced with original spare parts from Fissler. Simple repairs such as the replacement of wear parts, valves and handles or the tightening of screws can be performed independently (see the manufacturer's user instructions) as all of the components required can be purchased separately.

POT AND LID CARE

Stainless steel care: regularly treat the pot and lid (without attachments) with a stainless steel care product to retain their attractive appearance.

Thanks to their special conical shape, multiple Fissler pressure cookers of the same diameter can be stacked inside each other for compact storage.

Food preparation and information about cooking times

Pressure cooking preserves food's nutrients and flavor. The successful use of the method depends on both a little knowledge and high-quality produce.

Preparing vegetables: different cooking times for vegetables and other foods (e.g., meat) can, can be balanced out by the size of the pieces. Anything that takes longer to cook can simply be chopped up smaller and vice versa. For example, meat can be chopped into very small pieces and vegetables into very large ones.

Before vegetables, poultry, meat or fish can be placed in a pressure cooker, there are a few things that have to be considered. Although food preparation is essentially the same as with conventional cooking, there are several things to note when pressure cooking due to the high pressure and higher temperatures. The next few pages explain these in detail.

PRESSURE COOKING WITH QUALITY PRODUCE

Successful results when cooking, and in particular pressure cooking, start with the grocery shop. It is important to focus on good quality and look out for high-quality produce in markets and supermarkets or from a trusted fishmonger or butcher. Those who opt for crisp seasonal vegetables, legumes from an organic store, sustainably caught or organically raised fish or finely marbled meat from grass-fed animals will be rewarded with wonderfully flavorsome, delicious and perfectly cooked food.

PRESSURE COOKING IS HEALTHIER

The results will also be far healthier and quicker than with 'normal' cooking. As nothing leaches out of vegetables when they are pressure cooked, they retain far more vitamins and minerals than when conventionally boiled. Meat is far more tender, while also cooking up to 70% quicker. This applies in general, but especially for sinewy cuts, which otherwise have to cook for hours.

COOKING TIME SPECIFICATIONS ARE GUIDE VALUES ONLY

The cooking times can differ greatly depending on the species, breed and age of the animals. Meat from a young deer cooks far quicker than that from an older one. Carrots that have been stored for a while take 1–2 minutes less than freshly harvested ones. Dried borlotti beans from the previous year's harvest cook more evenly and quickly than lentils and beans that have not yet reached their expiry date but have already sat on a shelf for two or three years. As such, the times quoted on the next few pages, in the recipe section and in the cooking time reference tables are merely guide values. However, through 'learning by doing,' you will gain experience and get a feel for how long things take.

BALANCING OUT COOKING TIMES

When pressure cooking food like vegetables with different cooking times, these can be balanced out by chopping them into larger and smaller pieces.

Vegetables particularly benefit
from being pressure cooked

Pressure cooking offers major benefits: thanks to the shorter cooking times in steam with practically no atmospheric oxygen, broccoli, carrots and other vegetables retain far more vitamins and minerals than when conventionally cooked.

Scientific studies (Justus Liebig University Giessen and the University of Koblenz, 2012; ipi Institute für Produkt-Markt-Forschung and the University of Hohenheim, 2022) prove that pressure cooking vegetables delivers better results with regard to nutrient preservation and sensory quality than boiling them without pressure in a conventional pot. This means that broccoli, potatoes and carrots not only cook quicker but also offer greater nutritional value.

VEGETABLES ARE HEALTHIER

With pressure cooking, vegetables benefit from very short cooking times in steam or little water with almost no atmospheric oxygen. Sensitive vitamins are better preserved. For example, broccoli, carrots and potatoes retain about 90% of their vitamin C. At 88%, pressure cooked potatoes retain a significantly higher vitamin B1 content (thiamine) than when boiled (49%). The level of beta-carotene (provitamin A), for example in carrots and broccoli, even increases with pressure cooking as it is made more accessible to the body. As such, conventionally cooked carrots contain 156% compared to pressure cooked ones, which contain 190%. With broccoli, the provitamin A content after pressure cooking is even higher, at 213% compared to 174% when boiled.

Minerals such as calcium, potassium or iron are less sensitive to heat and oxygen but water-soluble. When food is boiled, they are rinsed out and no longer available to the body unless the cooking water is put to use.

UP TO 100% NUTRIENT PRESERVATION

This is not the case in a pressure cooker: when gently pressure cooking in steam, up to 100% of the minerals found in vegetables and other foods are preserved. The flavor and taste of foods, such as carrots, are also intensified. Furthermore, the color of vegetables is positively influenced be-

VITAMIN C PRESERVATION COMPARED TO WHEN RAW

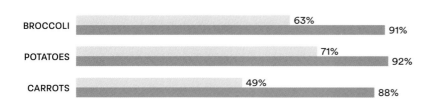

- BROCCOLI: 63% / 91%
- POTATOES: 71% / 92%
- CARROTS: 49% / 88%

MINERAL PRESERVATION COMPARED TO WHEN RAW

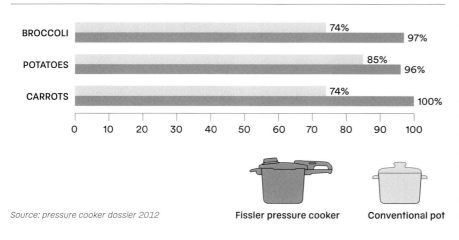

- BROCCOLI: 74% / 97%
- POTATOES: 85% / 96%
- CARROTS: 74% / 100%

Fissler pressure cooker | Conventional pot

Source: pressure cooker dossier 2012

cause their natural dyes are pressed into the outer layers when under pressure, making them brighter and more vibrant.

COOKING DELICATE VEGETABLES IN A PRESSURE COOKER

Delicate vegetables such as broccoli and cauliflower are also suitable for pressure cooking as their color, shape and natural taste are fantastically preserved. Despite this, like leafy vegetables (e.g., spinach or Swiss chard), they should only be briefly subjected to a low amount of pressure so as not to overcook them.

For al dente florets and leaves, the gentle cooking setting 1 is recommended for more delicate vegetables. This cooking setting is also ideal when pressure cooking chopped vegetables with soft flesh, such as eggplant and zucchini. The cooking times are generally very short and range from 1–4 minutes.

PREPARATION TIPS

- Cook delicate or thinly sliced vegetables on the lowest pressure setting (gentle cooking) or by steaming them without pressure in the Vitavit® Premium.
- Precisely observe the cooking times; delicate vegetables quickly overcook.

PRESSURE COOKING SETTING 1 IS FOR

Eggplant, chopped	Swiss chard
Cauliflower florets	Spinach
Broccoli	Zucchini

Even delicate vegetables such as broccoli can be successfully cooked in a pressure cooker. So as not to overcook the florets, they should be placed in the pot using the perforated insert and cooked on setting 1. This takes only a few minutes and preserves their beautiful color.

Cooking spiralized zucchini: use a spiralizer to cut young zucchini into long, thin strips, place them in the perforated insert and cook them on pressure cooking setting 1 or the pressure-free steaming setting.

Stuffed vegetables: halved peppers or eggplant are ideal for filling with couscous, rice and ground meat. When multilevel cooked, they are often placed in an insert.

Fresh from the market: kohlrabi, tubers, root vegetables, artichokes, peas, tomatoes, sweet potatoes and Brussels sprouts all benefit from short, rapid heating with pressure as they retain their fresh color and most of their valuable vitamins and minerals.

Robust vegetables

Most vegetables can withstand a little more pressure and higher temperatures, plus they benefit from the shorter cooking times. The highest pressure cooking setting is ideal for extremely robust root vegetables, tubers or cabbage.

Flavoring the cooking liquid: to flavor vegetables, such as corn on the cob, simply add the desired spices to the liquid in which they are cooked.

With their high content of vitamins, minerals, fiber and antioxidants, vegetables are regarded as particularly healthy. For example, kale contains high levels of vitamins K, C and A as well as magnesium. Bell peppers have a high vitamin C and A content. Tomatoes are a good source of vitamins C and K as well as potassium and lycopene. Beet is rich in vitamin B, potassium and iron, etc. When cooked in a pressure cooker, these constituent substances are far better preserved than with conventional cooking. The minimum amount of liquid required to produce steam is low. This means that nothing leaches out of vegetables when they are pressure cooked, even if placed directly in the pot. Kohlrabi, carrots, parsnip and sweet potatoes can be cooked even more gently in the perforated insert as this prevents them from coming into direct contact with the liquid.

PREPARING VEGETABLES

Prior to being cooked, vegetables are washed to remove any dirt and pollutants. To reduce the risk of harmful substances, it is usually best to peel carrots and other root vegetables. This should ideally be done with a peeler as the outer layer of many vegetables contains important constituent substances. In the case of young organic produce, it usually suffices to brush them thoroughly under running water. Green asparagus needs only to be

about one-third peeled whereas white asparagus should be fully peeled. Potatoes that have been stored for longer should always be peeled, whereas new potatoes can simply be thoroughly washed. The vegetables should then be trimmed to remove all hard parts that would feel unpleasant when eating them – for example, stems (cucumbers, eggplant, zucchini), woody sections (kohlrabi, asparagus) or tough strings (green beans, celery).

TIP: as most vegetables take only a few minutes to cook, the use of a timer is recommended!

COOKING SETTINGS AND TIMES

Most robust vegetables are very suitable for pressure cooking. With the Vitavit® Premium, setting 2 is the ideal choice for vegetables. The Vitaquick®, on the other hand, should be set to setting 1. With these settings, the temperature reaches approx. 235°F (113°C) (Vitavit® Premium) and approx. 228°F (109°C) (Vitaquick® Premium). As such, the cooking times with the Vitaquick® are slightly longer. Particularly robust vegetables, such as potatoes, squash wedges, thick carrots or cabbage, can be express cooked at higher temperatures and greater pressure (Vitavit® Premium: setting 3/approx. 241°F/116°C, Vitaquick® Premium: setting 2/approx. 243°F/117°C). The cooking times lie between 2 and 10 minutes or 15 and 25 minutes in the case of root vegetables and tubers (e.g., beet).

Tip: place stuffed vegetables such as peppers or eggplant in the perforated insert and cook them on setting 2 (pressure regulator, cooking indicator: 1st ring) for 8–10 minutes. Further guidance on cooking times for vegetables can be found in the tables on pages 298 and 299.

Cooking asparagus in an insert: wash green asparagus, peel the lower third, trim as required and cook in the perforated insert on setting 2 for 3–6 minutes depending on the thickness.

PREPARATION TIPS

- Vegetables cook perfectly on setting 2 of the Vitavit® Premium or setting 1 of the Vitaquick® Premium.
- Always observe the minimum amount of liquid and the maximum fill level.
- Note the cooking time and release the steam as soon as this has passed.

Cooking coloring food in an insert: when multilevel cooking, place the peeled beet or other coloring vegetables like red cabbage in the unperforated insert.

PRESSURE COOKING SETTING 2 IS IDEAL FOR:

Artichokes	Parsnips
Cauliflower (whole)	Brussels sprouts
Fennel (halved)	Beet
Green beans	Black salsify
Green peas	Asparagus
Kohlrabi	Celery
Squash (cubed)	Sweet potatoes
Leeks	Tomatoes
Corn on the cob	Savoy cabbage
Bell peppers	Sugar snap peas

PRESSURE COOKING SETTING 3 IS IDEAL FOR:

Potatoes	Carrots
Celeriac	Red/white cabbage
Squash (wedges)	Sauerkraut

Legumes cook even better with pressure

Red, black, white, green or orange: beans, lentils and chickpeas come in many different varieties but all have one thing in common – they can be beautifully pressure cooked, and in less time than normal.

Legumes particularly benefit from pressure cooking as they take less than half the usual amount of time to cook, plus they cook through evenly. Before cooking, they should be sorted and rinsed in cold water in a sieve.

TO SOAK OR NOT TO SOAK?

Larger legumes, such as dried lima beans, lentils that have been stored for longer, or chickpeas, should be soaked in cold water before being cooked (see the figures on the right).

Depending on the variety, they absorb their own weight in water over 3 (lentils) to 24 hours (dried whole peas or large white beans), which slightly reduces the cooking time. However, this is only by 4–5 minutes, so the difference is not so great that soaking is a must. If time is of the essence or you suddenly need some hummus, chickpeas and other legumes can also be placed directly in the pressure cooker with cold unsalted water. Legumes are cooked on the highest pressure setting (Vitavit®: setting 3; Vitaquick®: 2nd ring).

Not soaked, they need between 10 (lentils) and 20 minutes (kidney beans, white beans, lima beans). About 4 to 6 cups (1 to 1.5 L) of water are needed to cook 10 to 14 oz (300 to 400 g) dried legumes. About two-thirds of this amount suffice for well-soaked chickpeas or beans.

LEGUMES IN AN INSERT

Although often cooked directly in the pot, chickpeas, lentils and beans can also be multilevel cooked providing the pressure cooker has a large enough capacity (at least 4½ quarts/4.5 L, ideally 6 quarts/6 L).

When cooking them with other foods, the legumes should be placed in the unperforated insert and sufficient water added at a ratio of 1:2.

PURCHASING AND PREPARATION TIPS

- When grocery shopping, always look for quality produce and check the filling date on the packaging. Legumes that have been stored for a while cook unevenly and take longer to be done.
- Soaking is not imperative but reduces the cooking time by several minutes, thereby further reducing the energy consumption.
- The pressure cooker must be only one-third filled.
- Cook legumes on the highest setting, without seasoning them with salt beforehand.
- Remove the pot from the heat at the end of the cooking time and slowly release the steam (see p. 63).

As legumes swell up and foam when cooked, the pressure cooker should only ever be one-third or at most one-half filled, plus no salt should be added to the water before cooking them.

Colorful and healthy: dried legumes such as lentils, beans, peas or chickpeas are ideal for making in a pressure cooker as they cook far quicker, even when they have not been soaked.

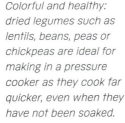

1. Soak the beans: rinse the dried beans, tip into a large bowl, fully cover with cold water and let soak for 12–24 hours.

2. Once soaked, the beans will have clearly increased in size as they have already absorbed water. This makes them quicker to cook.

3. Once cooked, slowly release the steam from the beans and season with salt. Their volume has significantly increased and they can be served directly or used for a recipe.

PRACTICAL INFORMATION ≫ BASIC PREPARATION

Basic preparation of meat: beef, veal and pork

Boiled, braised or fried – meat always benefits from being cooked in a pressure cooker, and delivers an instant sauce to boot. Even sinewy cuts become wonderfully tender – and in a fraction of the normal time.

Whether goulash, beef brisket, pork fillets or spare ribs, quick, tender and succulent results are easy to achieve when using pressure.

PREPARING MEAT

A few steps are necessary before cooking the meat: allow chilled meat to come to room temperature for about 30 minutes. During this time, dab the meat dry with paper towels and remove the silver skin, sinews and excess fat, as shown below in the example of a pork fillet.

Depending on the dish, the meat must then be portioned into slices or cubes (see below). If, as with involtini or roulades, the meat is to surround a filling, the

PREPARING MEAT: REMOVING SINEWS, PORTIONING AND DICING

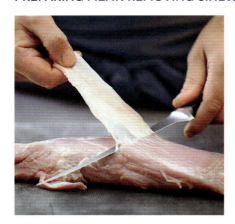

Removing sinews: hold a sharp knife blade flat against the meat and carefully separate the silver skin from the surface.

Cutting meat into medallions: use a sharp knife to cut the meat (fillet) across the grain into 1¼ to 1½-inch (3 to 4 cm) thick pieces.

Dicing meat: smaller cubes of meat cook faster. When making ragouts and goulash, meat is usually diced into 1¼ to 1½-inch (3 to 4 cm) pieces.

slices should ideally be tenderized in advance. To do this, wrap the meat in plastic wrap and pound it flat with a meat tenderizer or a large, heavy pan until it has an even thickness all over.

STEWING AND BRAISING MEAT USING PRESSURE

Cuts intended for boiling, such as rump or brisket, are more succulent when placed in simmering liquid (stock). Meat intended to release its flavor is prepared with cold water. When pressure cooking leg meat, shin or oxtail, start by covering the bones and soup greens with cold water and slowly bringing them to the boil in the uncovered pot. Add the meat, seal the pressure cooker with the lid and cook on the highest setting for 30–40 minutes. It can also help to sear meat rolls or cubes in a little fat in advance as the roasting juices created during this process further enhance the flavor of the braised dishes (see the example on the right).

Tip: start by cooking meat (spare ribs, brisket) in an insert using pressure or, if the cuts are too large, directly in the pot, then brown them in the oven (or on the grill).

PREPARATION TIPS

- When buying meat, ensure that it is of good quality and finely marbled.
- Always add stewing meat to simmering liquid (stock).
- Briefly sear meat for roulades and ragouts in the pressure cooker before cooking it.
- Meat can be deglazed with the minimum amount of stock or a mixture of stock and red or white wine.
- If meat should retain its brown color or be browned later on, pressure cook it in an insert or with as little contact with the cooking liquid as possible.
- When filling the pot, always observe the maximum fill level.

SEAR MEAT BEFORE BRAISING:

1. Add a little hot oil to a pressure cooker or pressure skillet, then sear and brown the meat (involtini, goulash, etc.).

2. Deglaze everything with liquid (minimum amount), seal the pot and cook the meat on the highest setting for 20 to 25 minutes.

Cooking spare ribs in an insert: fill the pot with the minimum amount of water. Place the ribs (curvature outward) in the insert.

Cooking ribs directly in the pot: if the spare ribs are too long, they can be cooked upright (with the curvature outward).

PRACTICAL INFORMATION » BASIC PREPARATION

Basic preparation of meat: lamb and game

Both offer high-quality meat that is tender and succulent when cooked with pressure. Larger shoulder or leg cuts are just as suitable for pressure cooking as smaller pieces intended for lamb curry or venison stew/goulash.

TIP: entire legs or saddles are often too large for the pressure cooker. These should therefore be cut into portions so that they fit in the pot without exceeding the maximum fill level.

The meat from grass-fed animals (lamb) and game is low in fat and contains far higher levels of nutrients (omega-3 fatty acids, B vitamins) and minerals (such as iron, zinc, selenium, potassium and magnesium) than that from conventionally raised animals (such as cattle or pigs). This is primarily because animals that are reared on meadows or in the wild are able to find and use far more diverse sources of food.

WHICH CUTS SHOULD BE USED FOR WHAT?

The most tender cuts generally stem from the hindquarters of an animal, where the muscles are worked less. They contain less sinew and cook quicker. These include the saddle with the tenderloin and the legs. These cuts are very popular and therefore more expensive than the sinewy forequarter cuts, in part because the latter have to cook for a long time to achieve the desired tenderness when using conventional methods.

This is where a pressure cooker comes into its own: while this can naturally also be used to perfectly prepare legs of lamb or wild boar or saddles of venison, its strengths particularly shine through when cooking cheaper shoulder cuts or using pressure to braise lamb shanks.

To achieve evenly cooked and beautifully tender lamb and game, the meat needs to be carefully tenderized first. This takes a little patience but produces far more tender results.

Dicing venison leg: when making goulash or ragout, use a sharp knife to cut the meat into evenly sized cubes measuring 1¼ to 1½ inches (3 to 4 cm).

Removing sinew from venison shoulder: holding the knife flat so as not to damage the meat, remove all silver skin and sinews.

Lamb can be prepared in a pressure cooker in a range of different ways: larger cuts (shoulder or leg) taste particularly delicious as conventional or rolled roasts. Shanks become beautifully tender when braised using pressure. Diced lamb, which is obtained from young animals up to 12 months old, is ideal for Asian curries or braised Middle Eastern dishes with chickpeas.

COOKING LAMB AND GAME

Use a sharp knife (e.g., a boning knife) to remove the silver skin and sinews. Pat the meat dry and sear it in a little clarified butter or oil in the pressure cooker before deglazing it with the minimum amount of liquid (wine, stock or, in the case of game, often a combination of game stock, red wine and port).

Next, cook the lamb or game on the highest pressure setting. This usually takes 15–30 minutes.

TIPS AND TRICKS

- Carefully remove the sinew from the meat before cooking it.
- With large cuts (shoulder, leg), remove the bones and cut the meat into 2 to 3 larger pieces, taking care to ensure they all have the same thickness.
- Alternatively, roll up the meat, tie it into shape with kitchen twine like a rolled roast and slice it in half across the middle if necessary.
- To enhance the flavor, sear and brown the meat before pressure cooking it.

Preparing and pressure cooking poultry and rabbit

Poultry such as chicken, turkey, duck or goose becomes tender and succulent when cooked using pressure and is usually done in 15 to 20 minutes. However, it is rare for it to fit in the pot whole. The same applies to rabbit.

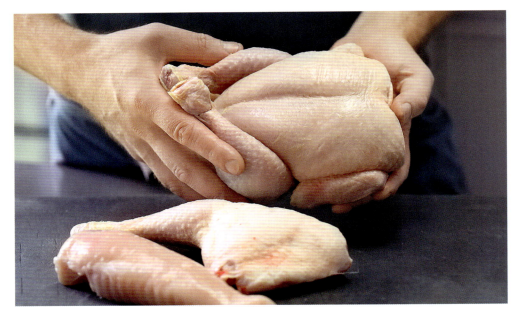

Whole chickens can be easily cut into pieces with the aid of a sharp knife, poultry shears or a kitchen cleaver. Start by separating the legs and wings, then remove the breast fillets. Do not throw away the carcass. Instead, cook it with some chicken giblets to make a delicious stock (see p. 96).

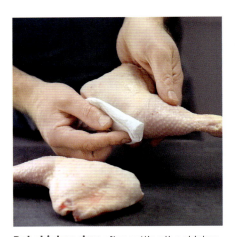

Pat chicken dry: after cutting the chicken (or removing the chicken from the packaging), use paper towels to pat them dry all over.

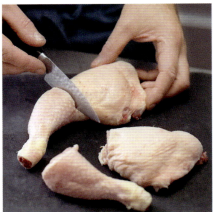

Joint the legs: feel for the joint with your fingers and use a sharp knife to separate the drumstick from the thigh.

Marinate with spices: placing chicken in a marinade made of soy sauce, ginger, garlic and spices for at least 30 minutes enhances the flavor.

When cooked conventionally, duck legs take a long time to become soft and tender. This is achieved far quicker in a pressure cooker using the highest pressure setting.

Chicken, turkey, duck and goose are used in many different ways in curries, stews or soups, especially for traditional Asian cuisine. Chefs have a whole array of tips and tricks on how to enhance the subtle flavor of chicken and make the meat more tender – for example, by marinating it in milk.

CUTTING AND MARINATING POULTRY AND RABBIT

It is cheaper to buy poultry and rabbit whole and cut it up yourself than to buy cuts. When making soups and one-pot dishes, chickens are usually cut up into 6 to 8 portions and rabbits into 10 to 12. This should be done using a sharp knife (e.g., a boning knife) so that the sinews and joints can be smoothly severed.

The excess fat should then be removed and the cuts should be thoroughly dabbed dry. When cooked on the highest setting using pressure, poultry and rabbit usually take between 15 minutes (chicken) and 25–30 minutes (duck and rabbit) to cook.

ENHANCING THE FLAVOR

The flavor of poultry and rabbit can be enhanced by placing them in a spiced marinade (e.g., an Asian marinade based on soy and/or fish sauce with ginger, chile peppers and garlic or a Mediterranean marinade with olive oil, rosemary, thyme, garlic and mild chile peppers). Searing the produce before cooking it generates roasting juices that further enhance the flavor.

TIPS AND ADVICE

- When buying poultry and rabbit, always ensure good quality.
- Cut both into pieces before pressure cooking so as not to exceed the maximum fill level.
- To enhance the flavor, place chicken and rabbit pieces in a spiced marinade (e.g., consisting of soy sauce, ginger, garlic and other seasoning ingredients, for 30 minutes to 2 hours before cooking).
- Sprinkle diced chicken (breast) with cornstarch before searing it to keep it more succulent.
- Briefly sear and brown the poultry and rabbit in the pressure cooker, deglaze with 1¼ cups (300 ml) liquid and cook on the highest setting for 10–30 minutes.

Searing rabbit legs: to enhance their flavor, season rabbit legs with salt and pepper, then sear and brown them in a little vegetable oil before pressure cooking them.

Deglazing the cooking juices: remove the legs and set aside briefly. Use 1¼ cups (300 ml) stock (or stock and wine) to deglaze and loosen the cooking juices on the base of the pot.

Pressure cooking fish and seafood

Fish fillets and delicate types of seafood such as prawns or mussels cook best when only briefly subjected to low pressure. Other types of seafood such as cuttlefish, calamari or octopus require a little more pressure.

Fish has tender flesh and cooks extremely quickly under pressure due to its protein structure. As such, the (very short) cooking times should be carefully observed when pressure cooking fish and many types of seafood.

Even with conventional methods, fish and seafood cook quickly. When using pressure, this often takes far less than 5 minutes. When pressure cooking seafood, the cooking times should therefore be adhered to as precisely as possible and the use of a timer (e.g., on a cell phone) is recommended.

COOKING FISH IN A PRESSURE COOKER

Fish is usually cooked on the lowest pressure setting. Delicate trout, flounder or sole fillets are often ready after just 2, 3 or 4 minutes, as are entire fish that have been sliced into pieces. Ragouts and stews with larger pieces take 3–4 minutes. Fleshy fish (e.g., haddock, cod, sea bass, ocean perch or monkfish) are slightly more robust and require 4–8 minutes. Gentle cooking in the perforated insert – for example, on a bed of vegetables (see the example on the right), which will then be served as a side, is also recommended.

Tip: the perforated insert can be used to gently steam fish and seafood without pressure (Vitavit®) with especially succulent results, even when cooking on multiple levels.

Delicate fillets of sole, flounder or trout can also be cooked on a bed of vegetables. To this end, wash, trim and slice carrots, parsnip, leeks or green onions. Grease the perforated insert with a little oil or butter, then add the vegetables. Season with aromatic herbs and spices, place the fish on top and steam without pressure for 4–10 minutes depending on the thickness.

PRESSURE COOKING OCTOPUS, MUSSELS AND PRAWNS

Octopus can be prepared on a higher pressure cooking setting. They cook beautifully in a pressure cooker in just a fraction of the time needed with conventional methods. Please note that the cooking times (see right) are again for guidance only as they depend on the age and size of the animal. More delicate types of seafood are also suitable for pressure cooking. These can be cooked on setting 1. Prawns take 2–3 minutes to cook and mussels 1–3 minutes depending on their size.

PREPARATION TIPS

- When purchasing fish and seafood, ensure good quality and freshness.
- Ask the fishmonger for the carcasses as well and use them to make a flavorsome stock (see p. 293).
- Wash fish fillets before cooking them and remove any remaining bones.
- Observe the minimum amount of liquid and maximum fill level.
- Precisely adhere to the cooking times when pressure cooking fish and seafood and release the steam quickly.
- Discard any mussels that are still closed at the end of the cooking process.

Octopus can be beautifully prepared in a pressure cooker: add enough water (approx. 4 cups/1 L) to the pressure cooker to just cover the washed octopus, followed by 1 tbsp salt and 2 tbsp white wine vinegar, then pressure cook on the highest setting for 5–6 minutes or on setting 2 (Vitavit®) for 7–8 minutes. Release the steam slowly.

Cooking fish fillets in an insert: fish fillets (e.g., salmon), cook in 5–8 minutes on a bed of vegetables (or directly in the insert) on the lowest pressure level. Delicate fillets of sole and flounder take just 2–3 minutes.

Preparing mussels: thoroughly brush and wash the fresh mussels. Discard any mussels with damaged shells or open shells that will not close when tapped with a finger.

Different rice varieties and how to cook them in a pressure cooker

Rice is a popular side dish both in Asia and worldwide as well as the basis for many dishes such as risotto, paella or pilaf. It can be beautifully prepared in a pressure cooker, where it (fascinatingly) cooks in just 3–5 minutes.

Cooking basmati rice as a side: when placed in the unperforated insert with the right amount of water (at a ratio of 1:1) and a little salt, the rice cooks on the highest setting at the same time as the remaining food for the last 5 minutes of the cooking process – saving time and energy, reducing cleanup and ensuring that everything is ready at the same time.

Of the over 100,000 varieties found worldwide, only a few are sold in North America. But even here, the amount of choice available in supermarkets is growing steadily. Depending on the grain length, retailers differentiate between long-grain (over 6 mm), medium-grain (5.2–6 mm) and short-grain rice (usually 5–5.2 mm). The shorter, thicker grains of Japonica rice tend to be sticky when cooked due to their starch composition and are easy to eat with chopsticks. Indica rice varieties have longer, slimmer grains, stick together less when cooking and retain their consistency. There are also multiple varieties of brown rice, which has the hull removed but retains the bran and germ. Long-grain brown rice varieties of both types, from which the bran layers and germ are not removed, contain particularly high levels of nutrients and fiber, such as red or black long-grain rice from Thailand, which is now also cultivated in Europe (France, Italy).

SHOULD RICE BE WASHED?

Barring a few exceptions, white or colored rice should ideally be washed before it is cooked in order to remove any dirt and excess starch (sticky rice dust). This makes the rice looser and stops the grains from sticking together as much when cooking. To wash the rice, either place it in a sieve and hold it under cold running water until the water runs clear, or cover it with cold water in a bowl, swish it around and pour the water away before repeating the process another two or three times.

The process differs in the case of creamy rice dishes such as risotto: here, the starch on the rice grains is desired as it helps to bind the dish and make the risotto beautifully creamy.

COOKING RICE SEPARATELY

In Asia, rice is far more than 'just' a side dish; it is at the very heart of many meals. It is therefore with good reason that the word 'rice' can also mean 'meal' in countries such as Korea, Thailand, Vietnam, China or Japan. And this is no wonder as rice contains complex carbohydrates and valuable B vitamins. When cooked using pressure, these are well preserved and the rice grains come out of the pressure cooker perfectly cooked.

PREPARATION TIPS

- Most varieties of rice, with the exception of risotto rice, should be thoroughly washed before being cooked.
- If rice is made as a side, a rice-to-water ratio of 1:1.2 is ideal. When cooked in an insert, a ratio of 1:1 is also possible.
- As rice swells when cooked, do not put too much rice (or water) in the unperforated insert and only half-fill the pot.

COOKING BASMATI RICE DIRECTLY IN THE PRESSURE COOKER

1. Place the basmati rice in a sieve and hold it under cold running water until the water runs clear and no further starch is stuck to it, then allow it to strain.

2. Add the rice to the pressure cooker, season with salt and pour in the water at a ratio of 1:1.2 (or 1:1). Seal the pot and heat on the highest setting.

3. Pressure cook the rice on the highest setting for approx. 5 minutes. Release the steam, then divide the rice into four crosswise and fluff it slightly.

The cooking time of rice can vary depending on the variety, the desired consistency and personal preference. Hulled white rice (basmati rice, sushi rice) takes only 3–5 minutes on the highest pressure setting while long-grain brown rice takes slightly longer (7–9 minutes). A rice to water ratio of 1:1.2 should ideally be used. Depending on the moisture content and maturity, this ratio can vary slightly. Rice that has been stored for 1 year or more is drier than freshly harvested rice.

When making rice as a side, apart from adding a little salt, it can simply be cooked 'as is.' In Asia, however, people know many ways of giving the grains a little color when cooking them (e.g., with turmeric) and enhancing the flavor of the rice by cooking it with ingredients that add seasoning.

PRESSURE COOKING SUSHI AND SPICED RICE

Even sushi rice can be perfectly prepared in a pressure cooker. This means that nothing stands in the way of you making nigiri, maki or temaki sushi, especially as the rice cooks in just 3 minutes and simply has to be fluffed again after leaving it to cool for 10 minutes. There is no need to flavor the cooked rice as the seasoning ingredients – a mix of sugar, salt and rice vinegar – already form part of the cooking process.

The same applies when making spiced rice. To this end, fry various spices in a little fat (ghee, clarified butter or vegetable oil) until they become fragrant.

Only then should the other ingredients (ginger, garlic, etc.) be added together with the washed and strained rice. Cooked on the highest pressure setting, the spiced rice is ready in just 3 minutes. Remove the pot from the heat and leave it to cool for 10 minutes before opening it. For a Chinese version, add 8 oz (250 g) washed basmati rice, 1¼ cups (300 ml) vegetable stock, 1 tsp five-spice powder, 2 tbsp sesame oil and 2 tbsp soy sauce to the pressure cooker and cook the rice as described.

COOKING RICE FOR RISOTTO, PAELLA AND PILAF

From southern Europe to Central Asia and the Middle East, there are many dishes where rice grains are cooked with other ingredients and absorb the flavorful stock as they swell. These include paella in Spain and Portugal, risotto in Italy, the only major rice-producing country in Europe, and all variations of pilaf further to the east. To make such dishes, start by briefly searing onions and the other ingredients in a little oil. Next, add the rice and the minimum amount of liquid and pressure cook everything on the highest setting for 5–7 minutes.

When making pilaf, paella and risotto, the rice is not cooked separately but together with an array of vegetables, seafood or meat. Even these kinds of rice dishes can be made in a pressure cooker with outstanding results.

COOKING SUSHI RICE IN A PRESSURE COOKER

1. Optionally place an approx. 2-inch (5 cm) piece of kombu (seaweed) on the base of the pressure cooker and top with 15 oz (450 g) of washed and strained sushi rice.

2. Measure out 2 cups + 3 tbsp (540 ml) cold water and pour into the pressure cooker with the rice. Stir in ¼ cup (60 ml) rice vinegar.

3. Add 2 tbsp sugar and 1½ tsp salt, mix well and then seal the pot. Cook the rice on the highest pressure setting for 3–5 minutes, release the steam and fluff (see p. 87).

MAKING RICE PUDDING

Pressure cooking rice pudding: cook 7 oz (200 g) short-grain rice on the lowest pressure cooking setting for 15 minutes with 3 times the amount of milk and 1.5 times the amount of water.

Preparation tips:

- Lightly salt the rice and water before starting the cooking process (1 tsp to 7 oz/200 g rice) and cook on the highest setting for 3–5 minutes.
- Many Koreans love their rice to be slightly sticky. To achieve this consistency, cook the rice and water at a ratio of 1:1 in the pressure cooker on the highest pressure cooking setting for 10 minutes.
- In Europe, many people prefer rice to be looser. To this end, pressure cook 8 oz (250 g) long-grain rice with 1 tsp salt and 1¼ cups (300 ml) water for 5 minutes on the highest pressure setting.

COOKING SPICED RICE IN A PRESSURE COOKER

1. Heat 1 tbsp ghee in a pressure cooker, add 1 stick of cinnamon, 3 cloves and 4 cardamom pods and sauté for 1–2 min, stirring regularly, until the spices become fragrant.

2. Peel and chop 1 clove of garlic and 2 cm ginger, add to the pot together with 10 oz (300 g) basmati rice plus 1 cup + 3 tbsp (300 ml) water. Cook everything on the highest setting for 3 minutes, then allow to cool for 10 minutes.

PRACTICAL INFORMATION » BASIC PREPARATION

Pasta and cereals
The basis for one-pots and bowls

Pasta can be pressure cooked with outstanding results and benefits from being cooked in a flavorsome environment when making one-pot dishes. The same also applies to cereals.

Pasta and cereals absorb water and soften when cooking. As the starch grains swell, their texture changes, including when cooked using pressure. When making these types of food, the pressure cooker must be filled only to the halfway mark.

Pasta and spaetzle are ideal for one-pot dishes with tomato sauce or cheese and sit steaming on the table after just a few minutes. Smaller amounts of short pasta are ideal for multi-level cooking in inserts.

PRESSURE COOKING PASTA

A pressure cooker is a great way to cook dried pasta made from durum wheat semolina, which is particularly popular in the south of Italy. Using conventional methods, orecchiette and calamarata take at least 12–15 minutes to cook, as does Sardinian fregula: depending on the manufacturer, when conventionally boiled, these little balls of semolina dough take up to 20 minutes to cook. Pressure cooking, on the other hand, takes just 8–10 minutes. A further advantage: when making a pasta sauce (e.g., Bolognese), the steam can simply be released from the pressure cooker 5 minutes before the end of the cooking time. The pasta (and some liquid if necessary) can be mixed in and thus absorb additional flavor while cooking.

Smaller amounts of pasta with the required amount of salted water can also be successfully cooked in an insert at the same time as other items in the pressure cooker.

PREPARATION TIPS

- When pressure cooked, pasta requires sufficient cooking liquid (usually at a ratio of 1:2) and salt. As a general rule of thumb, this means ¾ cup + 2 tbsp to 1 cup (200 to 250 ml) liquid per 3.3 oz (100 g) of pasta.
- Note the cooking time shown on the packaging. When pressure cooked on the highest setting, this is halved (+/-1 minute) for durum wheat pasta and reduced to about a third for faster-cooking egg pasta.

Ideal as a basis for bowls and salads: cereals and pseudo-cereals (e.g., quinoa, amaranth and buckwheat) do not need to be soaked and are ready in minutes.

Always add sufficient liquid when pressure cooking pasta and cereals as they absorb water and swell while cooking. They can also be multilevel cooked in the unperforated insert providing the maximum fill level is observed.

Buckwheat: a pseudo-cereal with a nutty flavor that can be intensified by toasting it in a little fat prior to pressure cooking.

Millet: the fine-grained, gluten-free cereal has a slightly nutty flavor and can be pressure cooked in an instant.

- When pressure cooked, pasta often has a cooking time of 4–5 minutes.
- Short pasta (orzo, ditali, orecchiette) is ideal for directly cooking in a sauce.
- Long pasta (spaghetti, fettucine) should be snapped in half or broken into short lengths before being pressure cooked.

PRESSURE COOKING CEREALS

Cereals and pseudo-cereals such as quinoa provide important nutrients and fiber. Their mild flavor and pleasantly granular texture also enable their versatile use. For example, they enrich salads (bulgur, quinoa, couscous, wheat, spelt) or can be used like rice (e.g., for risotto and paella). Thanks to their very short cooking times, they are done in 1–9 minutes. Once the steam has been released from the pressure cooker and it has been opened, fluff the grains with a fork to prevent them from clumping together. Do not allow fast-cooking varieties to continue to swell after the end of the cooking time.

PREPARATION TIPS

- Before cooking, place the cereals in a sieve, rinse with cold water and allow to strain.
- When pressure cooking types of cereals that swell, always add sufficient salted water or stock. About 2 to 2.5 times the volume of liquid is usually required.
- On the highest setting, cereals usually take 8–9 minutes to cook.
- The cooking time is shorter for millet (2–3 minutes) and buckwheat (4–5 minutes).
- Quinoa or precooked cereals such as bulgur (cracked durum wheat) and soft wheat cook in 1–2 minutes.
- The cooking time reference tables at the end of the book provide good guidance.

PRACTICAL INFORMATION » BASIC PREPARATION

Side dishes and baby food
cooked with and without pressure

Pressure cookers enable popular sides such as potatoes, loose or stuffed dumplings, dim sum or purées to be prepared in a time – and energy-saving manner, plus they allow baby food to be gently cooked.

When using pressure to cook side dishes and baby food, always add the necessary minimum amount of liquid and observe the maximum fill level, especially when multilevel cooking with inserts.

Potatoes are a much-loved side dish and contain valuable vitamins and minerals. These are preserved far better with pressure cooking than with conventional methods as the tubers are simply surrounded by steam rather than sitting in the cooking water. Instead of being washed away, almost 100% of the potatoes' original content of water-soluble minerals such as iron and calcium are retained.

COOKING POTATOES

Cooking potatoes in a pressure cooker is extremely simple.

Cooking unpeeled potatoes: wash the potatoes and place them unpeeled directly in the pot together with the necessary minimum amount of liquid (see right). Alternatively, place them in the perforated insert and position this on the tripod in the pressure cooker. It is important not to release the steam too quickly as this can cause the potatoes and their skin to burst.

Cooking peeled potatoes: peel and wash the potatoes, cut into equal-sized pieces, place in the perforated insert and season with salt. Fill the pot with the minimum amount of water, put the insert on the tripod and cook the potatoes on the highest setting for 6–8 minutes.

COOKING DUMPLINGS

Potatoes also taste great in the form of dumplings. In the perforated insert over the minimum amount of liquid, they cook in approx. 5 minutes. Dumplings made of raw potato usually take 1–3 minutes longer.

Pressure cooking bread dumplings: using damp hands, shape the bread mixture into equal-sized dumplings and place them in the perforated insert. Fill the pressure cooker with the minimum amount of water and place the insert on the tripod over the water in the pot. Cook the dumplings either on the highest setting for approx. 5 minutes or with slightly less pressure on setting 2 (Vitaquick®: 1st ring) for 12–15 minutes. Smaller dumplings cook in just 10–12 minutes.

COOKING POLENTA

Pressure cookers can also be used to cook polenta. To this end, add the polenta and water to the pressure cooker at a ratio of 1:4, stir well, season with salt and pressure cook on the highest pressure setting. Depending on whether precooked instant polenta or regular polenta is used, this takes as little as 1–2 minutes or up to 10 minutes. Set the pot aside, shake it gently and slowly release the steam.

COOKING DUMPLINGS AND DIM SUM

In Asia, stuffed dumplings are extremely popular when celebrating various occasions and at different times of day. They are usually cooked in the perforated insert. Dumplings made from yeast dough can withstand a little pressure and can

Peeled potatoes are a much-valued side for fish, meat or cabbage dishes and extremely easy to cook. One important consideration is that the potatoes should be cut into equal-sized pieces so that all of these are ready at the same time. The cooking time can vary slightly depending on the age, potato variety and size of the pieces.

be cooked in 12–14 minutes on the lowest pressure cooking setting. Larger yeast dumplings (baozi) and stuffed dumplings (gyoza, dim sum) are better steam cooked without pressure (12–20 minutes).

MAKING BABY FOOD

Babies need baby food from 5–6 months of age. Using pressure to make this is highly recommended from a nutritional perspective as the baby food then contains more nutrients, and the natural taste of foods (carrots, potatoes, etc.) is more pronounced. This makes it possible to deliberately avoid adding salt or sugar.

Polenta: mix polenta with water and salt and then cook on the highest setting for 1–2 minutes (instant polenta) or 6–10 minutes (regular polenta).

Unpeeled potatoes: add unpeeled potatoes to the pressure cooker with the minimum amount of liquid and cook on the highest setting for 8–12 minutes. Release the steam slowly.

Potato dumplings: place in the perforated insert and either cook on the highest pressure setting for approx. 5 minutes or steam without pressure for 12–15 minutes.

Sweets and desserts from the pressure cooker

Not only can pressure be used to cook hearty meals, but also sweet dishes such as rice pudding, pastries, proper puddings, delicious custard dishes and fine clafoutis. Even cheesecakes, brownies and cakes are possible.

Ripe solid fruits such as peaches, nectarines or pears can be quickly cooked in a pressure cooker with wine or apple juice and spices.

A surprising number of sweet dishes and/or popular classic desserts such as crème brûlée or crème caramel can be made in a pressure cooker with fantastic results and an astonishingly smooth and even consistency. In principle, there is no difference between pressure cooking sweet dishes and hearty meals. The prescribed minimum amount of fluid and maximum fill level still have to be observed, although a few other things also need to be considered.

RICE PUDDING AND FRUIT

Rice pudding is extremely easy to make and can be varied in many ways. Essentially, short-grain rice and liquid (usually a mixture of milk and water) are added to the pressure cooker or unperforated insert at a ratio of 1:6 together with any other ingredients for adding flavor. Everything is then cooked for approx. 15 minutes at low pressure (Vitavit® and Vitaquick®: setting 1).

Firm fruits (for example, tree fruits like quinces, apples and pears or stone fruits such as peaches or nectarines) are particularly ideal for cooking in a pressure cooker. They retain their shape when briefly cooked (5–6 minutes) on the lowest pressure setting in flavorsome liquid (white wine, red wine, juice).

Soft fruit varieties, berries with a high water content and overripe fruit are not suitable for pressure cooking as they can disintegrate into a viscous pulp that tends to bubble and spatter and can therefore impair the pressure cooker's safety features (see the manufacturer's specifications).

SWEET DUMPLINGS

Sweet dumplings made from quark, potato or yeast dough are cooked in an insert using low pressure (Vitavit® and Vitaquick®: setting 1). The cooking time depends on the diameter but is usually 10–15 minutes. In the Vitavit®, yeast dumplings (for example, filled with plum jam), can also be pressure-free steamed in approx. 20 minutes. To stop them from sticking, the insert should be thoroughly brushed with melted butter before use.

PUDDINGS AND CUSTARD DISHES

Sweet cake mixtures that contain egg benefit from being cooked in a pressure cooker. Proper puddings and egg-based custard desserts cook particularly evenly under low pressure (Vitavit® and Vitaquick®: setting 1). To this end, they are either placed in the unperforated insert (which should be thoroughly greased with butter – see right) or in suitable, smaller molds. To give them enough stability for them to be sliced once cooked, 1 heaping tsp agar-agar is added to the mixture. In an insert, puddings take 15–20 minutes and custard desserts approx. 20 minutes to cook.

CLAFOUTIS AND CAKES

Doughs and mixtures can withstand a little more pressure and are usually cooked in a mold on a medium setting (Vitavit®: setting 2, Vitaquick®: 1st ring) for approx. 25 minutes. A suitable unperforated insert, greased with butter as described below, is an ideal choice for this. If custard desserts, puddings or cakes are cooked without pressure, the insert also has to be well greased or sprayed with a baking release spray. A little condensation usually drips onto the surface when cooking and releasing steam. Prior to serving, the finished clafoutis or cake should therefore be dusted with confectioners' (icing) sugar or cocoa powder or topped with fruit, fruit sauce or jam.

PREPARATION TIPS

- When 'baking,' thoroughly grease the unperforated insert with melted butter, a neutral vegetable oil or baking release spray.
- Dust the surface of the finished clafoutis or cake with confectioners' (icing) sugar. Alternatively, top with jam or fruit compote.

Greasing the unperforated insert: to prevent custard desserts and doughs from sticking, thoroughly brush melted butter all over the base and sides of the insert prior to filling it and dust with flour if necessary.

The following basic rules also apply when 'baking' cake mixtures in the pressure cooker: always add the minimum amount of liquid, place the insert on the tripod and never exceed the maximum fill level.

Flavorsome stock
made quickly and easily

They are the basis for soups and one-pot meals or can be used to infuse paella, pilaf and risotto or to cook braised dishes: homemade stock improves the taste of many meals.

TIP: freeze stock in small 1 to 1¼ cups (250 to 300 ml) portions so you always have easy access to the minimum amount of liquid required.

Even instant or jarred stock can be used to deglaze base ingredients such as onions, garlic, ginger and chile pepper or well-browned meat. However, soups and sauces, curries and braised dishes taste even better when made with homemade stock. This is easy to make and no problem for pressure cookers: it takes little time to prepare the food, which is simply added to the pot directly with water and a few herbs and spices. Fifteen to 30 minutes later, everything is ready. The only important thing to ensure is that the pressure cooker is big enough, as the usual basic rule applies: the maximum fill level must not be exceeded. Pressure cookers with a capacity of between 6 and 10 liters are therefore the best choice when making stock.

VEGETABLE STOCK

2 Spanish onions | 1 garlic clove | 10 oz (300 g) carrots | 3.3 oz (100 g) broccoli stalks | 7 oz (200 g) celery | 8 oz (250 g) leek | 5 oz (150 g) zucchini | 4 tsp (20 g) butter | ⅔ cup (150 ml) dry white wine | 1 sprig of thyme | 1 sprig of rosemary | 1 bay leaf | 1 browned onion (see p. 103) | salt | 10 white peppercorns | 1 clove | freshly ground pepper

1. Peel the Spanish onions and garlic and cut the onions into rings. Wash and trim or peel the rest of the vegetables and cut them all into ½- to ¾-inch (1 to 2 cm) pieces or slices.
2. Melt the butter in the pressure cooker and sauté the onions until translucent. Add and briefly sauté the remaining vegetables, stirring regularly, then deglaze with white wine and pour in 8 cups (2 L) water. Add the garlic, herbs, browned onion, 1 pinch of salt, peppercorns and clove. Seal the pot and cook the stock on setting 3 (cooking indicator: 2nd ring) for 10–15 minutes.
3. Slowly release the steam and open the pot. Strain the stock (see p. 98) and reduce it uncovered to approx. 6 cups (1.5 L). Season to taste with salt and pepper.

POULTRY STOCK

1 stewing hen | 1 garlic clove | 1 carrot | ½ leek | 1 stalk of celery | ½ browned onion (see p. 103) | 1 sprig of thyme | 1 bay leaf | 1 clove | salt

1. Remove any visible fat from the chicken. Re-rinse the stewing hen, place it in a large pressure cooker (6–8 L) and cover it with 8 to 12 cups (2 to 3 L) water. Peel the garlic and carrot, wash and trim the leek and celery and cut everything into ½- to ¾-inch (1 to 2 cm) pieces. Add the vegetables and garlic to the pot with the other ingredients and 1 pinch of salt.
2. Seal the pressure cooker and cook the stock on setting 3 (cooking indicator: 2nd ring) for 30–40 minutes. Slowly release the steam from the pressure cooker and open the lid. Remove the stewing hen and make use of it elsewhere. Strain the stock through a sieve (see p. 98), remove the fat (see pp. 98–9) and season to taste.

LIGHT BEEF STOCK

2 lbs 7 oz (1.2 kg) beef bones (or beef ribs), in small pieces | 4 lbs (2 kg) short ribs | 1–2 tbsp sea salt | 4 oz (125 g) celeriac | 2 finger-thick carrots | 1 parsnip | 1 celery heart | 3.3 oz (100 g) leek | 1 sprig of lovage | 5 sprigs of parsley | 5 sprigs of thyme | 1 browned onion (see p. 103)

1. Rinse and blanch the bones and short ribs as shown in step 1 below. Rinse the bones and meat. Clean the pressure cooker, then follow the instructions in step 2.

2. Wash the vegetables and herbs. Peel or trim the vegetables, tie together with the herbs to form a bouquet and then follow the instructions in step 3.

HOW TO MAKE LIGHT BEEF STOCK (MEAT STOCK)

1. Bring plenty of water to the boil in the pressure cooker (or another pot), add the bones, meat and 2 pinches of salt, cook uncovered for 5 minutes, then strain.

2. Add the bones and short ribs to the pot, pour in 12 cups (3 L) water (note the maximum volume mark) and season with salt. Bring to the boil and skim several times.

3. Add the bouquet garni and the browned onion. Seal the pot, set the pressure regulator to setting 3 (cooking indicator: 2nd ring) for 30–40 minutes, then strain (see p. 98).

Stock: straining, removing the fat and clarifying

Homemade stock makes the ideal tasty basis for soups, stews and braised dishes made in a pressure cooker. The following tricks help to achieve particularly good results.

Pressure cooking always requires a minimum amount of liquid. Stock, often in combination with wine or tomatoes, is ideal for this as it already provides a great deal of flavor and taste. This also benefits potatoes, pasta or rice. If bones, carcasses, meat and vegetables are cooked with water using pressure, proteins dissolve and tarnish the result. This is irrelevant with regard to braised dishes with a dark sauce. If a clear stock is desired, however, the food should be blanched first (see pp. 102–3).

STRAINING STOCK

Another very simple way of separating liquids and solids is to strain them after cooking (see left). If the sieve is lined with a cloth when doing this, many constituent substances that can make the stock cloudy can also be filtered out.

STRAINING OFF THE FAT AND CLARIFYING THE STOCK

Stewing hens and stewing meat have a great deal of flavor but also contain a lot of fat, which dissolves during the cooking process. There are various ways in which this can be subsequently removed from stock (see right and p. 99, top). All of these are based on the principle that fat is lighter than water and always settles on the top.

If a very clear stock is desired, it can be clarified after cooking as shown in steps 1–6 on the right. As a vegetarian alternative, add 1 egg white to the pot per 4 cups (1 L) of stock, heat the contents slowly, stirring regularly, skim the liquid several times and then strain the stock through a cloth.

Tip: for a clear, vegan stock, allow the liquid to strain through a Superbag (filter bag, nut milk bag) to remove the finest suspended particles.

MAKING DARK STOCK

Stock (e.g., veal or game, see p. 293) is particularly flavorsome when the bones and vegetables are placed in a roaster, drizzled with a little oil and roasted in the oven at 350°F to 400°F (180°C to 200°C) for 20–30 minutes prior to their use. Next, drain off the fat, transfer everything to the pressure cooker and make the stock as described.

Straining stock: line a sieve with a clean tea towel or straining cloth and pour in the contents of the pot.

For clear stock: do not press the contents through the sieve or straining cloth; instead, allow the liquid to slowly run through on its own.

Straining the fat off stock when cold: allow the stock to cool in the pot or a glass jar, then simply use a spoon to remove the fat.

Straining the fat off stock when hot: use a ladle or flat spoon to carefully remove the liquid fat from the surface.

... using paper towels: lightly touch the stock with a piece of paper towel to absorb the fat from the surface.

... using a fat separator: the fat will settle on the top after a few minutes and the stock can be carefully poured out.

CLARIFYING STOCK WITH MEAT AND EGG WHITE

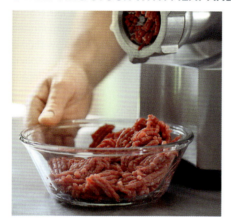

1. To clarify approx. 6 cups (1.5 L) stock, pass 11.6 oz (350 g) clarifying meat (e.g., beef shank) through the coarse disk of a meat grinder.

2. Put the clarifying meat into the pressure cooker together with 1–2 handfuls of ice cubes. Add 3 egg whites and mix well.

3. Pour in approx. 6 cups (1.5 L) stock with the fat strained off (e.g., veal or beef stock) and season with 1 pinch of salt and 1 tsp peppercorns.

4. Heat everything in the uncovered pot, using a spatula to constantly stir the base of the pot to prevent the egg white from sticking.

5. Once brought to the boil and the egg white is sufficiently bonded, stop stirring and simmer uncovered for approx. 30 minutes.

6. Set everything aside, let rest for 10 minutes, lift off the solidified egg white and strain the stock in portions through a cloth.

Reducing liquids
Thickening and perfecting sauces

Unlike with a normal pot, no steam can escape when cooking using pressure so cooking juices remain thinner than with conventional braising. With a few tricks, though, these are quick and easy to turn into a deliciously creamy sauce.

Enhancing the flavors: reducing flavorsome liquids (cooking juices) in an uncovered pot lowers the amount of water contained and creates the ideal basis for a good sauce.

The cooking juices that remain on the base of the pot once the steam has been released and the lid has been opened are often ideal as a basis for sauces.

REDUCING THE COOKING JUICES

To give the sauce the desired consistency, the first step is to reduce the water content. Depending on the dish, the vegetables and/or meat are removed from the pot and briefly kept warm (e.g., in an oven at 170°F/80°C). If the pot also contains bones from meat or fish, the stock should first be passed through a sieve to remove these from the liquid and the pressure cooker should be cleaned. Return the collected liquid to the pressure cooker (or a casserole dish) and reduce by one-third or half uncovered(!) over a high heat. The water evaporates during reduction, leaving a flavorsome liquid, which can either be thickened or further refined with a little cream or butter.

THICKENING THE LIQUID

There are also several other ways to improve the consistency of cooking

Cornstarch, flour or a grated potato are all viable options for thickening the cooking juices created when pressure cooking. A little cream rounds off the sauces, and a few cubes of cold butter rapidly mixed in at the end improve the taste and consistency.

juices: add a grated, starchy potato or a little mashed potato for 10–15 minutes during the reduction process and then finely blend the sauce. An aromatic purée of soft-cooked root vegetables, onions and a little garlic is also suitable for thickening sauces, but is not as effective as flour or cornstarch.

THICKENING SAUCES WITH FLOUR AND CORNSTARCH

Sauces can also obtain a good texture when thickened with flour or cornstarch. However, sauces thickened with flour need to simmer for 15–20 minutes to get rid of the floury taste. To thicken reduced cooking juices that should not be cooked for much longer, it is best to stir in a little cold starch, as described on the bottom right.

REFINING AND PERFECTING SAUCES

Once almost ready, the reduction can be improved by adding single or double cream. Both thicken sauces easily and give them a creamy consistency. Butter is also a great choice for refining sauces: either in the form of a beurre manié (soft butter mixed with flour at a ratio of 1:1), after which the sauce needs to simmer for a while, or by whisking in a few little ice-cold cubes of butter, after which the sauce can be instantly served.

Thickening with starch: stir 1–2 tsp starch into a little (2–3 tbsp) cold water until smooth, pour into the hot liquid and simmer for another 2–3 minutes, stirring regularly.

Precooking food
to enhance flavor

Prior to cooking using pressure, it is sometimes useful to briefly blanch food, toast individual ingredients such as spices or sear meat in order to enhance the flavor.

Cooking in a pressure cooker basically requires the addition of a minimum amount of liquid. This often means the use of stock, which is extremely easy to make in the pressure cooker itself (see pp. 96–7). If bones and meat are placed in the pot with the other ingredients, protein and other particles dissolve when these are heated and rise to the top in the form of a brownish foam, which can make the stock cloudy. Although this does not impair the taste, a clear stock is sometimes desired. In the case of light-colored rice dishes such as risotto, the particles look unappetizing. If it needs to be completely clear, stock can naturally be clarified with egg white (see p. 99) but this takes time and requires more ingredients. A quicker and easier way to make clear stock or soup is to blanch protein-rich ingredients such as bones, meat or green beans in boiling water beforehand.

BLANCHING PROTEIN-RICH INGREDIENTS

Blanching means briefly immersing food in boiling water, as described in the steps below. During this process, proteins are denatured on the surface so that they can no longer make the stock cloudy. Important: when blanching items in a pressure cooker, always thoroughly clean this af-

1. Blanching bones: bring plenty of water to a boil in the pressure cooker or a large pot) and add the bones. Return to a boil and blanch the bones uncovered for 5 minutes.

2. Repeatedly skim off the foam that rises to the surface. Strain the bones using a colander or remove them with a slotted spoon, rinse well under cold running water and let strain.

Blanching green beans: blanch trimmed, washed beans in the uncovered pot for 2–3 minutes. Remove with a slotted spoon and immerse in iced water to stop the cooking process.

Briefly toasting spices intensifies their flavor. This is a trick that is used in many traditional Asian dishes, such as when making spice pastes for curries.

terwards, taking special care to ensure that all substances stuck to the rim that could cloud the stock are removed. Thoroughly dry the pot and then continue as per the instructions in the relevant recipe.

TOASTING SPICES

Gently heating spices such as coriander, cumin, cloves, mustard seeds or star anise releases the essential oils contained, further enhancing and strengthening their flavors. In most cases, these flavor-enhancing ingredients are toasted in no or little fat (vegetable oil, ghee or clarified butter) until they become fragrant. They are then left to cool slightly before being crushed in a mortar or spice grinder. Important: do not toast spices for too long or over too high a heat as they burn quickly and then become bitter.

BROWNING ONIONS

Another way of increasing the depth of flavor of stock or soups while also giving them a beautiful color is to add a browned onion or shallot while making them. Doing so is easy: cut off the onion's root, peel off the skin and slice the bulb in half. Place both halves cut-side-down in a frying pan or pressure cooker and toast over a medium heat without fat, as shown on the right. Add the browned onion halves to a pressure cooker with the remaining ingredients and continue to follow the instructions in the relevant recipe.

SEARING MEAT

Pressure cooking is possible only with sufficient liquid, which prevents ingredients from being browned as they cook. However, it is still easy to give braised dishes the much-loved roasted undertones that develop when searing meat, game or poultry. Simply sear the ingredients in the base of the pressure cooker before adding the liquid. This preserves all of the roasted undertones for a fabulous taste.

Toasting onions: place the halved onion cut-side-down in a hot pot (pressure cooker with a smooth base or even a frying pan) and slowly toast without fat until golden to dark brown.

Searing meat: add a little frying oil or clarified butter to the pressure cooker and sear smaller pieces of meat for goulash or ragouts until well-browned all over.

Seasoning and flavoring
to taste

A pinch of salt here, a few herbs there – as the phrase infers, seasoning to taste is primarily a matter of (personal) taste. With a little practice, it is also something that is very easy providing you follow a few basic principles.

Do not be conservative with salt, but do not be too liberal either. When pressure cooking soups, stews and stock, 1–2 pinches are enough to start with. Vegetables, fish and smaller cuts of meat are seasoned with fine salt and have a few flakes of fleur de sel added as a finishing touch.

The higher pressure used when pressure cooking intensifies the flavor of spices and better preserves the ingredients' natural taste. As such, the amounts of herbs and spices that need to be added before cooking may vary slightly compared to those used in 'conventional' cooking. For example, fresh bay leaves develop a very pronounced flavor and can quickly dominate a dish and cover up other flavor nuances. The same applies to cumin and smoked spices. When used correctly, however, they perfectly round off dishes. As such, it is best to start by adding spices and dried herbs conservatively and then season the food to taste once it is cooked. It is always easier to add a little more salt, pepper or chili powder to a dish than it is to save an over-seasoned or overly spicy one.

USING SALT

Sea salt or rock salt? Pink or black? Fine or coarse? The range of options is huge but few varieties are actually suitable for seasoning and flavoring purposes. Finely ground and (preferably) unrefined salt without anticaking agent or other additives is ideal for seasoning as it dissolves quickly and is easy to distribute. Large cuts of meat should ideally be rubbed with coarse sea salt 30–45 minutes before they are seared. This gives the salt time to absorb slightly, which is beneficial in view of the shorter cooking times in a pressure cooker. Fish, on the other hand, needs little salt before cooking. Sea salt flakes containing minerals are the best choice as a finishing touch for cooked dishes as their special texture adds both taste and crunch.

Tip: add plenty of salt to water for blanching food (approx. 2 tsp per 4 cups/1 L) as this prevents minerals from leaching out of vegetables or meat.

PERFECT SEASONING

Spices can have a milder or more pronounced taste depending on their origin

Herbs, spices and chiles add flavor to dishes. Most of the seasoning ingredients used in this book are available from supermarkets. The rest can be found in Asian or Turkish food stores or online.

and storage time. It is therefore difficult or impossible to provide specific information in this regard. The amounts specified in the recipes are therefore more for guidance than a must. Personal preferences also come into play. For example, those who do not like cumin and fresh cilantro should reduce the quantity or simply leave them out entirely – and instead add their own favorite herbs or spices.

FINISHING TOUCHES FOR DISHES

- A pinch of nutmeg gives a nutty taste to vegetables and sauces.
- Mild pepper flakes, sweet paprika, a little sugar or honey adds pleasant finishing touches to dishes.
- Lemongrass and lime leaves should be cooked with the other ingredients. They add a touch of freshness to Asian dishes.
- Season Asian dishes with ponzu (citrus-flavored soy sauce) or fish sauce instead of salt.
- If smoked pepper flakes are unavailable, they can be substituted with mild chili flakes and 1 pinch of smoked salt. Don't be afraid to improvise!

FLAVORING WITH FRESH HERBS

Mediterranean herbs such as rosemary, thyme, sage or bay leaves are robust and release their flavor when cooked. Most other herbs have thinner leaves and are added only at the end of the cooking process. To do this, wash parsley, chives, basil or cilantro and shake them dry. Only chop or cut up the leaves just before adding them, to prevent the essential oils and other constituent substances from evaporating prematurely. In the case of young herbs (parsley, thyme) or delicate-leafed varieties (cilantro), the stems can also be used.

TIP: it is best to buy spices in small quantities and store them in an airtight container away from the light. Ground spices last for up to 6 months while whole spices retain their flavor for about a year.

PRACTICAL INFORMATION >> TIPS & TRICKS   **105**

Frequently asked questions (FAQs):

What can a pressure cooker do that a normal pot cannot?

Use pressure to cook food faster and particularly gently. Benefits: shorter cooking times (by up to 70%), energy savings of up to 50% and a higher content of vital substances (see pp. 16–17 + 73 onward).

How does pressure cooking work?

The steam produced when preheating the pressure cooker displaces the atmospheric oxygen. The valves close, pressure builds up and the boiling temperature rises to up to 243°F (117°C) (see p. 13 onward).

How safe are pressure cookers?

Fissler pressure cookers are safe when used correctly. This is ensured by safety features with patented technology (see pp. 36–7) and the highest-quality standards 'Made in Germany.'

For what burner types is my pressure cooker suitable?

Modern Fissler pressure cookers with a CookStar® (Vitavit® Premium) or Superthermic (Vitaquick® Premium) base are suitable for all burner types, including induction.

For what should the different cooking settings be used?

The gentle cooking setting (1) is suitable for fish and leafy vegetables, cooking setting 2 (Vitavit®) is ideal for vegetables, and the quick cooking setting (Vitavit®: 3/Vitaquick®: 2nd ring) is suitable for meat and stews (see pp. 54–5).

What is special about the traffic light indicator?

The traffic light indicator makes it possible to optimally monitor the cooking process: it shows when the selected cooking setting has been reached and when the heat should be reduced or increased (see p. 62 onward).

How do I know how long to cook my ingredients for?

The Fissler cooking time reference tables provide you with guidance. As a rule of thumb, conventional cooking times should be reduced by up to two-thirds when pressure cooking on setting 3 (Vitaquick®: 2nd ring) (see pp. 54–5 + p. 294 onward).

When should I start measuring the cooking time?

The specified cooking time begins once the cooking setting has been reached – i.e., when the green ring is visible on the Vitavit® Premium or the appropriate white ring is visible on the Vitaquick® (see p. 61 onward).

What is the purpose of the inserts?

Suitable perforated and unperforated inserts with spacers (tripods) make it possible to gently cook dishes with and without pressure, including on multiple levels one above the other (see pp. 46–7, p. 57 + p. 66 onward).

What cannot be placed in a pressure cooker?

Apple sauce, compotes and thick sauces should not be made in pressure cookers as steam bubbles can form, which spray out when the lid is opened (see p. 60 onward). Refer to the manufacturer's instructions in this regard.

How should I clean my pressure cooker?

The pot and lid (without the pressure regulator/cooking indicator, handle and sealing ring) are dishwasher safe. The cooking valve, lid handle and sealing ring must be washed by hand (see pp. 70–1).

Do I need to service my pressure cooker, and if so, how often?

Wear parts such as the sealing ring and elastomer parts must be replaced with Fissler original spare parts after a maximum of 400 cooking processes or two years, whichever comes first (see p. 36 onward + pp. 70–1).

My pressure cooker is no longer shiny – what can I do?

This is usually caused by limescale or other marks that can develop during use. These can be easily removed using Fissler stainless steel care products (see p. 71).

My pressure cooker no longer works properly – what can I do?

The user instructions for the Fissler pressure cooker provide extensive information and guidance on how to correctly use the device. If you still require further assistance, please contact Fissler customer service.

How do the Vita® models differ?

The Vitavit® Premium fulfills every need with four cooking settings, including a pressure-free steaming setting. The Vitaquick® Premium has two cooking settings to provide an introduction to pressure cooking.

Where can I buy spare parts for my pressure cooker?

All original spare parts are available in the Fissler online shop, Fissler stores, leading specialist stores and specialist areas in department stores.

The golden rules of pressure cooking

When using a pressure cooker, both the **minimum amount of liquid** and the **maximum fill level** must be observed. The maximum volume mark must be particularly heeded in the case of **food that expands when cooking**. Here, the **fill level should not exceed the halfway mark**.
The pressure cooker lid features several safety mechanisms that must not be blocked, touched, covered or clogged. As such, food in the pressure cooker should never be covered with tinfoil or baking paper as these could come loose during the cooking process. Some foods tend to foam or spatter and can potentially affect the safety features.

These are therefore not suitable for cooking in a pressure cooker. Any accessories used (e.g., baking tins), must be suitable for use in a pressure cooker. The relevant manufacturer's specifications must be observed.

The pressure cooker must be regularly serviced and maintained using the manufacturer's **original spare parts** only.

Always observe the manufacturer's user instructions. These contain further important information about the safe use of the pressure cooker.

Recipes for pressure cookers

Pressure cooking is not only healthy but also saves time and energy. Many dishes can be whipped up and served in a matter of minutes. The recipe ideas in the following chapters show that The Healthy Cooker® can do far more than just perfectly cook potatoes and stews. They reflect the full diversity of pressure cooking, from spicy to sweet, from simple to refined.

Quick & easy

Much-loved dishes like paella and risotto take little more than 5 minutes to cook in a pressure cooker – without having to stir them – and can be varied in a multitude of ways, as the following chapter shows. The same applies to Bolognese sauce, whether as a classic or vegan version, or hot and fiery chiles both 'con' and 'sin' carne. Newcomers to the world of pressure cooking are certain to find several new favorite dishes.

COOKING LEVEL VITAVIT®

COOKING LEVEL VITAQUICK®

COOKING TIME

Herby soups with lentils & peas

MAKES: 4 PORTIONS   **PREP TIME:** 15–20 MIN.

Red lentil soup (1)

1 onion | 1 garlic clove | 1½ cups (300 g) red lentils | 2 tbsp olive oil | 1 cup + 2 tbsp (150 g) diced carrots | 1 cup + 2 tbsp (150 g) peeled diced potatoes | 2 tsp tomato purée | 1 good pinch each of sweet paprika, turmeric, ground cumin, pepper and chili flakes | 1 tsp each of chopped thyme and rosemary | salt | 6 tbsp + 2 tsp (100 ml) heavy or whipping (35%) cream | lemon juice | mint leaves

1. Peel and finely dice the onion and garlic. Rinse the red lentils and let strain.
2. Heat the oil in the pressure cooker and sauté the onion until translucent. Add the carrots, potatoes and garlic and cook briefly.
3. Stir in the tomato purée, lentils, spices and half of the herbs and cook for 1–2 minutes. Pour in 6 cups (1.5 L) water and seal the pressure cooker. Turn the pressure regulator to setting 3, heat the pot on the highest setting and, once the green ring (cooking indicator: 2nd ring) appears, cook for 12–15 minutes.
4. Remove the pot from the heat, release the steam and open the lid. Remove one-third of the soup for the topping and finely blend the rest. Add the topping back in and stir in 1 tsp salt and the cream. Briefly reheat everything in the uncovered pressure cooker and season to taste.
5. Spoon the lentil soup onto deep plates, grind with pepper, sprinkle with the remaining herbs and serve garnished with mint leaves.

Vegan green pea and coconut soup (2)

4 cups (600 g) frozen peas | 1 large onion | 1 garlic clove | ½ chile pepper | 2 green bell peppers | 1–2 tbsp olive oil | salt | pepper | 4 cups (1 L) vegetable stock | 1 cup (250 ml) coconut milk | 1⅔ cups (80 g) finely chopped flat-leaf parsley | 1–2 tbsp lemon juice | 1 handful of pea sprouts

1. Allow the peas to thaw for 5 minutes. Peel and finely dice the onion and garlic. Wash, trim and chop the chile pepper. Wash and trim the green peppers, then cut into strips.
2. Heat the oil in the pressure cooker and sauté the onion until it starts to brown. Add the green pepper, chile and garlic and cook briefly. Season with salt and pepper and cook for 3–4 minutes, stirring regularly, then pour in the stock. Seal the pot, set the pressure regulator to setting 3 and heat on the highest setting. Cook the soup for 12–15 minutes from the time the green ring (cooking indicator: 2nd ring) appears.
3. Release the steam from the pot and open the lid. Add the coconut milk, chopped parsley and peas. Return to the boil and simmer for another 2–3 minutes in the uncovered pressure cooker.
4. Blend the soup, season to taste with lemon juice, divide between four deep plates, grind with pepper and serve garnished with pea sprouts.

(1)

Mixed vegetables
cooked with and without pressure

MAKES: 4 PORTIONS **PREP TIME:** 15 MIN.

COOKING LEVEL VITAVIT® COOKING TIME 5

Spiralized zucchini with chicken (1)

2 zucchini | 8 oz (250 g) boneless skinless chicken breast | 1 red chile pepper | 2 green onions | 2–3 firm apricots, as desired | salt | pepper | 1 tbsp curry powder | 2 tbsp ponzu (or soy sauce) | 2 tbsp vegetable oil | 2 tsp mirin (or sherry or white wine) | 2–3 tbsp toasted sesame seeds

1. Wash and trim the zucchini, then cut into long strips (noodles) with a spiralizer. Pat the chicken dry and cut into approx. ¾-inch (2 cm) cubes. Wash and trim the chile pepper and green onions. Finely dice the chile pepper and cut the green onions diagonally into rings. Set the green and white portions aside separately. Quarter and pit the apricots.
2. Season the spiralized zucchini with salt and pepper. Season the chicken with curry powder, salt, pepper and ponzu.
3. Heat the oil in the pressure cooker, sear the chicken briefly, then remove it. Briefly sear the diced chile and white portion of green onions in the remaining oil, then deglaze with the mirin.
4. Add the zucchini and apricots. Seal the Vitavit® pressure cooker, set the pressure regulator to the steam symbol (steaming setting) and steam for approx. 5 minutes. Season the zucchini, arrange on plates, garnish with the remaining green onions and sesame seeds and serve.

COOKING LEVEL VITAVIT® COOKING LEVEL VITAQUICK® COOKING TIME 1

Asian squash stew (2)

1 lb (500 g) winter squash, such as butternut | 1 red onion | 2 green onions | 2⅔ oz (80 g) pork back fat (lard) | 7 oz (200 g) ground beef | 2–3 tbsp soy sauce | ¼ cup (60 ml) mirin (or sherry or white wine) | 1 tbsp cornstarch | salt | pepper | ¾ cup (40 g) chopped fresh cilantro leaves and stems | 1–2 tsp liquid honey

1. Peel, wash and seed the squash, then cut the flesh into approx. ¾-inch (2 cm) cubes. Peel and slice the onion, then dice into approx. ½-inch (1 cm) cubes. Trim and wash the green onions, then chop them into rings.

2. Dice the pork back fat and render it in the pressure cooker. Sear the ground meat in the fat until browned. Add the onion and green onions and briefly cook, then mix in the diced squash. Mix 2 tbsp soy sauce and mirin with 1 cup (250 ml) water and use to deglaze the contents.
3. Seal the pressure cooker with the lid and set the pressure regulator to setting 3. Heat the pot on the highest setting. When the yellow ring appears (cooking indicator: 1st ring), reduce the heat. As soon as the green ring becomes visible (cooking indicator: 2nd ring), switch off the burner and allow the pressure cooker to slowly cool down.
4. Once fully depressurized, open the pressure cooker. Mix the cornstarch with 2 tbsp water and stir until smooth, then add to the pot. Return the uncovered pot to the boil and briefly thicken the contents over a medium heat. Season the squash stew with salt, pepper and fresh cilantro, add soy sauce and honey to taste, plate up and serve.

TIP: solid white pork back fat is ideal for rendering. Originally from Asia, it is rarely available in North America but Italian Lardo di Colonnata makes a good substitute.

COOKING LEVEL VITAVIT®

COOKING LEVEL VITAQUICK®

COOKING TIME

Potato salad: traditional, vegan or Mediterranean

MAKES: 4 PORTIONS   **PREP TIME:** 15–20 MIN.   **WAITING TIME:** APPROX. 30 MIN.

Potato salad
with stock

2 lbs (1 kg) firm potatoes | 1¼ cups (300 ml) meat stock (or vegetable stock) | salt | freshly ground pepper | 2 tbsp mustard | ¼ to ⅓ cup (60 to 75 ml) white wine vinegar | 2 small onions | 2 gherkins | 2 tbsp canola or sunflower oil | 3 tbsp (9 g) sliced chives

1. Peel the potatoes and cut them into about ⅛-inch (3 mm) thick slices. Put the potatoes, stock, salt, pepper, mustard and vinegar into the pressure cooker.
2. Seal the pressure cooker with the lid. Set the pressure regulator to setting 2 and heat the pot on the highest setting. When the yellow ring appears (cooking indicator: 1st ring), reduce the heat. As soon as the green ring becomes visible (cooking indicator: 1st ring), the 5–7-minute cooking time begins.
3. Peel the onions, cut them in half and chop them into thin strips. Slice the gherkins.
4. Remove the pressure cooker from the heat, release the steam and open the lid.
5. Mix the onion and oil into the potatoes and allow to sit in the uncovered pressure cooker for another 5 minutes or so.
6. Season the potato salad to taste, spoon into bowls or onto plates and garnish with chives and gherkins.

Styrian
potato salad

2 lbs (1 kg) firm potatoes | 1 red onion | 1 tbsp butter | ¼ to ⅓ cup (60 to 75 ml) white wine vinegar | 1¼ cups (300 ml) fish stock (or vegetable stock) | 1 tbsp mustard | salt | freshly ground pepper | ¼ cup (60 ml) sunflower oil | 1.6 oz (50 g) smoked bacon | 2 handfuls of mâche or corn salad, trimmed | 3 tbsp (30 g) toasted green pumpkin seeds | 2–3 tbsp pumpkin seed oil

1. Peel the potatoes and cut them into about ⅛-inch (3 mm) thick slices.
2. Peel the onion, cut it in half and chop it into thin strips. Sauté in the butter in the pressure cooker until translucent and then deglaze with the vinegar and stock. Stir in the mustard, add the potatoes and season with salt and pepper.
3. Seal the pressure cooker with the lid. Cook the potatoes on setting 2 (pressure regulator: 1st ring) for 5–7 minutes. Remove the pressure cooker from the heat, release the steam, open the lid and stir in the sunflower oil.
4. Finely dice the bacon, brown it in a frying pan and place it on paper towels to strain off the fat. Wash and spin-dry the mâche, then stir into the potato salad with the bacon. Season the potato salad to taste, spoon into bowls, grind with pepper, top with pumpkin seeds, drizzle with pumpkin seed oil and serve.

Vegan
potato salad

1.9 lbs (900 g) firm potatoes | ½ cucumber | ½ bunch of radishes | ⅓ cup (75 ml) vegan mayonnaise (from a jar) | ⅓ cup (75 ml) vegetable stock | 2 tbsp apple cider vinegar | 2 tbsp canola oil | salt | pepper | 1 tsp mustard | 2–3 tbsp finely chopped parsley

1. Wash and cook the potatoes, then release the steam (see pp. 92–3).
2. Wash and trim the cucumber, cut it in half lengthwise and remove the seeds, then slice it crosswise. Wash, trim, pat dry and finely slice the radishes.
3. Peel and slice the potatoes, then mix with the cucumber and half of the radishes. Stir together the vegan mayo, stock, vinegar and oil, then season with salt, pepper and mustard.
4. Taste test the mayo and add further seasoning if necessary. Add to the potato mixture and mix well. Spoon the potato salad into bowls or onto plates, top with the remaining radishes and garnish with parsley.

Greek
potato salad

2 lbs (1 kg) firm potatoes | 5 anchovy fillets | 2 tbsp capers, as desired | 3 tbsp (25 g) each of green and black olives, pitted (e.g., kalamata) | 3 tbsp (9 g) chopped herbs (parsley, rosemary, thyme) | 3 tbsp (45 ml) red wine vinegar | 2 pinches of granulated sugar | 1 red onion | ¾ cup (125 g) red and yellow cherry tomatoes | ½ cup (125 ml) olive oil (approx.) | salt | pepper

1. Cook the potatoes and release the steam as described on pp. 92–93.
2. Peel the potatoes, cut into thick slices and place in a bowl. Strain the anchovies and capers (as desired), chop coarsely and add to the potatoes. Slice the olives into rings and mix in together with 2 tbsp of the chopped herbs.
3. Briefly heat the vinegar and sugar in a pot. Peel the onion, cut it in half, slice it into strips and add it to the pot, then set to one side and allow to cool.
4. Wash and pat dry the tomatoes. Mix the quick-pickled onions (including the sauce), oil (as needed), salt and pepper into the potatoes. Season the salad to taste, serve onto plates and top with the remaining herbs and tomatoes.

COOKING LEVEL VITAVIT®

COOKING LEVEL VITAQUICK®

COOKING TIME

Spain's national dish
Variations on paella

MAKES: 4 PORTIONS   **PREP TIME:** 20–25 MIN.

(1)

Classic paella (1)

½ tsp saffron threads | 2 cups (500 ml) poultry stock | 1 onion | 2 garlic cloves | 1 red bell pepper | 10 oz (300 g) boneless skinless chicken breasts | ¼ cup (60 ml) olive oil | 1¼ cups (250 g) paella rice (e.g., bomba) | 1 tsp sweet paprika | 6 tbsp + 2 tsp (100 ml) tomato passata | salt | freshly ground pepper | 14 oz (400 g) each of cleaned mussels and clams | 8 uncooked king prawns, ready to cook | ⅔ cup (100 g) frozen peas | 1 pinch of cayenne pepper | 2 tbsp chopped parsley

1. Soak the saffron threads in ¼ cup (60 ml) stock. Meanwhile, peel and finely dice the onion and garlic. Wash, trim and finely dice the red pepper. Pat the chicken dry and cut it into approx. 1-inch (2.5 cm) cubes.
2. Heat 2 tbsp oil in a pressure cooker, briefly sear the red pepper and chicken until lightly browned, then remove and set aside.
3. Heat the remaining oil in the pressure cooker, add the diced onion and garlic and sauté lightly. Add the rice and cook briefly. Next, stir in the sweet paprika, tomato passata and the saffron together with the liquid in which it was soaked. Season with salt and pepper, then pour in the remaining stock.
4. Seal the pressure cooker, turn the pressure regulator to setting 3 and heat the pot on the highest setting. When the yellow ring appears (cooking indicator: 1st ring), reduce the heat. As soon as the green ring becomes visible (cooking indicator: 2nd ring), the 5-to-6-minute cooking time begins.
5. Meanwhile, rinse and strain the mussels, clams and prawns. Remove the pressure cooker from the heat, release the steam and open the lid. Mix the mussels, clams, prawns, peas, chicken and diced red pepper into the rice and cook on setting 1 (cooking indicator: 1st ring) for another 2–3 minutes.
6. Remove the pot from the heat and let stand for 2–3 minutes, then release the steam and open the lid. Season the paella with a little cayenne pepper to taste, sprinkle with chopped parsley and serve.

Seafood paella
with mild chile peppers (2)

1 lb (500 g) seafood (shrimp, octopus, mussels, precooked) | 1 onion | 2 garlic cloves | 1 red bell pepper | 2 mild red chile peppers | ¼ cup (60 ml) olive oil | salt | pepper | 1¼ cups (250 g) paella rice | 6 tbsp + 2 tsp (100 ml) white wine | ¾ cup + 2 tbsp (200 ml) fish stock | ½ tsp saffron threads | 2¼ cups (400 g) chopped tomatoes | ¾ cup + 2 tbsp (200 ml) tomato passata | ⅔ cup (100 g) frozen peas | juice of 1 lime | 2 tbsp chopped parsley

1. Rinse and strain the seafood. Peel and finely dice the onion and garlic. Wash and trim the red pepper and the mild chile peppers, then cut the pepper into pieces and the mild chile peppers into rings.
2. Heat the oil in the pressure cooker, sear the seafood briefly, then season with salt and pepper. Add the onion, garlic, red pepper, chile peppers and rice and cook briefly. Deglaze with wine and fish stock, then mix in the saffron, the chopped tomatoes and the tomato passata.
3. Seal the pot, cook the paella and add the peas towards the end of the cooking time as described in steps 5 and 6 on the left. Season with lime juice to taste and sprinkle with parsley.

Vegetarian paella
with quinoa (3)

1 onion | 2 garlic cloves | 1 red bell pepper | 1 orange bell pepper | 1 young green zucchini | 1 young yellow summer squash | 2 tbsp olive oil | 1 cup (200 g) quinoa | 1⅔ cups (400 ml) vegetable stock | ½ tsp saffron threads | salt | pepper | 8 oz (250 g) colorful tomatoes | 2 tbsp chopped herbs (parsley, basil) | basil leaves for garnish, optional

1. Peel and finely dice the onion and garlic. Wash, trim and finely dice the bell peppers, zucchini and summer squash.
2. Heat the oil in the pressure cooker and sauté the diced ingredients lightly. Rinse the quinoa, allow to strain and add together with the stock, saffron, salt and pepper.
3. Seal the pot and cook on setting 3 (cooking indicator: 2nd ring) for 1–2 minutes, then release the steam.
4. Halve or quarter the colorful tomatoes and mix in with the chopped herbs. Season the paella to taste, garnish with basil as desired and serve.

COOKING LEVEL VITAVIT® 2

COOKING LEVEL VITAQUICK® 1

COOKING TIME 1–6

Fish slices and fillets
cooked in an instant

MAKES: 4 PORTIONS **PREP TIME:** 15–20 MIN.

Mackerel in chili sauce (1)

1–2 mackerels, ready to cook | 1 lb (500 g) daikon radish (or mild white radish) | 2 green onions | 1–2 large mild red chile peppers (or sweet chile peppers) | salt | pepper | 1 tsp sesame seeds | herbs, for sprinkling | **For the sauce:** 2 tsp Korean chili paste (gochujang, alternatively Thai chili paste) | $\frac{1}{2}$–1 tsp red chili flakes | $\frac{1}{2}$ tsp granulated sugar | 2 tsp mirin | $\frac{1}{2}$ tsp liquid honey

1. Wash the mackerel(s) inside and out, slice them crosswise into pieces and re-rinse. Peel the radish and cut crosswise into thin slices. Wash and trim the green onions. Cut the light parts into approx. 2½-inch (6 cm) long pieces, then into strips, and cut the greens diagonally into rings. Wash, halve and trim the chile peppers, then cut them crosswise into strips.
2. To make the sauce, add 1 cup (250 ml) water to the pressure cooker and stir in the chili paste, chili flakes, sugar, mirin and honey.
3. Add the fish slices to the sauce in the pressure cooker together with the radish and the chile strips, then seal it with the lid. Set the pressure regulator to setting 2 and heat the pot on the highest setting. When the yellow ring appears (cooking indicator: 1st ring), reduce the heat. When the green ring becomes visible (cooking indicator: 1st ring), remove the pot from the heat and gradually release the steam (see p. 63).
4. Add the green onion strips, boil down for a short while uncovered and then season with salt and pepper. Season the fish dish to taste, arrange on plates, garnish with green onion rings, sesame seeds and herbs and serve.

Cod with ginger (2)

4 pieces cod fillet, 3.3 to 4 oz (100 to 125 g) each | 2 red bell peppers | 1¼-inch (3 cm) piece gingerroot | 1⅔ cups (150 g) julienned leek (light green part only) | 1 tsp diced chile | 1 tsp organic lime zest | 5 oz (150 g) bean sprouts, blanched | 3 tbsp (45 ml) sesame oil | salt | pepper | 4 thin organic lime slices | 2 tbsp toasted sesame seeds | 2 tbsp chopped cilantro

1. Rinse the fish and pat it dry. Wash, trim and julienne the peppers. Peel and finely dice the ginger.
2. Briefly sear the peppers, leek, chile, ½ tsp ginger, lime zest and bean sprouts in 2 tbsp oil in the pressure cooker, season with salt and pepper, then clean the pot.
3. Grease the perforated insert with the remaining oil. Spoon half of the vegetable mixture into the insert, dividing it into four portions. Place a cod fillet in the center of each portion and cover with the remaining vegetable mixture. Top each portion with 1 lime slice, sesame seeds, ginger and fresh cilantro.
4. Fill the pressure cooker with the minimum amount of water, put the insert on the tripod and seal the pot. Set the pressure regulator to the steam cooking symbol and steam the contents without pressure for approx. 6 minutes. Remove the vegetables and cod, arrange on plates and serve.

COOKING LEVEL VITAVIT®

COOKING LEVEL VITAQUICK®

COOKING TIME

An Italian classic
Mushroom risotto

MAKES: 4 PORTIONS   **PREP TIME:** APPROX. 25 MIN.

FOR THE RISOTTO
15 oz (450 g) mixed mushrooms (e.g., cremini, oyster, king)
2 shallots
1 garlic clove
1 tbsp butter
1½ cups (300 g) short-grain rice (e.g., arborio, carnaroli)
6 tbsp + 2 tsp (100 ml) dry rosé (or white wine)
1¾ cup + 2 tbsp (450 ml) veal stock (or poultry stock)
salt
freshly ground pepper

TO FINISH
3.3 oz (100 g) mascarpone cheese
¾ cup + 2 tbsp (80 g) grated Parmesan cheese
1 green onion

FOR THE RISOTTO: brush clean and trim the mushrooms. Avoid washing them if possible; instead, briefly rinse if necessary and thoroughly pat dry. Next, halve, quarter or slice the mushrooms depending on their size. Peel the shallots and garlic, finely dice the shallots and cut the garlic in half.

Melt the butter in a pressure cooker and lightly sauté the shallots and garlic. Add and briefly sauté the mushrooms, turning them occasionally **(1)** until the water released from them has evaporated and they are lightly browned. Remove half of the mushrooms and keep them warm.

Add the risotto rice **(2)** and briefly cook until the tips of the rice grains become translucent. Deglaze with the rosé wine and simmer until it has almost fully dissolved, stirring regularly. Pour in the veal stock **(3)** and lightly season with salt and pepper.

Seal the pressure cooker with the lid, turn the pressure regulator to setting 3 and heat the pot on the highest setting. When the yellow ring appears (cooking indicator: 1st ring), reduce the heat. As soon as the green ring becomes visible (cooking indicator: 2nd ring), the 5-to-6-minute cooking time begins.

TO FINISH: remove the pressure cooker from the heat, release the steam and open the lid. Fluff the risotto, stir in the mascarpone and half of the Parmesan and leave the risotto to steep briefly.

In the meantime, wash and trim the green onion, then chop into thin rings. Season the risotto to taste, spoon onto preheated deep plates and top with the remaining fried mushrooms.

Grind a little pepper over the mushroom risotto, sprinkle with a little Parmesan and serve garnished with green onion rings. Serve the rest of the Parmesan separately in a small bowl.

TIP: the Italian national dish comes in countless different versions. For a vegetarian version, substitute the veal stock with strong vegetable stock. Alternatively, stir in some full-flavored Swiss-style cheese instead of Parmesan. Instead of mushrooms, risotto also tastes great with spring vegetables such as asparagus or peas, summer vegetables (bell peppers, tomatoes) or autumn vegetables (squash) – several suggestions in this regard can be found on pp. 124–125.

  COOKING LEVEL VITAVIT® | COOKING LEVEL VITAQUICK® | COOKING TIME

  COOKING LEVEL VITAVIT® | COOKING LEVEL VITAQUICK® | COOKING TIME

Pea risotto

MAKES: 4 PORTIONS   **PREP TIME:** APPROX. 15 MIN.

3 tbsp (45 ml) olive oil | 2 tbsp butter | 6 tbsp (50 g) diced shallots | 1½ cups (300 g) short-grain rice (e.g., arborio, carnaroli) | ⅔ cup (150 ml) white wine | 2 cups (500 ml) vegetable stock | salt | white pepper | 2 cups (300 g) peas (fresh or frozen) | ¾ cup (40 g) chopped flat-leaf parsley leaves and stems | ½ cup + 1 tbsp (50 g) grated Parmesan

1. Heat 1 tbsp oil and the butter in the pressure cooker and sauté the shallots until translucent. Add the rice, sauté briefly, then deglaze with the wine and stock. Season with salt and pepper.
2. Seal the pot and cook the risotto on setting 3 (cooking indicator: 2nd ring) for 5–6 minutes. Meanwhile, blanch the peas in salted water. Release the steam from the pot and stir in the peas, parsley and ⅓ cup (30 g) Parmesan. Season the risotto to taste, top with the remaining oil and Parmesan and serve.

Squash risotto

MAKES: 4 PORTIONS   **PREP TIME:** APPROX. 20 MIN.

1 onion | 1 garlic clove | 4 to 5 tbsp (60 to 75 g) butter | 1 cup + 6 tbsp (200 g) each of cubed (½ inch/1 cm) peeled hokkaido pumpkin (red kuri squash) and butternut squash | 1½ cups (300 g) short-grain rice (e.g., arborio, carnaroli) | ⅔ cup (150 ml) white wine | 2 cups (500 ml) vegetable stock | salt | pepper | ⅔ cup (60 g) grated Parmesan | 1 tbsp sliced green onion | chopped parsley

1. Peel and finely dice the onion and garlic. Melt 2 tbsp (30 g) butter in the pressure cooker, then sauté the onion, pumpkin and squash and garlic for approx. 4 minutes. Add the rice and briefly sauté, then pour in the wine and stock, season with salt and pepper and seal the pot.
2. Cook the risotto on setting 3 (cooking indicator: 2nd ring) for 5–6 minutes. Release the steam from the pot. Stir in the remaining butter and half of the Parmesan, season the risotto to taste, top with the remaining ingredients and serve with the remaining Parmesan.

COOKING LEVEL VITAVIT® | COOKING LEVEL VITAQUICK® | COOKING TIME ... COOKING LEVEL VITAVIT® | COOKING LEVEL VITAQUICK® | COOKING TIME

Risotto with green asparagus

MAKES: 4 PORTIONS   **PREP TIME:** APPROX. 20 MIN.

14 oz (400 g) green asparagus | 6 tbsp (180 g) butter | 6 tbsp (50 g) diced shallots | 1½ cups (300 g) short-grain rice (e.g., arborio, carnaroli) | 1 cup (250 ml) white wine | 2 cups (500 ml) veal stock (or poultry or vegetable stock) | salt | pepper | 7 tbsp (40 g) grated Parmesan | microgreens or fresh herbs | toasted sunflower seeds

1. Chop the ends off the asparagus, peel the lower third, wash and diagonally cut into pieces. Melt 3 tbsp (45 g) butter in the pressure cooker and sauté the shallots until translucent. Add the rice and asparagus and sauté briefly. Pour in the wine and stock, season with salt and pepper and seal the pressure cooker.

2. Cook the risotto on setting 3 (cooking indicator: 2nd ring) for 5 minutes, then release the steam. Stir in the remaining 3 tbsp (45 g) butter and the Parmesan. Season the risotto to taste, top with the microgreens and sunflower seeds and serve.

Pearl barley risotto

MAKES: 4 PORTIONS   **PREP TIME:** APPROX. 20 MIN.

1 lb (500 g) soup vegetables (carrots, parsnip, leek, celery) | 1 red onion | 2 garlic cloves | 2 tbsp olive oil | ¾ cup + 2 tbsp (200 g) pearl barley | 6 tbsp + 2 tsp (100 ml) white wine | 1⅔ cups (400 ml) vegetable stock | 1 bay leaf | salt | pepper | ¾ cup + 2 tbsp (80 g) grated Parmesan | 2 tbsp chopped parsley

1. Peel or wash the soup vegetables, trim and finely dice. Peel and finely dice the onion and garlic. Heat the oil in the pressure cooker and lightly sauté the prepared ingredients. Add the pearl barley and continue to sauté for another 2 minutes or so. Pour in the wine and stock, then add the bay leaf. Season with salt and pepper and seal the pot.

2. Cook the pearl barley risotto on setting 3 (cooking indicator: 2nd ring) for another 8–9 minutes, then release the steam from the pot and open the lid. Remove the bay leaf. Stir in the Parmesan, season the pearl barley risotto to taste, sprinkle with chopped parsley and serve.

COOKING LEVEL VITAVIT® 2

COOKING LEVEL VITAQUICK® 1

COOKING TIME 5–7

Well-known dishes
Pilaf, pilau, palaw & plov

MAKES: 4 PORTIONS   **PREP TIME:** APPROX. 25 MIN.

Delicate and aromatic
Mussel pilaf (1)

2 lbs (1 kg) clams (or other small mussels) | 1 onion | 2 garlic cloves | 2 tbsp olive oil | ¾ cup (175 ml) white wine | 5 sprigs of parsley | 5 white peppercorns | coarse sea salt | 1⅔ cups (300 g) long-grain white rice | 2 green onions | 1 young leek | 2–3 green asparagus stalks | 1 zucchini | 2 tbsp butter | salt | freshly ground pepper | 3 tbsp (9 g) chopped parsley

1. Rinse and clean the mussels, discarding any that are already open. Peel and dice the onion and 1 garlic clove. Heat the oil in a pressure cooker, briefly sauté the onion and diced garlic, deglaze with 6 tbsp + 2 tsp (100 ml) white wine and pour in 2 cups + 6 tbsp (600 ml) water. Add the sprigs of parsley, peppercorns and sea salt. Bring to the boil, add the mussels and cook on setting 2 (cooking indicator: 1st ring) for 2 minutes. Remove with a slotted spoon and discard any mussels that are still closed. Strain the cooking juices through a sieve. Remove the meat from half of the mussels and keep the other half warm.

2. Rinse and strain the rice. Wash and trim or peel the vegetables. Cut the green onions and leek in half lengthwise, then slice into half rings. Cut the asparagus diagonally into short pieces and the zucchini into small cubes. Peel and finely dice the remaining garlic.

3. Melt the butter in the pressure cooker and lightly sauté the vegetables. Stir in the garlic and sauté for another 1 minute. Season with salt and pepper, then add the rice. Pour in the strained cooking juices from the mussels and the remaining ⅓ cup (75 ml) wine.

4. Seal the pot and cook the pilaf on setting 2 (cooking indicator: 1st ring) for 5 minutes. Remove the pot from the heat and leave the contents to rest for 1–2 minutes. Release the steam from the pot, cover the pilaf with a towel and let sit for 10 minutes.

5. Mix in the loose mussel meat and chopped parsley. Season the pilaf to taste, spoon onto plates, top with the remaining mussels and serve.

Pilaf with tomatoes (2)

2 tbsp butter | 1 tbsp olive oil | 1¾ cups (350 g) short-grain rice (e.g., baldo, arborio, bomba) | 3 large tomatoes (or 2¼ cups/400 g chopped tomatoes) | ½ cup (125 ml) poultry stock | 2 tbsp white balsamic vinegar | 2 tsp salt | 1 tsp pepper | 1 tsp granulated sugar | 7 oz (200 g) colorful cherry tomatoes | 2–3 tbsp chopped parsley

1. Heat the butter and oil in a pressure cooker, then sauté the rice, stirring regularly.
2. Wash the large tomatoes, remove the cores, coarsely dice and blend in a mixer with the stock, 1 tbsp vinegar, 1 tsp salt, pepper and sugar. Top up the tomato mixture to 2 cups + 1 tbsp (525 ml) with water and pour it into the rice in the pressure cooker.
3. Seal the pot, cook the pilaf and release the steam as described in the recipe on the left.
4. Wash and quarter the colorful tomatoes, then season them with the remaining salt and the remaining vinegar. Spoon the pilaf onto the plates, top with the tomatoes, sprinkle with parsley and serve.

(2)

Bulgur pilaf with vegetables (3)

1 Italian eggplant | salt | 6 tbsp (90 ml) olive oil | 2 onions | 4 garlic cloves | 1 mild banana pepper | 1 green bell pepper | 1 tbsp butter | 1 tsp tomato paste | 2 tsp tomato paste | black pepper | 1 tsp confectioners' (icing) sugar | 1 tsp vinegar | 2 tsp dried oregano | 1 tsp dried mint | 1 cup + 6 tbsp (250 g) coarse bulgur | 1 large tomato | 2¼ cups (550 ml) poultry stock | 1 tsp chopped fresh mint | mint sprig, to garnish

1. Wash and trim the eggplant, cut into approx. ½-inch (1 cm) cubes, season with salt and let sit for 10 minutes. Pat the cubes dry, sear in 3 tbsp (45 ml) oil in the pressure cooker, remove and place on paper towels to soak up the excess oil. Peel and finely dice the onions and garlic. Wash, trim and finely dice the peppers.
2. Heat the remaining oil and butter in the pressure cooker and briefly sear the onions and peppers. Add the garlic and sear for another minute or so. Stir in the tomato paste, season with 1½ tsp salt, 1 tsp pepper, sugar, vinegar and dried herbs, then add the bulgur. Coarsely chop, then blend the tomato in a blender. Add the mixture to the stock and mix well.
3. Seal the pot and cook the pilaf on setting 2 (cooking indicator: 1st ring) for 7 minutes. Let rest for 1–2 minutes and then release the steam from the pot. Stir in the eggplant, season the pilaf to taste, sprinkle with chopped fresh mint, garnish with a sprig of mint and serve.

(3)

COOKING LEVEL VITAVIT® — COOKING LEVEL VITAQUICK® — COOKING TIME

Bolognese sauce with meat & vegan

MAKES: 4–6 PORTIONS   **PREP TIME:** APPROX. 25 MIN.

Bolognese sauce with beef (1)

2 onions | 2 garlic cloves | 2 carrots | 3 tbsp (45 ml) olive oil | 14 oz (400 g) ground beef | salt | pepper | 1 tsp dried thyme | 1 tsp dried oregano | 1 tbsp tomato paste | ¾ cup + 2 tbsp (200 ml) beef stock | ¾ cup + 2 tbsp (200 ml) tomato juice | 2¼ cups (400 g) canned chopped tomatoes | ½ tsp ground cinnamon | 1 tbsp honey | fresh basil | ½ cup + 1 tbsp (50 g) grated Parmesan

1. Peel and finely dice the onions and garlic. Peel the carrots and cut into small cubes. Heat the oil in a pressure cooker, then sear the ground meat for 4–5 minutes until browned. Add the onions, garlic and carrots and cook for another 1–2 minutes. Season with salt, pepper and the dried herbs. Stir in the tomato paste and cook briefly. Deglaze with the stock and tomato juice, then stir in the chopped tomatoes.

2. Seal the pot, set the pressure regulator to setting 2 and heat on the highest setting. When the yellow ring appears (cooking indicator: 1st ring), reduce the heat. As soon as the green ring becomes visible (cooking indicator: 1st ring), cook for 10 minutes.
3. Release the steam from the pot. Refine the sauce with cinnamon and honey, season to taste and serve with pasta of your choice, garnished with basil. Serve the Parmesan separately.

Vegan Bolognese (2)

2 onions | 2 garlic cloves | 2 carrots | 2 stalks celery | 3 tbsp (45 ml) olive oil | 2 tbsp tomato paste | 4½ cups (800 g) canned chopped tomatoes | 1¼ cups (300 ml) vegetable stock | 1 cup (200 g) dried brown lentils | 1 bay leaf | 4 sprigs of thyme | salt | freshly ground pepper | 14 oz (400 g) short pasta, such as Vesuvio, cavatappi | 8 oz (250 g) baby carrots | 1⅔ cups (200 g) diced peeled sweet potato | 1 pinch of ground cinnamon

1. Peel the onions, garlic and carrots. Wash and trim the celery. Finely dice the onions and garlic and cut the carrots and celery into small cubes. Heat the oil in the pressure cooker and sauté the prepared vegetables for 3–4 minutes. Stir in the tomato paste and continue to cook for another minute or so.
2. Add the chopped tomatoes and stock. Rinse and strain the lentils, then mix them in. Add the bay leaf and thyme and lightly season with salt and pepper.
3. Seal the pot, set the pressure regulator to setting 2 and heat the pot on the highest setting. As soon as the yellow ring appears (cooking indicator: 1st ring), reduce the heat. When the green ring becomes visible (cooking indicator: 1st ring), cook for 10 minutes.
4. Meanwhile, cook the pasta in salted water until al dente. Release the steam from the pot, add the vegetables and ground cinnamon and cook on setting 2 for another 3–4 minutes until fully done. Release the steam from the pot and open the lid. Strain the pasta and divide between four plates. Remove the bay leaf. Season the vegan Bolognese to taste, spoon onto the pasta and serve.

(1)

RECIPES >> QUICK & EASY

COOKING LEVEL VITAVIT® | COOKING LEVEL VITAQUICK® | COOKING TIME 10–20

Beautifully spiced and gently stuffed

MAKES: 4 PORTIONS **PREP TIME:** APPROX. 20 MIN.

Curried lentils with lamb (1)

4 pieces lamb tenderloin (approx. 4 oz/125 g each) | salt | ¼ cup (60 ml) olive oil | 1 garlic clove | 1 green onion | 1¼ cups (250 g) dried brown lentils | 1½ cups (200 g) diced shallots | 1½ cups (200 g) diced carrots | 1 tsp chopped herbs (thyme and rosemary) | 2 tbsp curry powder | ½ tsp ground cumin | 2¾ cups (675 ml) lamb stock (or poultry stock) | salt | pepper | ¼ cup (12 g) basil leaves

1. Pat the meat dry and lightly season with salt. Heat 2 tbsp oil in the pressure cooker, sear the lamb all over until browned, then remove them. Peel and finely dice the garlic. Wash and trim the green onion, then cut into thin rings. Rinse the lentils and strain.

2. Heat the remaining oil in the pot and sauté the shallots, carrots, garlic and herbs. Add the lentils, curry powder and cumin, continue to sauté briefly, then deglaze with the lamb stock.

3. Seal the pot and cook the lentils on setting 2 (cooking indicator: 1st ring) for 10 minutes. Release the steam from the pot. Add the lamb fillets and heat briefly in the uncovered pot.

4. Season the lentils with salt and pepper. Finely chop and mix in 2 tbsp basil together with the green onion. Season the lentils to taste and divide between four plates. Diagonally slice the lamb fillets, arrange on top of the lentils, garnish with basil leaves and serve.

Stuffed peppers (2)

4 large bell peppers | 1 onion | 1 garlic clove | 1 handful of flat-leaf parsley | 1 lb (500 g) ground beef | ⅔ cup (150 g) cooked rice | 2 tbsp tomato paste | 1 egg | salt | pepper | 1 tsp paprika | 1 tbsp honey | 2 tsp Worcestershire sauce | 1 tsp finely chopped thyme | 2 cups (500 ml) vegetable stock | 2¼ cups (400 g) chopped tomatoes

1. Wash and dry the peppers, cut a lid off each one and set aside. Hollow out the peppers and remove the seeds. Peel and finely dice the onion and garlic. Wash, shake dry and finely chop the parsley, then set approx. 1 tbsp aside as a garnish.

2. Combine the ground meat, rice, tomato paste and egg in a bowl. Mix in the spices, honey, Worcestershire sauce, thyme and most of the parsley, then stuff the peppers with the mixture.

3. Put the vegetable stock and chopped tomatoes into a pressure cooker. Add the stuffed peppers and put on their lids.

4. Seal the pressure cooker, turn the pressure regulator to setting 2 and heat the pot on the highest setting. When the yellow ring appears (cooking indicator: 1st ring), reduce the heat. As soon as the green ring becomes visible (cooking indicator: 2nd ring), the 15-to-20-minute cooking time begins.

5. Release the steam from the pot and open the lid. Remove the stuffed peppers, keep them warm for a short while and allow the sauce to boil down a little more in the uncovered pot. Plate up the peppers with a little sauce and serve sprinkled with the remaining parsley.

(1)

COOKING LEVEL VITAVIT® 3

 COOKING LEVEL VITAQUICK® 2

 COOKING TIME 20

Hot and spicy: chili

MAKES: 4–6 PORTIONS **SOAKING TIME:** APPROX. 24 HRS **PREP TIME:** APPROX. 25 MIN.

Five-bean chili with ground beef

For the legumes: 1/2 cup (100 g) each of dried black beans, kidney beans, pinto beans, cannellini (white kidney) beans and chickpeas | **For the chili:** 1 small onion | 2 garlic cloves | 2 tbsp olive oil | 14 oz (400 g) ground beef | 1 tsp dried oregano | 1/2 tsp each of ground cumin, cayenne pepper and sea salt | 1 tbsp paprika | 2 tsp chili powder | 1/2 tsp ground cinnamon | 1 tsp cocoa powder (unsweetened) | 3/4 cup + 2 tbsp (200 ml) beef stock | 2 1/4 cups (400 g) chopped tomatoes | 1 2/3 cups (400 ml) tomato passata | 1 mild green chile pepper | 1/4 cup to 6 tbsp (60 to 90 g) sour cream | a little flat-leaf parsley, to garnish

1. For the legumes, soak all of the beans and the chickpeas in cold water for approx. 24 hours. Strain the legumes then place them in a large pressure cooker and cover with fresh water. The pressure cooker should only be one-third (max. half) full. Seal the pot with the lid and turn the pressure regulator to setting 3. Heat the pot on the highest setting. When the yellow ring appears (cooking indicator: 1st ring), reduce the heat. As soon as the green ring becomes visible (cooking indicator: 2nd ring), the 20-minute cooking time begins.
2. Meanwhile, peel and finely dice the onion and garlic. Release the steam from the pressure cooker, open the lid, and strain the legumes. Clean the pot.
3. Heat the oil in the pressure cooker, then sear the ground meat until browned. Add the oregano, spices and cocoa powder and cook briefly, then deglaze with the beef stock. Mix in the chopped tomatoes and tomato passata.
4. Seal the pot and cook the chili on setting 2 (cooking indicator: 1st ring) for another 10 minutes or so. Wash, trim, seed and finely dice the mild chile pepper. Release the steam from the pot and open the lid. Season the chili to taste and divide between four deep plates. Top each portion with 1 tbsp sour cream and a few pieces of diced chile pepper. Garnish with parsley and serve.

Chili sin carne

2 cups (400 g) dried red kidney beans | 1 large onion | 2–3 garlic cloves | 2 carrots | 1 red bell pepper | 1 green bell pepper | 1 cob corn | 2 tbsp olive oil | 2 1/4 cups (400 g) canned chopped tomatoes | 1–1 1/2 tsp ground cumin | 1–2 tsp paprika | 1–2 tsp chili powder | salt | black pepper | 2/3 cup (150 ml) vegetable stock | 1–2 tbsp agave syrup | 2 tbsp chopped cilantro | 1 pinch of ground fenugreek, as desired | 1 organic lime, cut into wedges | 1/2 handful of fresh cilantro

1. Soak the kidney beans and cook as described on the left. Peel and finely dice the onion and garlic. Peel the carrots, wash and trim the bell peppers and finely dice both. Wash the corn cob and cut the kernels off the cob.
2. Heat the oil in the pressure cooker and sauté the onion until translucent. Add the carrots, bell peppers and garlic and cook briefly, stirring regularly. Add the chopped tomatoes, kidney beans, corn and spices, then pour in the stock.
3. Seal the pot and cook on setting 2 (cooking indicator: 1st ring) for approx. 10 minutes. Release the steam from the pot and refine the contents with the agave syrup, chopped cilantro and ground fenugreek (as desired). Season the chili sin carne to taste, divide between four plates, garnish each portion with a little fresh cilantro and 1–2 lime wedges and serve. Rice tastes great as a side.

Salads, snacks & bowls

Colorful variety: you can prepare all sorts of salads in a flash in a pressure cooker, whether with vegetables or rice, or changing up the flavor profile. It's also a great way to prepare Mediterranean ingredients, such as white beans, lentils or chickpeas, which are essential for dips such as hummus, etc. By pressure cooking sushi rice or other ingredients for delicious bowls, not only do you save time, you also preserve vitamins.

COOKING LEVEL VITAVIT®

COOKING LEVEL VITAQUICK®

COOKING TIME

Warm bean salad
with olives and feta

MAKES: 4 PORTIONS   **SOAKING TIME:** 24 HRS   **PREP TIME:** APPROX. 25 MIN.

FOR THE BEANS
¾ cup (150 g) dried cannellini (white kidney) beans
½ cup (100 g) dried red kidney beans
1 red onion
2 garlic cloves
2 tbsp olive oil
2 cups + 6 tbsp (600 ml) vegetable stock
1 bay leaf

FOR THE SALAD
1⅔ cups (250 g) colorful cherry tomatoes
1 mild banana pepper
½ red bell pepper
½ orange bell pepper
2–3 green onions
½ handful of herbs (e.g., parsley, cilantro, mint)

FOR THE DRESSING
2 tbsp white balsamic vinegar
1 tsp grated zest and 2 tbsp juice of 1 organic lemon
1 tsp mustard
salt
freshly ground pepper
½ tsp liquid honey
¼ cup (60 ml) olive oil

TO FINISH
⅓ cup (50 g) black olives, pitted if desired
2.6 oz (75 g) feta
1 tsp mild chili flakes
basil, to garnish

FOR THE BEANS: rinse the dried cannellini (white kidney) beans and the kidney beans, put them in a bowl with plenty of cold water, cover and let soak for 24 hours.

The next day, put the beans in a colander and strain. Peel and finely dice the onion and garlic. Heat the oil in a pressure cooker, add the onion and garlic and sauté lightly. Add the strained beans, the stock and the bay leaf.

Close the pressure cooker with the lid and set the pressure regulator to setting 3. Heat the pot on the highest setting. As soon as the yellow ring appears (cooking indicator: 1st ring), reduce the heat. When the green ring becomes visible (cooking indicator: 2nd ring), the 12-minute cooking time begins.

Remove the pressure cooker from the heat, release the steam and open the lid. Strain the beans and let cool until lukewarm.

FOR THE SALAD: wash the cherry tomatoes, pat them dry and cut them in half. Wash, trim and chop the peppers. Trim and wash the green onions, then chop them into rings. Wash the herbs, shake them dry and chop the leaves.

FOR THE DRESSING: put the balsamic vinegar in a bowl with the lemon juice and zest, mustard, salt, pepper and honey and mix well. Add the olive oil, give the dressing a good stir and season to taste.

TO FINISH: put the beans and the prepared salad ingredients in a bowl and mix together. Stir in the olives and let marinate for another 10 minutes.

Season the salad to taste, divide between four plates and crumble some feta on top. Sprinkle with chili flakes, garnish with a couple of basil leaves and serve.

TIP: this Mediterranean bean salad also tastes great cold. In this case, leave it to marinate for longer before serving. Instead of chili flakes, you can also season the salad with pepper flakes or coarsely ground Espelette pepper from the Basque Country.

(1) (2)
(3) (4)

COOKING LEVEL VITAVIT® | COOKING LEVEL VITAQUICK® | COOKING TIME

Beluga lentil & pomegranate salad (1)

MAKES: 4 PORTIONS   **PREP TIME:** APPROX. 15 MIN.
2 small shallots | ¼ cup (60 ml) olive oil | ½ cup (100 g) beluga lentils (not soaked) | 1 bay leaf | 1 cup (250 ml) vegetable stock | 2 peeled garlic cloves | salt | 3 tbsp (9 g) chopped cilantro | 3 tbsp (45 ml) pomegranate syrup | freshly ground pepper | seeds from ½ pomegranate

1. Peel and finely dice the shallots. Heat 1 tbsp oil in the pressure cooker, add the shallots and sauté in the oil. Rinse the lentils and add them to the pot with the bay leaf and the stock.
2. Seal the pot and cook on setting 3 (cooking indicator: 2nd ring) for 10 minutes, then remove the pot from the heat, release the steam and leave the contents to cool.
3. Chop the garlic, sauté lightly in a frying pan in the remaining oil, season with salt, then add to the lentils together with the cilantro and the remaining ingredients. Season to taste and serve.

COOKING LEVEL VITAVIT® | COOKING LEVEL VITAQUICK® | COOKING TIME

Lima bean & tuna salad (2)

MAKES: 4 PORTIONS   **PREP TIME:** APPROX. 15 MIN. + 24 HRS
1 cup + 2 tbsp (200 g) dried lima beans (butter beans) | 2 cans (each 5 oz/142 g) tuna packed in oil | 1 red onion | ¼ cup (12 g) chopped herbs (flat-leaf parsley, oregano) | ¼ cup (60 ml) olive oil | 2 tbsp white balsamic vinegar | salt | pepper | oregano leaves

1. Soak the dried beans for approx. 24 hours in water. The next day, strain them, rinse them and then leave them to strain again.
2. Put the beans in a pressure cooker with approx. 2 cups + 6 tbsp (600 ml) fresh water and close the lid. Cook the beans on setting 3 (cooking indicator: 2nd ring) for 15 minutes. Release the steam from the pot, put the beans in a colander and strain.
3. Strain the tuna, then separate it into chunks. Peel the onion, cut it in half and chop into thin strips. Put the beans in a bowl with the remaining ingredients (except the oregano leaves) and mix together. Season the salad to taste and serve garnished with oregano.

COOKING LEVEL VITAVIT® | COOKING LEVEL VITAQUICK® | COOKING TIME

Black-eyed pea salad with cherry tomatoes (3)

MAKES: 4 PORTIONS   **PREP TIME:** APPROX. 15 MIN. + 1 HR
1⅓ cups (250 g) dried black-eyed peas | 4 garlic cloves | 1 bay leaf | 1 red onion | ⅔ cup (100 g) cherry tomatoes | 7 tbsp to ½ cup (105 to 125 ml) olive oil | 1 tbsp white wine vinegar | 3 tbsp (9 g) chopped flat-leaf parsley | salt | pepper | 1 pinch of paprika powder | 4 pieces of feta (approx. 1.6 oz/50 g each)

1. Soak the peas for about 1 hour in cold water. Peel the garlic, cut 1 clove in half and put it in the pressure cooker together with the peas, 3 cups (750 ml) water and the bay leaf. Cook on setting 3 (cooking indicator: 2nd ring) for 12 minutes.
2. Release the steam from the pot and strain the peas. Peel the onion and cut it into strips. Wash and halve the tomatoes, then finely dice the remaining garlic cloves. Put everything in a bowl with the remaining ingredients (except the feta) and mix together. Leave the salad to marinate for about 1 hour, then season to taste and serve with the feta.

COOKING LEVEL VITAVIT® | COOKING LEVEL VITAQUICK® | COOKING TIME

Chickpea & stockfish salad (4)

MAKES: 4 PORTIONS   **PREP TIME:** APPROX. 20 MIN. + 24 HRS
8 oz (250 g) dried Norwegian cod (stockfish) | ⅔ cup (120 g) dried chickpeas | 3 tbsp (45 ml) red wine vinegar | 1 pinch of sweet paprika | salt | pepper | 6 tbsp (90 ml) olive oil | ½ cup (60 g) diced red onion | 3 tbsp (9 g) parsley, chopped | 1 garlic clove, chopped | 2 hard-boiled eggs, in wedges

1. Soak the stockfish for 24 hours, changing the water 3 to 4 times. Rinse the chickpeas and cook them in the pressure cooker with the minimum amount of water on setting 3 (cooking indicator: 2nd ring) for 15 minutes, then release the steam. Clean the pot.
2. Put the stockfish in the pressure cooker with the minimum amount of water and cook it at the highest pressure cooking setting for 15 minutes. Remove the pot from the heat and release the steam. Remove the bones and skin from the fish, separate it into chunks, put it in a bowl, mix it with the other ingredients, season to taste and serve.

Vegetable salads with citrus flavors

COOKING LEVEL VITAVIT®

COOKING LEVEL VITAQUICK®

COOKING TIME

MAKES: 4 PORTIONS PER RECIPE   **PREP TIME:** 15–25 MIN. PER RECIPE

(1)

Asian-style
Brussels sprout salad (1)

MAKES: 4 PORTIONS   **PREP TIME:** APPROX. 25 MIN.
1–2 green onions | 1 red chile pepper | 2 tbsp liquid honey | 3 tbsp (45 ml) rice vinegar | 1 tbsp light soy sauce | 3 tbsp (45 ml) sesame oil | ½ handful of fresh cilantro | 1 red bell pepper | salt | **For the salad:** 1.5 lbs (750 g) Brussels sprouts | salt | 2 tbsp peanut oil | ⅓ cup (30 g) frozen cranberries | freshly ground pepper | freshly grated nutmeg | 1 organic lime, in wedges, for squeezing

1. Wash and trim the green onions and chile pepper and chop them into thin rings. Put the chile and green onion rings in a bowl with the honey, vinegar, soy sauce and sesame oil and mix together. Wash the cilantro, shake it dry and pluck the leaves. Wash, trim and finely dice the pepper and add it to the vinaigrette together with the cilantro. Season the vinaigrette to taste with salt.
2. To make the salad, trim, wash and halve the Brussels sprouts, then put them in an appropriate-sized perforated insert. Fill the pressure cooker with the minimum amount of water. Put the insert with the sprouts on the tripod and seal the pot. Set the pressure regulator to setting 2 and heat the pot on the highest setting. As soon as the yellow ring appears (cooking indicator: 1st ring), reduce the heat. When the green ring becomes visible (cooking indicator: 1st ring), the 2-minute cooking time begins.
3. Remove the pot from the heat, release the steam and open the lid. Remove the sprouts, plunge them immediately into ice-cold salted water, then strain.
4. Heat the peanut oil in a frying pan, add the sprouts and fry briefly. Add the cranberries and continue frying for 1–2 minutes, then set aside.
5. Put the warm sprouts in the vinaigrette, then season the salad with salt, pepper and 1 pinch of nutmeg. Plate up the salad and serve it while still warm or cold, with lime wedges for squeezing.

Moroccan carrot salad (2)

1.2 lbs (600 g) carrots (if possible, equal-sized) | sea salt | ½ mild red chile pepper | 2 young garlic cloves | 1 tsp ground cumin | ¼ cup (60 ml) lemon juice | ¼ cup (60 ml) olive oil | pepper | ½ handful of mint | ½ organic lemon, sliced

1. Peel the carrots and put them in the perforated insert. Fill the pressure cooker with the minimum amount of water and season the carrots with salt. Put the carrots in the insert on the tripod in the pot, and cook on setting 2 (cooking indicator: 1st ring) for 4–5 minutes. Release the steam from the pot and leave the carrots to cool slightly.
2. Wash and trim the mild chile pepper, peel the garlic and finely dice both of them. Toast the cumin in a frying pan without any fat, then let cool. Cut the carrots into sticks and mix them together with the remaining ingredients (except the mint and lemon). Season the salad to taste and serve garnished with mint and lemon slices.

Cauliflower salad (3)

1.6 lbs (800 g) cauliflower, trimmed, cut into florets (about 6 cups) | 4 juicy seedless oranges | 1 juicy organic lime | 3 tbsp (45 ml) maple syrup | 6 tbsp + 2 tsp (100 ml) mild olive oil | salt | 1–2 tsp crushed red peppercorns | 2⅓ cups (80 g) mixed salad greens | ½ cup (75 g) salted smoked almonds, coarsely chopped

1. Fill the pressure cooker with the minimum amount of water. Put the cauliflower in the perforated insert on the tripod and cook on setting 2 (cooking indicator: 1st ring) for 1–2 minutes (or on setting 1 for 2–5 minutes). Release the steam from the pot and open the lid.
2. Plunge the cauliflower immediately into cold water, strain, then put in a bowl. Peel 2 oranges, cut them into thin slices, cut each slice in half and add to the bowl.
3. Wash the lime in hot water, then dab it dry. Thinly peel the zest and cut it into fine strips. Squeeze the remaining oranges and the lime. Put the citrus juice and maple syrup in a small saucepan and reduce by half, then slowly pour in the oil, mixing it in with a hand blender. Season the dressing with salt and crushed red peppercorns and let cool. Tear the lettuce leaves into pieces and add them to the cauliflower together with the dressing and the strips of lime zest.
4. Briefly mix together. Season the salad to taste, plate it up and serve with a sprinkling of almonds.

(2)

(3)

COOKING LEVEL VITAVIT® 2 | **COOKING LEVEL VITAQUICK®** 1 | **COOKING TIME** 5–6

Octopus salad: Korean and Portuguese style

MAKES: 4 PORTIONS **PREP TIME:** 15–20 MIN. **COOLING TIME:** 3–4 HRS (NO. 1)

Portuguese-style octopus salad (1)

1.6 lbs (800 g) octopus, ready to cook (or just tentacles) | salt | 1 small onion | ½ each green and red bell pepper | ½ handful of flat-leaf parsley | ¼ cup (60 ml) olive oil | 3 tbsp (45 ml) white wine vinegar | 1 tbsp red wine vinegar | pepper | small basil leaves | 1 organic lemon, cut into wedges

1. Rinse the octopus, put it into the pressure cooker together with approx. 4 cups (1 L) water and 1 tbsp salt. Seal the pot, set the pressure regulator to setting 2 and heat the pot on the highest setting. As soon as the yellow ring appears (cooking indicator: 1st ring), reduce the heat. When the green ring becomes visible (cooking indicator: 1st ring), the 5-minute cooking time begins. Remove the pot from the heat and continue cooking the octopus for another 5–6 minutes, then slowly release the steam.
2. Open the pot, remove the octopus and let cool slightly. Remove the tentacles from the head using a sharp knife. Cut the head into approx. ¾-inch (2 cm) pieces and cut the tentacles at an angle into approx. ¾-inch (2 cm) pieces.
3. Peel the onion, wash and trim the pepper and finely dice both. Rinse the parsley, shake it dry and finely chop it. Put everything in a bowl, stir in the warm octopus pieces and season with oil, vinegars, salt and pepper. Mix the salad well, then refrigerate for 3–4 hours.
4. Remove the salad from the fridge about 30 minutes before serving it, then season to taste, arrange on plates, sprinkle with pepper and serve garnished with basil and lemon wedges.

(1)

Korean octopus salad (2)

1 to 1.2 lbs (500 to 600 g) octopus tentacles | 2 tbsp white wine vinegar | salt | 1 tbsp soy sauce | **For the salad:** 3.3 oz (100 g) daikon radish | 20 small cherry tomatoes, red and yellow | 1 mini cucumber | 2 tbsp soy sauce | 2 tbsp rice syrup | 1 tbsp lime juice | ¼ cup (60 ml) olive oil | salt | pepper | chili flakes | chervil

1. Rinse the octopus, put it into the pressure cooker, add enough water to just cover it, then add the vinegar, 1 tbsp salt and the soy sauce. Seal the pot and cook the octopus on setting 2 (cooking indicator: 1st ring) for 5 minutes, as described above. Then cook for another 5 minutes or so.
2. Remove the octopus, let it cool to room temperature, then cut it into ¾–1½-inch (2–4 cm) pieces.
3. To make the salad, peel and finely slice the radish. Wash and halve the cherry tomatoes. Wash and trim the cucumber, then cut it lengthwise into thin strips.
4. To make the dressing, mix together the soy sauce, rice syrup, lime juice, olive oil, salt and pepper in a bowl. Arrange the octopus pieces and the remaining salad ingredients on plates in a decorative way, drizzle with the dressing, sprinkle with chili flakes and serve garnished with chervil leaves.

RECIPES » SALADS, SNACKS & BOWLS 143

Spicy rice salad
with chicken

COOKING LEVEL VITAVIT®

COOKING LEVEL VITAQUICK®

COOKING TIME

MAKES: 4 PORTIONS **MARINATING TIME:** 30 MIN. **PREP TIME:** APPROX. 30 MIN.

FOR THE SALAD
3 chicken legs (approx. 1.2 lbs/600 g)
salt
1 tsp sweet paprika
juice of 1 lime
2 tbsp vegetable oil
freshly ground pepper
1 to 1¼ cups (250 to 300 ml) chicken stock
2 tbsp vegetable oil
1 red bell pepper
1 large green bell pepper
1 red chile pepper
1 cup + 2 tbsp (200 g) long-grain white rice (parboiled)
1⅔ cups (300 g) diced seeded tomatoes

FOR THE MARINADE
1 hard-boiled egg
1 onion
1 garlic clove
6 tbsp (90 ml) peanut oil
2 tsp (10 g) minced gingerroot
1–2 tbsp white wine vinegar
2 tbsp lime juice
salt
freshly ground pepper
1 pinch of chili powder
2 tbsp fresh cilantro, chopped

TO FINISH
8 large lettuce leaves
chili flakes, for sprinkling
cilantro, to garnish
2 organic limes, in wedges

FOR THE SALAD: pat the chicken dry and joint them (p. 82), then rub a mixture of salt, paprika and lime juice into them, cover and let marinate for 30 minutes.

Heat the oil in a pressure cooker, add the chicken pieces and sauté all over until browned. Season the meat with pepper and deglaze with the minimum amount of stock. Seal the pot, set the pressure regulator to setting 3 and heat on the highest setting. When the yellow ring appears (cooking indicator: 1^s ring), reduce the heat. When the green ring becomes visible (cooking indicator: 2nd ring), the 15-minute cooking time begins.

Wash, trim and finely dice both of the peppers. Wash and trim the chile pepper, then cut it into thin rings, discarding the seeds.

Put the rice in the unperforated insert with 1 cup (250 ml) water and 1 tsp salt. Remove the pressure cooker from the heat and release the steam. Put the insert with the rice on the tripod and seal the pot. Cook for another 5–7 minutes on setting 3. Remove the pot from the heat, release the steam and open the lid. Remove the chicken portions and the rice and let cool.

FOR THE MARINADE: peel and chop up the egg. Peel and very finely dice the onion and garlic. Heat up 2 tbsp peanut oil in a frying pan, add the diced onion and sauté lightly. Add the ginger and garlic and continue frying for another 1–2 minutes. Put the mixture aside and let cool.

Mix together the vinegar, lime juice, salt, pepper and chili powder, then fold in the egg, chopped cilantro and the remaining oil (¼ cup/60 ml).

TO FINISH: remove the chicken meat from the bones and remove the skin. Wash and spin-dry the lettuce leaves. Put the rice and the diced tomatoes and pepper in a bowl. Add the chile rings and the onion mixture and mix carefully.

Put some lettuce leaves on one side of each plate then fill them with rice salad. Slice the meat crosswise, then arrange a few slices in a fan shape next to the salad and drizzle with half of the marinade. Sprinkle some chili flakes over the salad, garnish with cilantro leaves and lime wedges and serve. Serve the rest of the marinade separately in a small bowl.

TIP: this recipe involves releasing the steam from the pressure cooker partway through the cooking process. At this stage, you add the rice one level above the chicken in an unperforated insert on the tripod in the pot and cook it with the meat for another 5–7 minutes. If you don't have an unperforated insert, simply cook the rice separately in the pressure cooker on the highest pressure setting beforehand, then leave it to cool.

RECIPES » SALADS, SNACKS & BOWLS

(1) (2)

146   **RECIPES** ›› SALADS, SNACKS & BOWLS

Aromatic & herbal tones
Salads with meat & seafood

| COOKING LEVEL VITAVIT® | COOKING LEVEL VITAQUICK® | COOKING TIME | | COOKING LEVEL VITAVIT® | COOKING LEVEL VITAQUICK® | COOKING TIME |

Chinese beef salad (1)

MAKES: 4 PORTIONS   **PREP TIME:** APPROX. 20 MIN.

1.6 lb (800 g) boneless beef rib roast | 4 oz (125 g) piece fresh gingerroot | 4 red chile peppers | 2 lime leaves | 6 tbsp + 2 tsp (100 ml) Shaoxing rice wine | ¼ cup (60 ml) light soy sauce | 3 tbsp (40 g) packed brown sugar | ½ to 1 tbsp salt | 2 tsp five-spice powder | 1 tbsp freshly ground pepper | 3 tbsp (45 ml) sesame oil | **For the dressing:** 1 garlic clove | 1 green onion | 1 red chile pepper | ⅓ cup (75 ml) light soy sauce | 2 tbsp rice wine | 1 tbsp minced fresh gingerroot | 1 tbsp sesame oil | **Other ingredients:** 2 handfuls of lettuce | ½ bunch of garlic chives (or chives) | chervil leaves, to garnish

1. Briefly blanch the meat in lightly salted water, then rinse and strain. Peel and finely slice the ginger. Wash the chile peppers and lime leaves. Put everything in a pressure cooker with the rice wine, soy sauce and ¾ cup + 2 tbsp (200 ml) water. Add the sugar, salt, spices and sesame oil. Seal the pot and cook on setting 3 (cooking indicator: 2nd ring) for 45–50 minutes.
2. Release the steam from the pot, open the lid, remove the meat, cover it and leave it to cool.
3. To make the dressing, peel and very finely dice the garlic. Wash and trim the green onion and chile pepper and chop them into thin rings. Mix together the soy sauce and rice wine in a small bowl. Add the ginger, garlic, chile, green onion and sesame oil. Give the dressing a good stir and season to taste.
4. Trim the lettuce, separate the leaves, wash them and spin them dry. Wash the garlic chives, shake them dry and cut them into rings. Remove any fat from the meat, cut it into thin slices and serve with the salad. Drizzle with the dressing, garnish with garlic chives and chervil and serve.

Asian salad with succulent pork fillet & shrimp (2)

MAKES: 4 PORTIONS   **PREP TIME:** APPROX. 25 MIN.

1.25 lb (625 g) pork tenderloin | 12 jumbo shrimp, with shells | 1 red chile pepper | 1 garlic clove | 1 lime | 2 tbsp liquid honey | 1 tsp curry powder | 1½ tbsp minced fresh gingerroot | ¼ cup (60 ml) light soy sauce | 1 small papaya | 2 green onions | 5 oz (150 g) sugar snap peas | 1¼ cups (150 g) shelled edamame (fresh or frozen) | 1 handful of fresh cilantro | 1 bunch of Thai basil (or basil) | 2 tbsp sesame oil | 3 tbsp (45 ml) peanut oil | salt | freshly ground pepper | toasted sesame seeds

1. Rinse the meat and shrimp, pat them dry and put them in the pressure cooker. Wash and trim the chile pepper, then cut it lengthwise into thin strips. Peel and finely dice the garlic. Squeeze the lime. Mix the juice with the honey, curry powder, garlic, ginger, chile, soy sauce and ¾ cup + 2 tbsp (200 ml) of water, then pour the liquid over the meat and shrimp.
2. Close the pressure cooker and cook on setting 2 (cooking indicator: 1st ring) for 6 minutes. Remove the pot from the heat and let stand by the stove for around 4 minutes.
3. In the meantime, peel and halve the papaya, remove the seeds and chop the flesh into pieces. Wash and trim the green onions, then cut into thin rings. Trim and halve the sugar snap peas, blanch them for approx. 1 minute with the edamame, then rinse them with cold water. Put everything in a large bowl. Wash the herbs, pluck the leaves and add them to the bowl.
4. Release the steam from the pot, remove the pork, cut it into slices and arrange the slices on plates with the shrimp. Mix together both of the oils with the cooking juices. Drizzle 3 tbsp (45 ml) of the vinaigrette over the salad and briefly mix together. Season the salad to taste with salt and pepper and divide between four plates. Drizzle the rest of the vinaigrette over the shrimp and meat and serve with a sprinkling of sesame seeds.

COOKING LEVEL VITAVIT®

COOKING LEVEL VITAQUICK®

COOKING TIME

Mezze: hummus & other delicious dips

MAKES: 4 PORTIONS   **SOAKING TIME:** 6–12 HRS   **PREP TIME:** 15–25 MIN.

Classic hummus

1 cup (200 g) dried chickpeas | 2–3 tbsp tahini | 1–2 garlic cloves | 1 tsp ground cumin | salt | 2 tsp lemon juice | 2–3 tbsp olive oil | 1 pinch of chili powder

1. Soak the chickpeas in cold water overnight. The next day, put them in a colander and strain. Fill a pressure cooker with the minimum amount of water, add the chickpeas, seal the pot and cook on setting 3 (cooking indicator: 2nd ring) for 15 minutes. Remove the pot from the heat, release the steam and open the lid. Put the chickpeas in a colander and strain and cool.
2. Set aside a few chickpeas for the garnish. Measure out 1 cup (250 ml) water. Blend the remaining chickpeas with some of the water. Add the tahini and stir in enough water to make a smooth purée.
3. Peel and finely dice the garlic and stir it into the purée together with the cumin and salt. Season the hummus to taste, then put it in a small dish.
4. Mix together the remaining chickpeas with the lemon juice and 1 tsp oil. Garnish the hummus with the chickpeas, drizzle generously with olive oil and sprinkle with chili powder.

Beet hummus

½ cup (100 g) dried chickpeas | 9 oz (270 g) beets | 1¼ cups (300 ml) vegetable stock | 3 tbsp (45 g) tahini | 2 tbsp olive oil | salt | pepper | 1 tsp ground cumin | 1 tsp toasted sesame seeds

1. Rinse the chickpeas, then leave them to soak in cold water overnight.
2. The next day, put them in a colander and strain. Peel and slice the beets. Put the chickpeas and beets in a pressure cooker. Pour in the stock and cook on setting 2 (cooking indicator: 1st ring) for 20 minutes.
3. Remove the pot from the heat and slowly release the steam. Leave the chickpeas and beets to strain, then blend them into a fine purée in a blender together with the tahini, olive oil, salt, pepper and cumin. Season the hummus to taste, put it in a bowl, sprinkle with toasted sesame seeds and serve.

Pepper hummus

¾ cup (150 g) dried chickpeas | 3 red bell peppers and 1 banana pepper, halved | 2 tbsp vegetable oil | ½ cup (120 g) oil-packed sun-dried tomatoes, oil reserved | 1 garlic clove, peeled and halved | 1 tbsp olive oil | 3 tbsp (45 g) tahini | ½ tsp hot paprika | 1 tsp ground cumin | 1 tsp salt | 1 tbsp lemon juice | pepper flakes, for sprinkling

1. Leave the chickpeas to soak overnight and cook them as described in the classic hummus recipe.
2. Heat up a grill (or the oven grill). Mix the pepper halves with 1 tbsp oil and grill them on an oiled rack until black patches appear on the skin. Leave the pepper to sweat briefly in a freezer bag, then remove the skin.
3. Strain the tomatoes, coarsely dice them together with the pepper halves and blend them into a fine purée with the tomato oil and the remaining ingredients (except the pepper flakes). Season the hummus to taste and sprinkle with pepper flakes.

Greek fáva

1⅓ cups (300 g) dried yellow split peas | 1 onion | approx. ½ cup + 1 tbsp (140 ml) olive oil | 1 bay leaf | salt | pepper | 1 tsp dried oregano | 5–6 tbsp (75–90 ml) lemon juice | 2 tbsp sliced green onion

1. Soak the peas for approx. 6 hours, then strain and rinse them. Boil the peas in a pot with 6 cups (1.5 L) water for approx. 10 minutes, skim off the foam, remove from the heat and let stand briefly.
2. Peel, quarter and chop the onion. Heat 3 tbsp (45 ml) oil in a pressure cooker, add the onion and sauté in the oil. Strain the peas, add them to the pot with the bay leaf, fill with the minimum amount of hot water (the pressure cooker should only be filled to ⅓). Cook the peas on setting 3 (cooking indicator: 2nd ring) for approx. 12 minutes until soft, then release the steam and let cool.
3. Remove the bay leaf. Add the remaining oil, salt, pepper, oregano and lemon juice and blend into a fine purée. Season the purée to taste and garnish with green onion.

Baba ganoush

Salt | 1.2 lbs (600 g) eggplant | ¼ cup (60 ml) olive oil | ½ bunch of parsley, chopped | 2 tbsp tahini | 2 tbsp lemon juice | 2 garlic cloves | smoked salt | pepper | ½ organic lemon, in wedges

1. Fill the pressure cooker with the minimum amount of salted water. Wash the eggplant, pat them dry, brush them lightly with some of the oil and stab several times with a fork. Put the eggplant in the perforated insert on the tripod and cook on setting 2 (cooking indicator: 1st ring) for 10 minutes.
2. Release the steam from the pot and open the lid. Remove the eggplant, let cool and cut in half. Scoop out the flesh with a spoon, blend it or chop it finely and put it into a bowl.
3. Stir in the parsley, tahini, lemon juice and 2 tbsp oil. Peel and crush the garlic and add it to the bowl. Season the purée with smoked salt and pepper, drizzle with the remaining oil and serve with lemon wedges.

COOKING LEVEL VITAVIT® — COOKING LEVEL VITAQUICK® — COOKING TIME

Simple and delicious
Nigiri sushi & nori maki

MAKES: 4 PORTIONS **PREP TIME:** APPROX. 45 MIN.

FOR THE SUSHI RICE
1²⁄₃ cups (300 g) sushi rice
2 tsp fine sea salt
1 kombu leaf
¼ cup to ⅓ cup (60 to 75 ml) rice vinegar
3 to 4 tbsp (45 to 60 ml) mirin

FOR THE NIGIRI SUSHI (12 PCS)
wasabi paste
12 slices of raw fish, sushi quality (e.g., tuna, mackerel, salmon, approx. ¾ inch x 2 inches/2 x 5 cm each)
½ of the cooked sushi rice

FOR THE NORI MAKI (24 PCS)
2 nori sheets
bamboo rolling mat
½ of the cooked sushi rice
strips (approx. ¾ inch x 4 inches/2 x 10 cm) of salmon, tuna, surimi, avocado, cucumber or kampyō (dried calabash), etc.

TO FINISH
Japanese soy sauce, to serve
pickled ginger, to serve

FOR THE SUSHI RICE: put the rice in a pressure cooker with 1½ cups (375 ml) water and the salt and mix well. Add the kombu leaf **(1)**, insert it beneath the rice and close the pressure cooker with the lid. Set the pressure regulator to setting 3. Heat the pot on the highest setting. As soon as the yellow ring appears (cooking indicator: 1st ring), reduce the heat. When the green ring becomes visible (cooking indicator: 2nd ring), the 4-to-5-minute cooking time begins.

Remove the pressure cooker from the heat, release the steam and open the lid. Remove the kombu leaf and leave the rice to cool slightly. Mix together the rice vinegar and mirin and carefully fold the mixture into the lukewarm rice using a spatula **(2)**.

FOR THE NIGIRI SUSHI: spread a very thin layer of wasabi on one side of each fish slice. Wet your hands and shape approx. 1 tbsp sushi rice into an oval-shaped mound.

Place a fish slice (with the wasabi side facing upwards) in your left hand. Put a rice mound on top and gently press it onto the fish.

Wet your fingers with vinegar water, turn the sushi over, carefully press it into an even shape and round off the edges slightly with your thumb and index finger.

Arrange the nigiri sushi on a serving board (right-hand side of the image) and serve with Japanese soy sauce, wasabi paste and pickled ginger.

FOR THE NORI MAKI: cut the nori sheets in half. Put half a nori sheet with the matt side facing upwards on a bamboo mat so that the top of the sheet aligns with the mat. Wet your fingers with water and spread a quarter of the sushi rice (thickness approx. ½ inch/1 cm) on the nori sheet, leaving a strip free along the top.

Make a groove in the front third of the rice and place the vegetable and/or fish strips on top. Carefully roll up the nori sheet evenly using the bamboo mat **(3)**. Remove the mat and press the roll onto the free edge of the nori sheet. Then wrap the roll in the mat once more and press it down slightly all over.

Remove the mat and slice each roll into 6 even pieces with a very sharp knife, dipping the knife into water between each slice.

Repeat with the remaining nori sheet halves and arrange on a board (left-hand side of the image). Serve the nori maki with Japanese soy sauce and pickled ginger.

TIP: when pressure cooking sushi rice, you can also add the spicy liquid – a mixture of rice vinegar and a sweet ingredient – before you cook it. That way, the cooked rice just needs to be fluffed afterwards to remove any lumps (p. 88).

1

2

3

Vegan and vegetarian
Quick rice and quinoa bowls

COOKING LEVEL VITAVIT®   **COOKING LEVEL VITAQUICK®**   **COOKING TIME**

COOKING LEVEL VITAVIT®   **COOKING LEVEL VITAQUICK®**   **COOKING TIME**

Thai Buddha Bowl
with tofu

MAKES: 4 PORTIONS   **PREP TIME:** APPROX. 20 MIN.

1 cup + 6 tbsp (250 g) long grain red rice (or whole-grain brown rice) | salt | 7 oz (200 g) sugar snap peas | 10 oz (300 g) firm or extra-firm tofu | 2 tbsp peanut oil | 4½ cups (400 g) thinly sliced red cabbage | **For the dressing:** 6 tbsp + 2 tsp (100 ml) vegetable stock | ¾ cup + 2 tbsp (200 ml) coconut milk | ¼ cup (60 g) peanut butter | 2 tsp Thai red curry paste | 2 tbsp lime juice | salt | pepper

1. Put the rice in the pressure cooker with 1¼ cups (300 ml) salted water. Seal the pot, set the pressure regulator to setting 3 and heat on the highest setting. As soon as the yellow ring appears (cooking indicator: 1st ring), reduce the heat. When the green ring becomes visible (cooking indicator: 2nd ring), cook the red rice for 8 minutes. Remove the pot from the heat, release the steam, open the lid and leave the rice to cool for around 10 minutes.
2. Wash and trim the sugar snap peas, blanch them for around 15 seconds in salted water, rinse with cold water, strain, then cut them lengthwise into narrow strips. Season with salt and knead vigorously with your hands for 2–3 minutes. Pat the tofu dry and cut into approx. ½-inch (1.5 cm) cubes. Heat the oil in a frying pan, add the tofu cubes and fry for approx. 5 minutes until golden brown, turning over occasionally, then remove them, cover and keep warm.
3. To make the dressing, bring the stock and coconut milk to the boil in a small saucepan. Stir in the peanut butter and red curry paste and simmer over a low heat for 2–3 minutes. Season the dressing to taste with lime juice, salt and pepper, then set aside.
4. Divide the rice between four bowls, top with sugar snap peas, red cabbage and tofu and drizzle with half of the dressing. Serve the rest of the dressing separately.

Cucumber ribbon bowl
with onions & egg

MAKES: 4 PORTIONS   **PREP TIME:** APPROX. 30 MIN.

2 red onions | 2 tbsp honey | ⅓ cup (75 ml) red wine vinegar | **For the wasabi cucumber ribbons:** 1 cucumber | ⅓ cup (75 ml) mayonnaise | ½ cup (125 g) crème fraîche | 2–3 tsp wasabi paste | salt | **Other ingredients:** 1 cup (200 g) quinoa | 1⅔ cups (400 ml) vegetable stock | salt | 4 large eggs | 2 small ripe avocados | juice of 1 lime | freshly ground pepper

1. Peel the onions, cut them in half and chop them into thin strips. Put the honey in a saucepan with the vinegar and ⅓ cup (75 ml) water and bring to the boil. Add the onions, boil with the lid on for approx. 2 minutes, set aside, then leave the onion strips to cool in the cooking juices.
2. In the meantime, put the quinoa and stock in the pressure cooker and add a little salt. Seal the pot and cook on setting 2 (cooking indicator: 1st ring) for 5 minutes. Then remove the pot from the heat, release the steam, open the lid and leave the quinoa to cool for around 10 minutes.
3. To make the wasabi cucumber ribbons, peel the cucumber and then use a peeler to slice it into thin strips with a width of approx. ½ inch (1 cm). Mix together the mayonnaise, crème fraîche and wasabi until smooth. Fold in the cucumber ribbons, season with salt and let marinate for approx. 10 minutes.
4. Soft-boil the eggs in a pan for approx. 6 minutes, rinse with cold water and let cool briefly. Carefully peel the eggs, then cut them in half. Cut the avocados in half, remove the pits and the skin, cut them crosswise into slices and drizzle with lime juice.
5. Strain the onions. Fluff the quinoa and divide it between four bowls, then top with the sweet-and-sour onions, the avocado, the cucumber ribbons and 2 egg halves per bowl. Season the egg and avocado with some salt and pepper and then serve.

COOKING LEVEL VITAVIT®: 3

COOKING LEVEL VITAQUICK®: 2

COOKING TIME: 20

Thai sweet chili pork bowl

MAKES: 4–6 PORTIONS   **PREP TIME:** APPROX. 20 MIN.

FOR THE MEAT
1.6 to 2 lbs (800 g to 1 kg) pork tenderloins
8 oz (250 g) small button mushrooms
1 large sweet onion
1 red bell pepper
2 limes
1 cup (250 ml) hoisin sauce (or teriyaki sauce)
¾ cup + 2 tbsp (200 ml) sweet chili sauce
¼ cup (60 ml) soy sauce
3 garlic cloves
1¼-inch (3 cm) piece gingerroot
1 tsp rice vinegar

FOR THE RICE
1 cup + 6 tbsp (250 g) basmati rice
1 tsp salt

TO FINISH
2 young green onions
1–2 tbsp cilantro leaves, chopped

FOR THE MEAT: pat the pork dry, remove any silver skin and cut into equal-size pieces that will fit flat in pressure cooker. Place pork in the pressure cooker. Trim and halve the mushrooms. Peel and finely dice the onion. Wash, trim and finely dice the pepper. Add the onion, pepper and mushrooms to the meat in the pot **(1)**.

Squeeze a lime. Put the juice in a small bowl together with the hoisin sauce, the chili sauce and the soy sauce and mix well. Peel and finely dice the garlic. Peel and finely chop the ginger and add it to the sauce with the garlic and vinegar. Pour the sauce over the ingredients in the pressure cooker and mix together well.

Seal the pressure cooker with the lid and set the pressure regulator to setting 3. Heat the pot on the highest setting. As soon as the yellow ring appears (cooking indicator: 1st ring), reduce the heat. When the green ring becomes visible (cooking indicator: 2nd ring), the 20-minute cooking time begins.

FOR THE RICE: in the meantime, put the basmati rice in a colander and rinse it with cold running water until the water runs clear. Put the rice in a saucepan with 2¾ cups (575 ml) water and the salt and cook as per the packet instructions.

TO FINISH: remove the pressure cooker from the heat, release the steam and open the lid. Remove the meat and shred it into large chunks with two forks **(2)**. Return the shredded chunks of pork to the pot **(3)** and briefly bring to the boil once again, without closing the lid.

Trim and wash the green onions, cut a piece (3 to 4 inches/8 to 10 cm long) from the light green part and slice it into thin strips. Cut the white part of the green onions at an angle into thin rings.

Fluff the rice and divide it between four to six bowls. Season the meat and mushroom mixture to taste and arrange it on top of the rice. Garnish the bowls with chopped cilantro leaves and green onion rings/strips and serve.

TIP: if using more than one pork tenderloin, choose two of the same thickness for even cooking.
To cook rice in the same pot as pork, remove the pressure cooker from the heat after approx. 15 minutes and release the steam. Put the rice and 1 cup + 6 tbsp (340 ml) water in an unperforated insert (ratio 1:1) and add some salt. Put the insert with the rice on a tripod in the pot (without exceeding the maximum volume mark). Heat up the pot again and cook everything on setting 3 (cooking indicator: 2nd ring) for another 5 minutes.

Soups & one-pot dishes

Creamy soups with herbs and vegetables, hearty soups with mushrooms and bacon or substantial bean or pearl barley soups work particularly well in a pressure cooker and can be whipped up in an instant. So, too, can aromatic stock as a basis for refined Asian noodle soups or hot and spicy goulash soups. One-pot dishes like mac and cheese, pasta with octopus or pasta al pomodoro are fully cooked and ready to serve in a matter of minutes.

COOKING LEVEL VITAVIT®   COOKING LEVEL VITAQUICK®   COOKING TIME

Creamy herb soup
with poached egg

MAKES: 4 PORTIONS   **PREP TIME:** APPROX. 30 MIN.

FOR THE VEGETABLE STOCK
2 shallots
2 carrots
5 small potatoes
1 small turnip
2 zucchini
1 celery stalk
½ fennel bulb
1 tomato
5 black peppercorns, crushed
1 clove
½ tsp salt

FOR THE SOUP
2 tbsp butter
3 tbsp (25 g) all-purpose flour
½ cup (125 ml) dry white wine (e.g., Riesling)
1 bunch of parsley
1 bunch of chives
¾ cup + 2 tbsp (200 ml) heavy or whipping (35%) cream
salt
freshly ground pepper

FOR THE POACHED EGGS
2 tbsp white wine vinegar
salt
4 fresh eggs

TO FINISH
2 tbsp finely diced red bell pepper
2 tbsp finely diced orange bell pepper
2 tbsp finely diced zucchini
salt
freshly ground pepper
chervil and chives

FOR THE VEGETABLE STOCK: peel the shallots, carrots, potatoes and turnip. Wash and trim the zucchini, celery and fennel. Cut the vegetables into large pieces. Wash and halve the tomato, remove the core, then chop into large pieces.

Put the prepared vegetables in a pressure cooker (minimum 4.5 Qts/4.5 L) and add the peppercorns, clove and salt together with 8 cups (2 L) cold water. Seal the pressure cooker with the lid and turn the pressure regulator to setting 2. Heat the pot on the highest setting. As soon as the yellow ring appears (cooking indicator: 1st ring), reduce the heat. When the green ring becomes visible (cooking indicator: 1st ring), the 10-minute cooking time begins. Remove the pressure cooker from the heat, release the steam and open the lid. Strain the stock into a pot through a sieve. Rinse the pressure cooker and rub it dry.

FOR THE SOUP: heat the butter in the pressure cooker until foamy, sprinkle in the flour, sauté lightly while stirring, then deglaze with the white wine. Gradually stir in half of the strained stock and simmer the contents in the uncovered pressure cooker for a few minutes.

Rinse the parsley and chives and shake them dry. Pluck and finely chop the parsley leaves and mince the chives. Remove 2–3 tbsp herbs and set aside for the garnish. Add the remaining herbs to the pressure cooker and blend the contents into a fine purée with a hand blender. Pour in the cream, reheat the soup and season with salt and pepper.

FOR THE POACHED EGGS: bring approx. 8 cups (2 L) water to the boil in a pot with the vinegar and 1 tbsp of salt, then reduce the heat. Crack the eggs into a cup one at a time and carefully slide them into the boiling water. Shape the egg white slightly with a spoon and poach the eggs for 3–4 minutes, then remove and strain.

TO FINISH: season the creamy herb soup to taste, spoon into deep plates and sprinkle on some diced pepper and zucchini. Place a poached egg in the middle of each portion, cut it open, sprinkle with salt and lightly grind with pepper. Garnish each portion with chervil leaves and chives, sprinkle with the herbs that were set aside and serve.

TIP: the remaining vegetable stock is ideal for freezing for use as a base for sauces and soups at a later date. Parsley and chives add a great deal of flavor to this soup but can also be complemented with other herbs. Dill provides freshness while chervil adds a subtle note of aniseed, and basil offers a Mediterranean touch. Particularly strong herbs such as lovage or mint can also be used, although restraint is recommended here. Simply experiment for yourself and see which combination you like the most.

(1) (2)

Colorful vegetable soup
refined with crème fraîche

COOKING LEVEL VITAVIT®   COOKING LEVEL VITAQUICK®   COOKING TIME

COOKING LEVEL VITAVIT®   COOKING LEVEL VITAQUICK®   COOKING TIME

Carrot soup
with orange (1)

MAKES: 4 PORTIONS   **PREP TIME:** APPROX. 25 MIN.

1 lb (500 g) carrots | ½ white onion | 1¼-inch (3 cm) piece gingerroot | 1 mild red chile pepper | 3 tbsp + 1 tsp (50 g) butter | 4 cups (1 L) vegetable stock | salt | freshly ground white pepper | 3 small oranges | 2 tbsp crème fraîche | marjoram leaves and tips, to garnish

1. Peel the carrots and diagonally cut them into ¾-inch (2 cm) pieces. Peel and finely dice the onion and ginger. Wash, trim and finely dice the mild chile pepper, then set about a third aside for the garnish.
2. Melt the butter in a pressure cooker and lightly sauté the diced onion and ginger. Add the carrots and mild chile pepper and cook for 3–4 minutes. Pour in the vegetable stock and lightly season with salt and pepper.
3. Close the pressure cooker with the lid, set the pressure regulator to setting 3 and heat the pot on the highest setting. When the yellow ring appears (cooking indicator: 1st ring), reduce the heat. As soon as the green ring becomes visible (cooking indicator: 2nd ring), the 5-to-6-minute cooking time begins.
4. Meanwhile, peel 1 orange and separate into segments. Squeeze the remaining 2 oranges. Remove the pressure cooker from the heat, release the steam and open the lid. Remove a third of the carrots and set aside for the topping.
5. Finely blend the pot contents, mix the orange juice and crème fraîche into the soup and briefly reheat everything in the uncovered pot.
6. Season the carrot soup to taste and spoon into bowls or deep plates. Top with carrots and fileted orange segments. Sprinkle with the remaining diced mild chile pepper and serve garnished with a little marjoram.

Squash soup
with ginger (2)

MAKES: 4 PORTIONS   **PREP TIME:** APPROX. 25 MIN.

1 hokkaido pumpkin (red kuri squash) (approx. 1.6 lbs/800 g) | 10 oz (300 g) diced peeled potatoes | 2 carrots | 1 large onion | 1 garlic clove | ½- to ¾-inch (1 to 2 cm) piece gingerroot | 2 tbsp (30 g) butter | salt | pepper | 1 tbsp curry powder | 1 pinch of chili powder | ½ tsp ground coriander | 6 cups (1.5 L) vegetable stock | 2 tbsp pumpkin seeds | 1 can (14 oz/400 ml) coconut milk | ¼ cup (60 g) crème fraîche | 1 tsp pumpkin seed oil | fresh basil

1. Wash, quarter, seed (do not throw away the seeds) and finely dice the squash. Peel and finely dice the potatoes, carrots, onion, garlic and ginger.
2. Melt the butter in the pressure cooker and lightly sauté the onion, garlic and ginger. Add the squash, potatoes and carrots. Cook briefly, stirring regularly. Lightly season with salt and pepper, stir in the remaining spices, then pour in the stock.
3. Close the pressure cooker, set the pressure regulator to setting 3 and heat the pot on the highest setting. When the yellow ring appears (cooking indicator: 1st ring), reduce the heat. As soon as the green ring becomes visible (cooking indicator: 2nd ring), the approx. 5-minute cooking time begins.
4. In the meantime, briefly toast the pumpkin seeds in a frying pan without fat until lightly browned, then remove, let cool and shell if desired.
5. Remove the pressure cooker from the heat, release the steam and open the lid. Finely blend the pot contents and stir in the coconut milk. Season the soup to taste, divide between four bowls or deep plates and add 1 tbsp crème fraîche to each portion, stirring it in slightly but not fully so as to create a beautifully decorative pattern. Drizzle the soup with a little pumpkin seed oil and serve garnished with the seeds and basil.

COOKING LEVEL VITAVIT® — COOKING LEVEL VITAQUICK® — COOKING TIME

Soups with mushrooms and chestnuts

MAKES: 4 PORTIONS PER RECIPE   **PREP TIME:** APPROX. 25 MIN. PER RECIPE

(1)

Porcini mushroom soup
with fried bacon (1)

14 oz (400 g) fresh small porcini or other exotic mushrooms | 2.6 oz (80 g) mild-smoked bacon | 2 shallots | 3 tbsp + 1 tsp (50 g) butter | salt | freshly ground pepper | freshly grated nutmeg | 4 cups (1 L) beef stock (see p. 97, or poultry stock, see pp. 96–7) | 2 tbsp chopped parsley

1. Trim the porcini mushrooms and briefly rinse if necessary, then pat dry. Cut the mushrooms into slices and the bacon into small cubes. Peel and finely dice the shallots.
2. Melt the butter in the pressure cooker and sauté the shallots and bacon until translucent. Add the mushrooms, continue to cook briefly until browned, then season with salt, pepper and 1 pinch of nutmeg. Remove one-third for the topping and keep warm, then add the stock to the remaining mushroom mixture.
3. Close the pressure cooker, set the pressure regulator to setting 2 and heat the pot on the highest setting. When the yellow ring appears (cooking indicator: 1st ring), reduce the heat. As soon as the green ring becomes visible (cooking indicator: 1st ring), the approx. 10-minute cooking time begins.
4. Remove the pot from the heat and release the steam. Finely blend the pot contents and simmer down a little more uncovered, as desired. Season the soup to taste, divide between four deep plates, add the topping and sprinkle with parsley. Sprinkle a little nutmeg over the top and serve the mushroom soup.

Chestnut soup
with Camembert quenelles (2)

1 small carrot | 1 large onion | 1 celery stalk | 2 tbsp butter | ½ cup (70 g) diced peeled russet potato | 8 oz (250 g) cooked chestnuts | 6 tbsp + 2 tsp (100 ml) white wine (or unsweetened grape juice) | salt | pepper | nutmeg | 3¼ cups (800 ml) vegetable stock | 3 tbsp + 1 tsp (50 g) crème fraîche | chervil | 1 tbsp minced chive | **For the quenelles:** ½ mild yellow chile pepper | 3.3 oz (100 g) mature Camembert | 2 tbsp minced chives | 1 pinch of blue fenugreek, if desired

(2)

1. Peel or wash the carrot, onion and celery, trim and cut into approx. ½-inch (1 cm) cubes. Heat the butter in the pressure cooker and sauté the onion and vegetables until lightly browned. Add the chestnuts and continue to cook briefly, then remove a third for the topping and keep warm. Deglaze the contents with white wine, lightly season with salt, pepper and nutmeg and pour in the vegetable stock.
2. Close the pressure cooker, set the pressure regulator to setting 2 and heat the pot on the highest setting. When the yellow ring appears (cooking indicator: 1st ring), reduce the heat. As soon as the green ring becomes visible (cooking indicator: 1st ring), the 7-to-10-minute cooking time begins.
3. Remove the pot from the heat, release the steam and open the lid. Finely blend the soup with an immersion blender and stir in the crème fraîche. Season the chestnut soup to taste and keep it warm.
4. To make the quenelles, wash, trim and finely dice the mild chile pepper. Mash the cheese in a bowl and add the mild chile pepper, chives and blue fenugreek, if using. Remove a little of the mixture at a time and use 2 spoons to shape it into quenelles.
5. Spoon the chestnut soup onto deep plates, add the topping and the Camembert quenelles, garnish with chervil and chives and serve.

Soups with beans, vegetables & bacon

COOKING LEVEL VITAVIT®

COOKING LEVEL VITAQUICK®

25 COOKING TIME

MAKES: 4 PORTIONS PER RECIPE **PREP TIME:** 25–30 MIN. PER RECIPE

Minestrone with pancetta (1)

1¼ cups (250 g) dried cannellini (white kidney) beans | 1 onion | 3 garlic cloves | ¼ savoy cabbage (or white cabbage) | 1 leek | 2–3 carrots | 1 red bell pepper | 1 orange bell pepper | 2–3 firm potatoes | 3 sage leaves | a few celery leaves | 2–3 tbsp olive oil | 1.6 oz (50 g) pancetta cubes | 4¾ cups (1.2 L) vegetable stock | salt | pepper | ½ cup + 1 tbsp (50 g) grated Parmesan | 1–2 tbsp chopped parsley

1. Rinse and strain the beans, then place in a pressure cooker and cover with 3 cups (750 ml) water. Seal the pot, set the pressure regulator to setting 3 and heat the pot on the highest setting. When the yellow ring appears (cooking indicator: 1st ring), reduce the heat. As soon as the green ring becomes visible (cooking indicator: 2nd ring), cook the beans for approx. 20 minutes, then release the steam and allow them to strain. Clean the pot.

2. Peel and finely dice the onion and garlic. Wash, trim or peel and finely dice the vegetables. Rinse the herbs and shake them dry. Heat the oil in the pressure cooker, then sear the pancetta cubes until lightly browned. Add the onion, garlic, beans and vegetables and continue frying briefly, then deglaze with the stock. Add the sage and celery leaves, lightly season with salt and pepper and seal the pot.

3. Cook the soup on setting 3 (cooking indicator: 2nd ring) for 5 minutes, then release the steam, simmer down a little uncovered if necessary and stir in ⅓ cup (30 g) Parmesan. Season the minestrone soup to taste and serve with parsley and the remaining Parmesan.

Ribollita with leek (2)

1 cup + 6 tbsp (250 g) dried lima beans | 1 onion | 2 garlic cloves | 1 leek | 1 sprig of sage | 2 sprigs of thyme | 3 tbsp (45 ml) olive oil | 3.3 oz (100 g) bacon, diced | ¾ cup (100 g) diced carrots | ⅔ cup (80 g) thickly sliced celery | 1 dried peperoncino | salt | pepper | ½ cup + 1 tbsp (50 g) grated Parmesan | 1 tbsp chopped parsley | 4 slices of toasted bread

1. Rinse the beans and allow them to strain. Peel and finely dice the onion and garlic. Wash and trim the leek, then cut into almost ½-inch (1 cm) thick rings. Wash the herbs, shake them dry and chop up the thyme.

2. Heat the oil in the pressure cooker, fry the bacon until browned, then remove it. Sauté the onion and garlic in the frying fat. Add the beans, sage and 8 cups (2 L) water, seal the pot and cook on setting 3 (cooking indicator: 2nd ring) for approx. 20 minutes, then release the steam and open the lid.

3. Add the vegetables, thyme and peperoncino, then season with salt and pepper. Seal the pressure cooker and cook the soup on setting 2 (cooking indicator: 1st ring) for another 5 minutes or so. Release the steam from the pot and open the lid.

4. Remove the peperoncino. Finely blend half of the soup, then stir back in with ⅓ cup (30 g) Parmesan. Season the ribollita to taste, spoon onto deep plates, sprinkle with parsley and serve with toasted bread and the remaining Parmesan.

RECIPES » SOUPS & ONE-POT DISHES   165

Warm & hearty
soups for cold days

MAKES: 4 PORTIONS **PREP TIME:** APPROX. 25 MIN.

(1)

Pearl barley soup (1)

½ cup to ⅔ cup (110 g to 140 g) pearl barley | 3.3 oz (100 g) smoked bacon | 2 carrots | 1 parsnip | 1 celery stalk | 1 young leek | 2 garlic cloves | 1 tbsp olive oil | 2 small onions, diced | 1½ cups (200 g) diced peeled potatoes | 4¾ cups (1.2 L) poultry stock | 1 bay leaf | salt | pepper | 1 tbsp chopped parsley | 2 tbsp minced chives

1. Rinse the pearl barley and let strain. Finely dice the bacon. Peel and dice the carrots and parsnip. Wash, trim and dice the celery and leek. Peel and finely chop up the garlic.
2. Heat the oil in the pressure cooker, fry the bacon until lightly browned, then remove it. Briefly sauté the onions and vegetables in the remaining fat until they start to color. Stir in the garlic and continue cooking for approx. 1 minute. Next, stir in the pearl barley and deglaze with the stock. Add the bay leaf and lightly season with salt and pepper.
3. Seal the pot, set the pressure regulator to setting 3 and heat the pot on the highest setting. When the yellow ring appears (cooking indicator: 1st ring), reduce the heat. As soon as the green ring becomes visible (cooking indicator: 2nd ring), the 8-to-10-minute cooking time begins.
4. Remove the pressure cooker from the heat, release the steam and open the lid. Depending on the desired consistency, simmer the soup down a little more (uncovered), or add stock.
5. Remove the bay leaf. Add the bacon to the pot and heat briefly. Season the pearl barley soup to taste, spoon onto plates and serve with a sprinkling of parsley and chives.

(2)

Caldo verde (2)

4 oz (125 g) cured chorizo | ¼ cup (60 ml) olive oil | 1 lb (500 g) russet potatoes | 2 small onions | 3 garlic cloves | 1½ tsp black peppercorns | 1 bay leaf | 8 oz (250 g) fresh kale | salt | freshly ground pepper | 1 tomato | 1 tbsp chopped flat-leaf parsley

1. Remove the skin from the chorizo and cut it into slices. Heat 1 tbsp oil in the pressure cooker, sear the chorizo slices, remove with the oil and set aside.
2. Wash, peel and quarter the potatoes. Peel and finely dice the onions and garlic. Heat 1 tbsp oil in the pressure cooker and sauté the onions until translucent. Add the garlic and potatoes, cook briefly, then add 6 cups (1.5 L) water, the peppercorns and the bay leaf.
3. Close the pressure cooker, set the pressure regulator to setting 3 and heat the pot on the highest setting. When the yellow ring appears (cooking indicator: 1st ring), reduce the heat. As soon as the green ring becomes visible (cooking indicator: 2nd ring), the 10-to-12-minute cooking time begins.
4. Release the steam from the pot, open the lid, remove and discard the bay leaf and coarsely blend the contents. Wash the kale, remove the thick leaf ribs, roll up the leaves and cut into thin strips. Add to the pressure cooker with the remaining oil and season the soup with salt and pepper. Seal the pot and cook the soup on setting 2 (cooking indicator: 1st ring) for another 3 minutes or so. Remove the pot from the heat, release the steam and open the lid.
5. Wash, quarter and seed the tomato, then finely dice the flesh. Lightly season the soup with salt to taste and spoon onto deep plates. Top the soup with sliced chorizo and diced tomato, sprinkle with parsley, drizzle with the cooking oil from the chorizo and serve.

COOKING LEVEL VITAVIT® — COOKING LEVEL VITAQUICK® — COOKING TIME

Beautiful potato soups
Thickened and clear

MAKES: 4 PORTIONS **PREP TIME:** APPROX. 25 MIN.

Creamy potato soup (1)

15 oz (450 g) russet potatoes | salt | ¼ cup (60 ml) milk | 4 tsp butter | white pepper | nutmeg | 3 cups (750 ml) beef stock (or vegetable stock) | ⅓ cup (75 ml) heavy or whipping (35%) cream | ¼ cup (60 g) crème fraîche | **For the topping (optional):** 6 small (size S) eggs or quail eggs, boiled, peeled and halved | 4 tsp seaweed caviar, as desired | 1–2 tbsp minced chives

1. Wash the potatoes and put them into the pressure cooker. Add the minimum amount of water and season the potatoes with salt.
2. Seal the pot and cook the potatoes on setting 3 (cooking indicator: 2nd ring) for 10–12 minutes. Remove the pot from the heat, release the steam and open the lid. Peel the potatoes and pass them through a ricer or food mill while still warm.
3. Heat the milk and butter in a pot, season with salt, pepper and 1 pinch of nutmeg, pour into the potatoes and stir to form a smooth mash. Bring the beef stock to the boil in the pressure cooker and stir in the mash and cream.
4. Seal the pot and cook on setting 1 (cooking indicator: 1st ring) for 4–5 minutes. Release the steam, season the soup to taste, refine it with crème fraîche, grind with pepper, top with chives and serve warm.
5. Alternatively, allow the soup to cool for about 4 hours without adding the crème fraîche and serve as vichyssoise. In this case, spoon the soup onto deep plates, stir 1 tbsp crème fraîche into each portion and top with the egg halves, the chives, and, if desired, 1 tsp seaweed caviar each.

Sweet potato dashi (2)

2 lemongrass stalks | 2 nori sheets | 2 tbsp soy sauce | 4 cups (1 L) vegetable stock | ¼ cup (60 ml) toasted sesame oil | 2 onions | 2 garlic cloves | 1¼-inch (3 cm) piece gingerroot | 1 yellow chile pepper | 2 green onions | 7 oz (200 g) silken tofu | 3¼ cups (400 g) cubed (½-inch/1 cm) peeled sweet potatoes | ½ cup (80 g) diagonally sliced green beans | salt | 2 tbsp toasted black sesame seeds | grated zest of 1 organic lime

1. Wash and trim the lemongrass, cut it in half lengthwise, press it and add it to the pressure cooker with the nori sheets, soy sauce, stock and oil. Seal the pot and cook on setting 3 (cooking indicator: 2nd ring) for 10 minutes.
2. Meanwhile, peel and finely dice the onions, garlic and ginger. Wash, trim and finely chop the chile pepper. Wash and trim the green onions, then cut them diagonally into rings; keep light and green separate. Cut the tofu into approx. ½-inch (1 cm) cubes.
3. Remove the pressure cooker from the heat, release the steam, open the lid and remove the lemongrass. Add the prepared vegetables, sweet potatoes and light green onion rings to the pot, reseal it and cook on setting 2 (cooking indicator: 1st ring) for another 5 minutes or so.
4. Release the steam from the pot and open the lid. Stir in the tofu cubes and infuse in the uncovered pot for another 2–3 minutes.
5. Season the sweet potato dashi with salt and soy sauce to taste, spoon into bowls, sprinkle with the green onion rings, sesame seeds and lime zest, then serve.

(1)

RECIPES » SOUPS & ONE-POT DISHES   169

Quick fish soup
with saffron and vegetables

170 RECIPES » SOUPS & ONE-POT DISHES

COOKING LEVEL VITAVIT®

COOKING LEVEL VITAQUICK®

COOKING TIME

MAKES: 4 PORTIONS **PREP TIME:** APPROX. 25 MIN.

FOR THE SOUP
½ small red bell pepper
8 oz (250 g) tomato (about 1 medium)
2 sprigs of flat-leaf parsley
3 sprigs of thyme
2 tbsp olive oil
¾ cup (100 g) diced onion
1–2 garlic cloves, finely diced
1 cup + 2 tbsp (150 g) diced peeled round (waxy) potatoes
1¼ cups (150 g) diced fennel bulb, with fronds reserved
⅔ cup (80 g) diced celery
4¾ cups (1.2 L) fish stock (see tip)
salt
15 saffron threads

FOR THE TOPPING
1.2 lbs (600 g) mixed fish fillets (e.g., sea bass, monkfish, sea bream, red mullet)
salt
freshly ground pepper

TO FINISH
2 tbsp chopped herbs (flat-leaf parsley and thyme)
fleur de sel
freshly ground pepper

FOR THE SOUP: wash and trim the pepper and finely dice the flesh.

Blanch and peel the tomato, remove the core and seeds, then finely dice the flesh. Rinse the parsley and thyme and shake them dry.

Heat the oil in a pressure cooker and sauté the diced onion until translucent. Add the garlic and continue to sauté briefly. Add the potatoes, pepper, fennel and celery and sauté for another 3–4 minutes. Deglaze with fish stock, lightly season with salt and add the parsley, thyme and saffron threads.

Close the pressure cooker with the lid, set the pressure regulator to setting 3 and heat the pot on the highest setting. When the yellow ring appears (cooking indicator: 1st ring), reduce the heat. As soon as the green ring becomes visible (cooking indicator: 2nd ring), the 3-to-4-minute cooking time begins.

FOR THE TOPPING: meanwhile, rinse the fish fillets, dab them dry and cut into large pieces. Remove the pressure cooker from the heat, release the steam and open the lid. Remove the parsley and thyme.

Season the soup with salt and pepper, add the diced tomato and pieces of fish, then reseal the pot.

Turn the pressure regulator to setting 1 and heat the pressure cooker on the highest setting. When the yellow ring appears (cooking indicator: 1st ring), reduce the heat. As soon as the green ring becomes visible (cooking indicator: 1st ring), cook for 2–3 minutes until done.

TO FINISH: meanwhile, roughly pluck the fennel fronds. Remove the pot from the heat, release the steam and open the lid. Season the fish soup to taste, spoon into deep plates, sprinkle with the chopped herbs, fennel fronds and 1 pinch of fleur de sel, grind with pepper and serve.

TIP: have the fishmonger fillet the fish when you buy it and ask to be given the carcasses (bones, fins and offcuts). These can be used to whip up a delicious fish stock in minutes (see p. 293), which is ideal as a tasty basis for this soup.

Asian chicken soup

COOKING LEVEL VITAVIT® 3

COOKING LEVEL VITAQUICK® 2

COOKING TIME 20

MAKES: 4 PORTIONS **PREP TIME:** APPROX. 1 HR

FOR THE CHINESE CHICKEN STOCK
1 whole chicken, approx. 2.4 lbs (1.2 kg)
2 green onions
¾ cup (35 g) sliced peeled gingerroot
1 tbsp salt
⅓ cup (75 ml) rice wine

FOR THE SOUP
4 cilantro roots
½ cup (25 g) sliced peeled galangal
½ cup (25 g) sliced peeled gingerroot
2 wild lime leaves
7 oz (200 g) boneless skinless chicken breast

FOR THE SPICE PASTE
2 red chiles
1 shallot
4 young garlic cloves
1 tbsp sesame oil

TO FINISH
1 tsp five-spice powder
1 tbsp light soy sauce
1 tbsp fish sauce
1 tsp granulated sugar
7 oz (200 g) medium rice noodles (or thin tagliatelle)
salt
1 tsp sesame oil
1 handful of fresh cilantro
4 green onions

FOR THE CHINESE CHICKEN STOCK: place the chicken in the pressure cooker. Wash and trim the green onions, then cut into rings. Put the green onion and ginger in a large pressure cooker (at least 6 L) with the salt. Add the rice wine and 3 L water. Seal the pressure cooker and turn the pressure regulator to setting 3. Heat the pot on the highest setting. When the yellow ring appears (cooking indicator: 1st ring), reduce the heat. When the green ring becomes visible (cooking indicator: 2nd ring), cook everything for 10–20 minutes. Set the pot aside and let the pressure release by itself. Remove the chicken and make use of it elsewhere (for example, for a poultry salad). Strain the stock and measure out 4 cups (1 L). Leave the rest to cool and freeze in portions for later use.

FOR THE SOUP: bring the 4 cups (1 L) stock to the boil in the uncovered pressure cooker. Clean the cilantro. Cut into thick slices and add to the stock, together with the galangal, ginger and lime leaves. Pat the chicken breasts dry and add to the stock. Seal the pot, heat on the highest setting, then cook on setting 2 (cooking indicator: 1st ring) for approx. 10 minutes.

FOR THE SPICE PASTE: wash and trim the chiles, then cut into rings, removing the seeds. Peel and finely dice the shallot and garlic. Briefly dry-fry in a hot frying pan with no fat, set aside, let cool, then coarsely crush in a mortar with the sesame oil.

TO FINISH: release the steam from the pressure cooker and open the lid. Remove the chicken, let cool briefly, then shred into strips just under ½ inch (1 cm) in width. Pass the soup through a sieve, then return it to the pot. Combine the five-spice powder, soy sauce, fish sauce and sugar and stir through the soup. Mix the chicken strips and two-thirds of the spice paste into the soup, then simmer uncovered for another 5 minutes. Cook the noodles in salted water according to the packet instructions, strain, rinse and mix with the oil. Rinse the fresh cilantro and shake dry. Set aside a few leaves for garnishing and finely chop the rest. Wash and trim the green onions, then diagonally slice into rings. Season the soup and briefly return to the boil. Spoon the noodles and green onions into preheated soup bowls, ladle on the hot soup, top with the fresh cilantro and the remaining spice paste and serve.

VARIATIONS: for a quick chicken soup, pat dry 1 lb (500 g) boneless skinless chicken breasts, and cut into pieces. Peel or trim and finely chop 3 carrots, 1 bunch of green onions, ⅔ cup (50 g) shiitake mushrooms, 1½ tbsp (20 g) minced ginger and 2¾ cups (250 g) Chinese (napa) cabbage. Put everything into the pressure cooker with 2 tsp salt, 2 tbsp rice wine or sherry and 6 cups (1.5 L) chicken stock. Seal the pot and cook the soup on setting 3 (cooking indicator: 2nd ring) for 5 minutes. Switch off the heat, leave the pot to stand for 2–3 minutes, then release the steam.

COOKING LEVEL VITAVIT® 3 | COOKING LEVEL VITAQUICK® 2 | COOKING TIME 5–7

Spicy chicken soups from Thailand

MAKES: 4 PORTIONS   **PREP TIME:** 20–25 MIN.

Red Thai curry soup (1)

2 boneless skinless chicken breasts (approx. 10 oz/300 g) | 1 lemongrass stalk | 2 green onions | 1 red chile pepper | 2 baby pak choi (bok choy) | salt | 2 shallots | 4 garlic cloves | 1¼-inch (3 cm) piece gingerroot | 2 tbsp vegetable oil | 2–3 tbsp Thai red curry paste | 4 cups (1 L) poultry stock | 1 can (14 oz/400 ml) coconut milk | 7 oz (200 g) rice noodles | 2–3 tbsp lime juice

1. Pat dry the chicken breast fillets. Wash and trim the lemongrass, green onions, chile pepper and pak choi. Cut the lemongrass, green onions and chile into thin rings and the pak choi into strips. Fill the pressure cooker with the minimum amount of water, season with salt, add the chicken and lemongrass and seal the pot.
2. Turn the pressure regulator to setting 3 and heat the pot on the highest setting. When the yellow ring appears (cooking indicator: 1st ring), reduce the heat. When the green ring becomes visible (cooking indicator: 2nd ring), cook the meat for 4–5 minutes. Remove the pot from the heat, release the steam and open the lid. Remove the meat and cut it into slices. Clean the pot.
3. Peel and finely dice the shallots, garlic and ginger. Heat the oil in the pressure cooker and lightly sauté the shallots, garlic and ginger. Stir in the curry paste, continue to sauté briefly, then deglaze with the stock and coconut milk. Season with salt and cook on setting 3 (cooking indicator: 2nd ring) for approx. 3 minutes, then remove from the heat and release the steam. Prepare the rice noodles as per the packet instructions.
4. Add the light green onion rings and pak choi to the soup, simmer uncovered for another 2 minutes, then season with salt and lime juice to taste. Remove the lemongrass stalk. Divide the noodles between four deep plates, ladle on the soup and top with the chicken, chile and onion greens.

Tom kha gai (2)

8 oz (250 g) boneless skinless chicken breasts | 2–3 shallots | 4 garlic cloves | 1¼-inch (3 cm) piece gingerroot | 4 mushrooms | 2 lemongrass stalks | 1 red chile pepper | 2 cups + 6 tbsp (600 ml) chicken stock | 1 can (14 oz/400 ml) coconut milk | 4 lime leaves | salt | 1 tbsp cane sugar | 2 tbsp each of lime juice and fish sauce | 1 tbsp red chile rings | 2 tbsp fresh cilantro, to garnish

1. Pat dry the chicken and cut it in half lengthwise. Peel and thinly slice the shallots, garlic and ginger. Trim and thinly slice the mushrooms. Wash and trim the lemongrass and chile pepper, then cut into rings.
2. Put everything except the mushrooms into the pressure cooker. Add the stock, coconut milk, lime leaves, salt and sugar. Seal the pot, cook the vegetables on setting 3 (cooking indicator: 2nd ring) for approx. 5 minutes, then release the steam and open the lid.
3. Remove the chicken and cut it crosswise into slices. Add the mushrooms to the soup and simmer uncovered for another 2–3 minutes, then re-add the chicken. Season with lime juice and fish sauce to taste, divide the soup between four bowls, garnish with the chile rings and fresh cilantro and serve.

COOKING LEVEL VITAVIT® 3

COOKING LEVEL VITAQUICK® 2

COOKING TIME 25

Substantial soups
Hearty and full-flavored

MAKES: 4 PORTIONS   **WAITING TIME:** APPROX. 30 MIN.   **PREP TIME:** 25–30 MIN.

(1)

Korean Gochujang (1)

Soup Ingredients: 2.4 lbs (1.2 kg) boneless beef chuck (blade) roast, cut into chunks | 1 cup (250 ml) dry red wine | 3 tbsp (45 ml) toasted sesame oil | salt | pepper | 5 white onions | 2 tbsp + 2 tsp (40 g) butter | 6 tbsp (50 g) all-purpose flour | 1–2 tbsp hot paprika | 4 garlic cloves | 2 tbsp + 1 tsp (30 g) finely chopped peeled gingerroot | 3 tbsp (45 ml) Worcestershire sauce | 1 tsp gochujang (Korean chili paste) | 3 cups (750 ml) chicken stock | **For the topping (optional):** 2 zucchini | 1 2/3 cups (250 g) cherry tomatoes | 3 tbsp (45 ml) sesame oil | 1 3/4 cups (250 g) cubed peeled winter squash | 2 tbsp soy sauce | 1 tbsp brown sugar | 2 green onions, cut into rings

1. Put the meat in a rimmed baking sheet with the red wine, sesame oil, 1 tsp salt and pepper, mix well, cover and let marinate for approx. 30 minutes. Peel the onions, cut them in half and chop them into thin strips.

2. Melt the butter in the pressure cooker and fry the flour until golden brown, stirring regularly. Sprinkle the paprika over the top and continue to fry for a few more seconds. Strain the meat and sear in the roux with the onions until browned. Peel and finely chop the garlic, then add to the pot with the other soup ingredients.

3. Close the pressure cooker, set the pressure regulator to setting 3 and heat the pot on the highest setting. When the yellow ring appears (cooking indicator: 1st ring), reduce the heat. As soon as the green ring becomes visible (cooking indicator: 2nd ring), cook for 20–25 minutes, then release the steam.

4. To make the optional topping, wash the zucchini and cut them into pieces. Halve the tomatoes. Heat the sesame oil in a frying pan and briefly sear the squash and zucchini until browned. Stir in the tomatoes and add the mixture to the pot together with the soy sauce and sugar. Reseal the pot and cook on setting 3 (cooking indicator: 2nd ring) for 3–5 minutes or until fully done. Release the steam from the pot, season the stew to taste, divide between four deep plates, sprinkle with green onions and serve.

Solyanka with debrecener (2)

1 each of celery root, leek, carrot and a large handful of parsley, washed, trimmed and coarsely chopped | 14 oz (400 g) boneless pork leg roast | salt | 1 bay leaf | 2 onions | 2 red bell peppers | 2 celery stalks | 3–4 gherkins + gherkin juice | 8 oz (250 g) young carrots, with leaves | 5 oz (150 g) debrecener sausage | 2 tbsp vegetable oil | 1 tbsp sweet paprika | 1 tsp hot paprika | freshly ground pepper | 1 cup (250 ml) tomato passata | 1/3 cup (85 g) tomato paste | 3/4 cup + 1 tbsp (200 g) sour cream | 2 tbsp chopped parsley

(2)

1. Put the soup vegetables in a pressure cooker. Pat the pork dry and add together with 1 pinch of salt, the bay leaf and 4 cups (1 L) water. Seal the pot and cook on setting 3 (cooking indicator: 2nd ring) for 15–20 minutes.

2. Remove the pot from the heat, release the steam, open the lid and leave the meat to cool in the stock. Once cool, remove the meat and cut it into slices. Strain the cooking juices and top them up to 4 cups (1 L) with water.

3. Peel and finely dice the onions. Wash and trim the peppers and celery, then cut into strips together with the gherkins. Peel the carrots and cut into approx. 1 1/4-inch (3 cm) long pieces. Diagonally slice the sausage into approx. 3/4-inch (2 cm) thick pieces.

4. Clean the pressure cooker. Heat the oil in it and sauté the onions until golden. Add the pepper and continue to cook briefly. Season with both types of paprika, salt and pepper, then pour in the cooking stock. Stir in the tomato passata and tomato paste. Add the pork, sausage, celery and carrots, then seal the pot. Cook on setting 3 (cooking indicator: 1st ring) for 4–5 minutes, then release the steam and open the lid.

5. Stir in the sour cream, season the soup with gherkin juice to taste, divide between four deep plates, top with slices of gherkin, sprinkle with parsley and serve.

COOKING LEVEL VITAVIT®

COOKING LEVEL VITAQUICK®

COOKING TIME

Thick oxtail soup

MAKES: 4 PORTIONS **PREP TIME:** APPROX. 30 MIN.

FOR THE SOUP
1.6 lbs (800 g) beef oxtail, cut into pieces
1.6 oz (50 g) cooked, mild-smoked bacon (pork belly)
1 onion
1 carrot
1 parsnip
1 garlic clove
2–3 tbsp vegetable oil
6 tbsp (50 g) diced peeled celeriac (celery root)
1 tsp tomato paste
2½ tbsp (20 g) all-purpose flour
1 cup + 6 tbsp (350 ml) full-bodied red wine (see tip)
2 tbsp + 2 tsp (40 ml) Madeira
salt
freshly ground pepper
6 white peppercorns
5 allspice berries
5 juniper berries
1 pinch of ground coriander
2 strips of zest from 1 organic lemon
1 sprig of thyme
1 small bay leaf
8 cups (2 L) beef stock

TO FINISH
½ handful of flat-leaf parsley
garlic oil
coarsely ground pepper

FOR THE SOUP: pat the oxtail dry. Cut the bacon into small cubes. Peel and coarsely dice the onion, carrot and parsnip. Peel the garlic and lightly crush with a wide knife blade.

Heat the oil in a pressure cooker, add the oxtail pieces and sauté all over until well browned. Add the diced vegetables together with the garlic and bacon cubes and sauté briefly until lightly browned.

Stir in the tomato paste and cook for another 1–2 minutes. Dust the pot contents with flour, deglaze with red wine and Madeira and allow the liquid to simmer down slightly. Season lightly with salt and pepper, add the spices, lemon zest, thyme and bay leaf, then pour in the beef stock.

Close the pressure cooker with the lid, set the pressure regulator to setting 3 and heat the pot on the highest setting. When the yellow ring appears (cooking indicator: 1st ring), reduce the heat. As soon as the green ring becomes visible (cooking indicator: 2nd ring), the 40-to-45-minute cooking time begins.

Remove the pressure cooker from the heat, release the steam and open the lid. Remove the oxtail pieces, let cool very slightly, then remove the meat from the bones while still warm. Pull the meat into small chunks and set aside on a plate.

Strain the stock through a colander, then a sieve, using a ladle to press all of the liquid out of the residues. Return the soup to a pot and simmer uncovered until the desired consistency has been achieved.

Strain the fat off the soup (see p. 98) and season to taste.

TO FINISH: add the chunks of meat back into the soup and briefly heat them up. Meanwhile, wash, shake dry and finely chop the parsley.

Divide the oxtail soup between four preheated deep plates and sprinkle with the parsley. Drizzle a few drops of garlic oil over each portion, sprinkle with coarsely ground pepper and serve.

TIP: the oxtail pieces should ideally be deglazed with a high-quality, full-bodied red wine with a fruity character and not too much acidity. Ideal choices include a soft, fruity Merlot, a Pinot Noir or a Syrah.

COOKING LEVEL VITAVIT® 3
COOKING LEVEL VITAQUICK® 2
COOKING TIME 5–90

Noodle soups made with meat and vegetables

MAKES: 4 PORTIONS   **PREP TIME:** APPROX. 30 MIN.

(1)

Asparagus ramen
with udon noodles (1)

6 shallots | 2 garlic cloves | 1 lb (500 g) green asparagus | 2 green onions | 3 tbsp to ¼ cup (45 to 60 ml) peanut oil | 1 tsp brown cane sugar | 3½ tbsp (52 ml) ponzu (or 3 tbsp/45 ml soy sauce with 1 tsp lemon juice) | 4 cups (1 L) vegetable stock | 10 oz (300 g) fresh or precooked udon noodles | salt | chili powder | 1½ handfuls of pea sprouts | 4 tsp toasted sesame seeds | grated zest of 1 organic lime

1. Peel the shallots and garlic, then chop into thin strips. Wash the asparagus, peel the lower third, remove the ends and cut in half on the diagonal. Wash and trim the green onions, then cut diagonally into rings.
2. Heat the oil in the pressure cooker and sauté the prepared ingredients for 3–4 minutes, stirring regularly, then sprinkle in the sugar and deglaze with the ponzu. Pour in the stock and mix in the noodles.
3. Seal the pot, set the pressure regulator to setting 3 and heat on the highest setting. When the yellow ring appears (cooking indicator: 1st ring), reduce the heat. When the green ring becomes visible (cooking indicator: 2nd ring), cook for 4–5 minutes.
4. Remove the pressure cooker from the heat, release the steam and open the lid. Season the soup with salt and chili powder to taste, divide between four bowls, garnish with pea sprouts, sprinkle with sesame seeds and lime zest, then serve.

Tonkotsu ramen
with broccolini and enoki (2)

1 pork hock and 14 oz (400 g) chicken wings (or 1.2 lbs/600 g pig's feet, 10 oz/300 g pig's tails and 10 oz/300 g chicken giblets) | 2-inch (5 cm) piece gingerroot | 5 green onions | 1 leek | 2 onions | ½ garlic bulb | 8 oz (250 g) shiitake mushrooms | 1 cinnamon stick | 2 star anise pods | 2 nori sheets | ¼ cup (60 ml) mirin | 2 tbsp + 2 tsp (40 ml) soy sauce | salt | pepper | chili oil | **For the topping:** 4 eggs | 10 oz (300 g) broccolini | 2 green onions | salt | 8 oz (250 g) dried ramen noodles | 1 nori sheet | 1 handful of enoki mushrooms | chili flakes

(2)

1. Pat dry the pork hock and chicken wings, place them in the pressure cooker and cover them with water. Briefly blanch (see p. 102) and skim, then pass through a sieve. Rinse the meat well and allow to strain.
2. Peel the ginger, wash and trim the green onions and leek, then cut into pieces. Wash and peel the onions and garlic. Trim the shiitake mushrooms and remove the stems.
3. Clean the pot. Briefly fry the prepared ingredients in the pressure cooker, then set them aside. Add the meat, spices and nori sheets. Pour in the mirin and soy sauce, cover with at least 8 cups (2 L) water (observe the maximum fill level) and seal the pot. Turn the pressure regulator to setting 3 and heat on the highest setting. When the yellow ring appears (cooking indicator: 1st ring), reduce the heat. When the green ring becomes visible (cooking indicator: 2nd ring), cook for 1 hour.
4. Meanwhile, prepare the topping by hard-boiling the eggs, immersing them in cold water, peeling them and cutting them in half. Wash and trim the broccolini and green onions. Cut up the broccolini and blanch in salted water. Cut the green onions into rings. Release the steam from the pressure cooker and open the lid.
5. Strain the stock through a sieve, simmer down uncovered by about a quarter and season with salt, pepper and a little chili oil to taste. Cook the noodles in salted water for 2–3 minutes. Cut the nori sheet into pieces and divide into four bowls with the noodles. Pour on the hot stock, top with the broccolini, enoki and egg halves, sprinkle with the chili flakes and green onion rings, then serve.

Global favorites
Soups from Vietnam

COOKING LEVEL VITAVIT®
COOKING LEVEL VITAQUICK®
COOKING TIME

MAKES: 4 PORTIONS **PREP TIME:** APPROX. 45 MIN.

Pho bo with rice noodles (1)

3.6 oz (110 g) gingerroot | 1 browned onion (see p. 103) | 2.4 lbs (1.2 kg) beef soup bones and 1 lb (500 g) beef brisket, blanched (see p. 102) | 5 star anise pods | 5 cloves | ½ cinnamon stick | 5 tbsp (75 ml) Vietnamese fish sauce | salt | pepper | 1 tbsp soy sauce | 1 tbsp miso paste | **For the topping:** 8 oz (250 g) banh pho (or other ribbon rice noodles) | 1 red onion | 1 tbsp vegetable oil | 2 green onions | 2.6 oz (80 g) bean sprouts | 1 bunch of herbs (fresh cilantro, Thai basil) | 2 red chile peppers | 1.6 oz (50 g) mushrooms (e.g., enoki mushrooms) | zest of 1 organic lime | 1 tsp white sesame seeds | 1 tsp black sesame seeds

1. Peel the ginger and add to the pressure cooker with the onion, beef bones and beef brisket. Pour in 8 to 12 cups (2 to 3 L) water (observe the maximum fill level), seal the pot and cook the stock on setting 3 (cooking indicator: 2nd ring) for 25–30 minutes. Release the pressure from the pot and add the spices, fish sauce and salt. Reseal the pot and cook on setting 3 (cooking indicator: 2nd ring) for another 15–20 minutes. Release the steam from the pot again, open the lid and strain the stock into a second pot (see p. 98). Allow the meat to cool and cut it into thin slices.

2. To prepare the topping, soak the noodles in cold water for approx. 30 minutes, then cook as per the packet instructions. Peel the onion, cut into eight pieces and briefly sauté in oil in a frying pan. Wash and trim the green onions, then cut into thin rings. Rinse the bean sprouts and herbs and shake them dry. Wash and trim the chile peppers, then cut into thin rings. Trim the mushrooms.

3. Heat the stock and season to taste with salt, pepper, soy sauce and miso paste. Divide the noodles, meat and spices from the sieve onto four plates, pour on the hot stock, sprinkle with herbs, chile rings, mushrooms, lime zest and sesame seeds, then serve.

Vietnamese noodle soup with chicken and seafood (2)

2 red onions | 6 tbsp (90 ml) rice vinegar | 3 tbsp (60 g) honey | **For the soup:** 5 oz (150 g) pork belly | 5 oz (150 g) squid, ready to cook | 8 jumbo shrimp, ready to cook, peeled except the tail segment |

(2)

1 red chile pepper | 3–4 green onions | 5 oz (150 g) boneless skinless chicken breast | 3¼ cups (800 ml) poultry stock | salt | pepper | fish sauce (nuoc mam) | 1 tbsp chopped cilantro | 3.3 oz (100 g) precooked egg noodles | chili flakes

1. Peel the onions and slice into thin rings. Heat the vinegar in a small pot, add the honey and onions and let sit until ready to use.

2. Rinse the pork belly. Fill the pressure cooker with the minimum amount of water, add the meat and cook on setting 3 (cooking indicator: 2nd ring) for 15–20 minutes.

3. Release the steam from the pot, open the lid, remove the pork belly and clean the pressure cooker. Rinse the squid and shrimp. Wash and trim the chile pepper and green onions, then cut the chile into pieces and the green onions into rings.

4. Add the chicken, squid, chile and stock to the pressure cooker and cook on setting 2 (cooking indicator: 1st ring) for another 3–4 minutes. Release the steam from the pot and open the lid.

5. Slightly simmer down the stock in the uncovered pressure cooker, then add the shrimp and cook for approx. 3 minutes until done. Season to taste with salt, pepper, fish sauce and fresh cilantro.

6. Cut the pork and chicken into slices and the squid into pieces, divide between four deep plates together with the noodles and shrimp and pour on the hot stock. Top each portion with the marinated onions and a sprinkling of green onions and chili flakes, then serve.

COOKING LEVEL VITAVIT® · COOKING LEVEL VITAQUICK® · COOKING TIME

Potatoes & pasta for
perfect octopus dishes

MAKES: 4 PORTIONS **PREP TIME:** 25–30 MIN.

Galician octopus (1)

1 octopus, ready to cook (2 to 3 lbs/1 to 1.5 kg or tentacles only) | 6 garlic cloves | 1 cup (250 ml) full-bodied Spanish red wine | 1 bay leaf | salt | ¼ to ⅓ cup (60 to 75 ml) olive oil | 4 large potatoes | 1 large onion | 1 handful of flat-leaf parsley | ¾ cup + 2 tbsp (200 ml) vegetable stock | freshly ground pepper | Padrón pepper powder (or another fruity, mild to medium paprika powder)

1. Rinse the octopus. Put 2 unpeeled garlic cloves into the pressure cooker together with 3 cups (750 ml) water and the red wine. Add the bay leaf, 2 tsp salt and 2 tbsp oil. Bring to the boil, then briefly dip the octopus in the red wine mixture 2–3 times to prevent the skin from coming off when cooked.
2. Seal the pot, set the pressure regulator to setting 2 and heat the pot on the highest setting. When the yellow ring appears (cooking indicator: 1st ring), reduce the heat. As soon as the green ring becomes visible (cooking indicator: 1st ring), cook the octopus for 7–10 minutes. Slowly release the steam from the pressure cooker and open the lid. Remove the octopus and let strain and cool. Pour away the liquid and clean the pot.
3. Cut the octopus into large pieces. Peel, wash and finely dice the potatoes. Peel the onion and remaining garlic. Chop the onion in half, then into slices. Chop the garlic in half or cut into large chunks. Wash, shake dry and chop the parsley.
4. Heat the remaining oil in a frying pan and slowly fry the potatoes and slices of onion until lightly browned. Add the vegetable stock. After 10–15 minutes, add the octopus and garlic and continue to cook for a few more minutes, then season with salt, pepper and Padrón pepper powder. Stir in half of the chopped parsley, season the octopus to taste, spoon onto plates, sprinkle with the remaining parsley and serve.

Octopus pasta (2)

1.6 lbs (800 g) octopus, ready to cook | salt | 14 oz (400 g) short pasta (e.g., ziti, ditalini) | 2 red onions | 2–3 garlic cloves | freshly ground pepper | 1⅔ cups (400 g) chopped canned tomatoes (or 2¼ cups/400 g chopped fresh tomatoes) | 6 tbsp + 2 tsp (100 ml) olive oil | 1 cinnamon stick, as desired | 1 pinch of bukovo (Greek smoked pepper flakes with a slight spiciness, or other pepper flakes) | ½ handful of chopped flat-leaf parsley | basil, to garnish

(2)

1. Rinse the octopus, put it into the pressure cooker together with 4 cups (1 L) water and 1 tbsp salt and cook on setting 2 (cooking indicator: 1st ring) for 7–10 minutes. At the same time, cook the pasta in a pot containing plenty of salted water as per the packet instructions until al dente. Strain and keep warm.
2. Peel the onions and garlic, then finely dice the onions. Release the steam from the pressure cooker and open the lid. Remove the octopus, allow it to strain and cool, then cut it into large pieces. Pour away the stock and clean the pot.
3. Put the onions, salt, pepper, chopped tomatoes, oil and, if desired, cinnamon stick into the pressure cooker, add the garlic by squeezing it through a press and seal the pot. Cook on setting 3 (cooking indicator: 2nd ring) for 10 minutes or so, then release the steam. Reduce the tomato sauce slightly in the uncovered pot. Stir in the octopus, bukovo and parsley, then season to taste. Plate up the pasta, divide the octopus between the plates and serve garnished with basil.

TIP: alternatively, for step 3, you can put the pasta into the pot together with the onions, 1⅔ cups (400 ml) tomato passata and 2 cups (500 ml) stock and cook on setting 2 (cooking indicator: 1st ring) for 5–7 minutes.

COOKING LEVEL VITAVIT® 3 | **COOKING LEVEL VITAQUICK®** 2 | **COOKING TIME** 5

One-pot comfort food
Pasta & cheese

MAKES: 2–4 PORTIONS   **PREP TIME:** APPROX. 15 MIN.

Mac 'n' cheese
with cheddar (1)

1 garlic clove | 2 tbsp + 2 tsp (40 g) butter | 1⅔ cups (400 ml) vegetable stock (or poultry stock) | ¾ cup + 2 tbsp (200 ml) milk | 8 oz (250 g) elbow macaroni (or other short pasta, cooking time at least 8 min.) | salt | freshly ground pepper | freshly grated nutmeg | 1 pinch of cayenne pepper | 1⅓ cups (150 g) grated cheddar cheese | ½ cup + 1 tbsp (50 g) grated Parmesan cheese | ¼ cup (60 ml) heavy or whipping (35%) cream | 1 tbsp chopped flat-leaf parsley

1. Peel and finely dice the garlic.
2. Melt the butter in a pressure cooker and briefly sauté the garlic. Add the stock, milk and pasta to the pot. Season the mixture with salt, pepper, nutmeg and cayenne pepper and mix well.
3. Close the pressure cooker with the lid, set the pressure regulator to setting 3 and heat the pot on the highest setting. As soon as the yellow ring appears (cooking indicator: 1st ring), reduce the heat. When the green ring becomes visible (cooking indicator: 2nd ring), cook the pasta for 5 minutes.
4. Remove the pot from the heat, release the steam and open the lid. Stir in both cheeses and the cream. Season the pasta to taste, sprinkle with parsley and serve.

Käsespätzle
with fried onions (2)

2 onions | ¼ cup (60 g) butter | salt | 1⅔ cups (400 ml) vegetable stock (or poultry stock) | ¾ cup + 2 tbsp (200 ml) milk | 8 oz (250 g) dried spaetzle-style or other egg noodles (cooking time 7 to 9 min.) | pepper | freshly grated nutmeg | 1¾ cups (200 g) grated Emmental cheese (or 1⅓ cups/150 g Emmental and 7 tbsp/50 g Alpine-style cheese) | 2 tbsp minced chives

1. Peel the onions. Finely dice 1 onion and cut the other onion in half, then into thin strips.
2. Melt 4 tsp (20 g) butter in a frying pan and slowly fry the onion strips until golden brown, then lightly season with salt.
3. Melt the remaining butter in a pressure cooker and sauté the diced onion, stirring regularly, until lightly browned. Add the stock, milk and spaetzle to the pressure cooker. Season with salt, pepper and nutmeg and mix well. Close the pressure cooker with the lid, set the pressure regulator to setting 3 and heat the pot on the highest setting. As soon as the yellow ring appears (cooking indicator: 1st ring), reduce the heat. When the green ring becomes visible (cooking indicator: 2nd ring), cook the spaetzle for 5 minutes.
4. Remove the pot from the heat, release the steam and open the lid. Stir the grated cheese into the spätzle and allow it to melt.
5. Season the käsespätzle to taste, divide between four plates and top with the fried onions. Sprinkle on the chives and serve.

RECIPES >> SOUPS & ONE-POT DISHES

One-pot pasta al pomodoro
Vegetarian and with meatballs

COOKING LEVEL VITAVIT® | COOKING LEVEL VITAQUICK® | COOKING TIME

COOKING LEVEL VITAVIT® | COOKING LEVEL VITAQUICK® | COOKING TIME

Rigatoni with pepper and tomato sauce (1)

MAKES: 4 PORTIONS   **PREP TIME:** APPROX. 20 MIN.
1 garlic clove | 2 tbsp olive oil | 1 tbsp butter | 1 diced bell pepper | 1²⁄₃ cups (400 ml) tomato passata | 1 tsp salt | 1 tsp freshly ground pepper | 1 tsp granulated sugar | ½ tsp chili powder | 4 cups (1 L) meat stock (or vegetable stock) | 10 oz (300 g) short pasta (e.g., rigatoni, macaroni) | 6 sprigs of basil | 3 sprigs of thyme | quality olive oil, for drizzling | 7 tbsp (40 g) grated Parmesan | fresh basil, to garnish

1. Peel and finely dice the garlic. Heat the oil and butter in a pressure cooker and briefly sauté the garlic until it starts to brown. Stir in the bell pepper and cook briefly, then mix in the tomato passata and cook for another 4–5 minutes. Season with salt, pepper, sugar and chili powder and pour in the stock.
2. Put the pasta in the pot and stir well. Seal the pressure cooker and turn the pressure regulator to setting 2. Heat the pot on the highest setting until the yellow ring appears (cooking indicator: 1st ring), then reduce the heat. As soon as the green ring becomes visible (cooking indicator: 1st ring), cook the pasta for 4–6 minutes (half the conventional cooking time) depending on the variety.
3. Meanwhile, rinse the basil and thyme, shake them dry and pluck the leaves. Finely chop the basil. Remove the pot from the heat, release the steam and open the lid. Stir in the herbs. Season to taste, spoon onto the plates and drizzle with a few drops of olive oil. Sprinkle on a little grated Parmesan and serve the rigatoni garnished with basil. Serve the remaining Parmesan on the side.

Pasta and polpette in tomato sauce (2)

MAKES: 4 PORTIONS   **PREP TIME:** APPROX. 35 MIN. + 20 MIN.
14 oz (400 g) mixed ground beef, veal and/or pork | ½ cup (50 g) dry breadcrumbs | 3 tbsp (45 ml) milk | ¼ cup (20 g) grated Parmesan | 1 egg | salt | freshly ground pepper | 1 tbsp chopped parsley | 1 tbsp oil | **For the sauce:** 1 onion | 1 garlic clove | 2 tbsp olive oil | 2¼ cups (400 g) chopped tomatoes | 1²⁄₃ cups (400 ml) tomato passata | approx. 1²⁄₃ cups (400 ml) poultry stock | salt | freshly ground pepper | 1 tsp dried herbs (thyme, oregano) | 8 oz (250 g) short pasta (e.g., penne) | 2 tbsp chopped herbs (parsley, basil)

1. Put the ground meat in a bowl. Add the breadcrumbs, milk, Parmesan and egg. Season with salt, pepper and parsley, mix well and work to form a malleable meat mixture. If necessary, add a little milk or more breadcrumbs, then let rest for approx. 20 minutes.
2. Use the meat mixture to create approx. 1-inch (2.5 cm) balls. Heat the oil in the pressure cooker, briefly sear a few polpette at a time all over until browned, then remove them. Clean the pressure cooker.
3. To make the sauce, peel and finely dice the onion and garlic. Heat the oil in the pressure cooker and lightly sauté both. Add the chopped tomatoes and tomato passata, then pour in the stock. Season with salt, pepper and dried herbs and simmer for 3–4 minutes. Stir in the polpette and the pasta. These should be covered with liquid, so add a little more stock if necessary, observing the maximum fill level.
4. Seal the pot and cook on setting 2 (cooking indicator: 1st ring) for another 6 minutes. Remove the pot from the heat, release the steam and open the lid. Plate up the pasta with the polpette and the sauce and serve sprinkled with fresh herbs.

COOKING LEVEL VITAVIT® 3
COOKING LEVEL VITAQUICK® 2
COOKING TIME 30

Mafé de poulet
with eggplant

MAKES: 4 PORTIONS **PREP TIME:** APPROX. 45 MIN. **WAITING TIME:** APPROX. 1 HR

FOR THE MAFÉ DE POULET
1 whole chicken, approx. 2.4 lbs (1.2 kg)
salt
6 cups (1.5 L) chicken stock
1½-inch (4 cm) piece gingerroot
1 small red chile pepper
7 oz (200 g) eggplant (about 1 medium)
1 lb (500 g) crookneck squash (or carrots)
1 lb (500 g) sweet potatoes
8 oz (250 g) thick green beans
¼ cup (60 ml) vegetable oil
¾ cup (100 g) chopped sweet white onion
4 garlic cloves, finely diced
3 tbsp (48 g) tomato paste
2 tbsp sweet curry powder
1–2 tsp chili powder

TO FINISH
¾ cup + 4 tsp (200 g) smooth peanut butter, unsweetened
1⅔ cups (400 g) chopped canned tomatoes
freshly ground pepper
celery leaves, to garnish
1 lime, quartered

FOR THE MAFÉ DE POULET: place chicken in a large pressure cooker, season with salt and pour in the chicken stock. Add enough water to cover the chicken (observe the maximum fill level). Seal the pot with the lid, turn the pressure regulator to setting 3 and heat on the highest setting. When the yellow ring appears (cooking indicator: 1st ring), reduce the heat. When the green ring becomes visible (cooking indicator: 2nd ring), the approx. 25-minute cooking time begins.

Meanwhile, peel the ginger, wash and trim the chile pepper and finely chop both. Wash and trim the eggplant, cut into approx. ½-inch (1 cm) thick slices and halve them crosswise or quarter if large. Peel and deseed the squash, then dice the flesh into approx. ¾-inch (2 cm) cubes. Peel and dice the sweet potatoes. Wash and trim the beans, then cut diagonally into small pieces.

Remove the pressure cooker from the heat, release the steam and open the lid. Allow the contents to cool, then remove and skin the chicken. Strip the meat off the bones, pull into large chunks and keep warm. Strain the chicken soup through a sieve and clean the pot.

Heat the oil in the pressure cooker and briefly sear the onion, garlic, ginger and chile. Add the tomato paste, curry powder and chili powder, and slowly fry over a low heat for approx. 10 minutes, stirring regularly, then pour in the chicken soup. Add the peanut butter and whiz with an immersion blender until smooth.

TO FINISH: add the prepared vegetables to the pressure cooker with the chopped tomatoes and mix well. Seal the pot with the lid, turn the pressure regulator to setting 3 and heat on the highest setting. As soon as the yellow ring appears (cooking indicator: 1st ring), reduce the heat. When the green ring becomes visible (cooking indicator: 2nd ring), the 3-to-5-minute cooking time begins.

Remove the pot from the heat, release the steam and open the lid. Depending on the desired consistency, simmer the soup down a little more or add more liquid (stock or water). Add the chicken and briefly reheat, but do not return to the boil. Season the stew to taste, spoon onto deep plates, grind with pepper, garnish with celery leaves and serve with the quarters of lime.

TIP: millet makes the perfect side. Rinse and strain 1 cup + 2 tbsp (200 g) millet, then add to the unperforated insert together with 1 tsp salt and 1⅔ cups (400 ml) water. Place the insert on the tripod in a pressure cooker and cook for 3–5 minutes.

Beef goulash with potatoes
and sour cream

COOKING LEVEL VITAVIT®

COOKING LEVEL VITAQUICK®

COOKING TIME

MAKES: 4 PORTIONS **PREP TIME:** APPROX. 25 MIN.

FOR THE GOULASH
1.2 lbs (600 g) boneless beef chuck (blade) roast
2 tbsp butter
2 cups (250 g) sliced or finely diced onions
1 tbsp sweet paprika
1 tsp hot paprika
1 tbsp tomato paste
1 tbsp red wine vinegar
salt
1 garlic clove, finely diced
1 pinch of ground cumin
½ tsp dried marjoram
2⅓ cups (300 g) cubed (½ inch / 1 cm) peeled russet potatoes

TO FINISH
½ bunch parsley
1 pinch of ground cinnamon
¼–½ tsp smoked paprika
6 tbsp (90 g) sour cream

FOR THE GOULASH: pat the meat dry and cut it into ¾-to 1-inch (2 to 2.5 cm) cubes.

Melt the butter in a pressure cooker and sauté the onions until translucent. Reduce the heat, sprinkle in both the sweet and hot paprika and briefly cook in the butter, stirring regularly. Stir in the tomato purée and cook for about 1 minute, then deglaze with the vinegar. Season the cubed beef with salt and add to the pot, followed by the garlic, cumin and marjoram. Pour in the minimum amount of cold water and simmer down slightly.

Seal the pressure cooker and turn the pressure regulator to setting 3. Heat the pot on the highest setting. As soon as the yellow ring appears (cooking indicator: 1st ring), reduce the heat again. When the green ring becomes visible (cooking indicator: 2nd ring), the 20-to-25-minute cooking time begins.

After 15–20 minutes of cooking time, remove the pressure cooker from the heat, release the steam and open the lid.

Add the potato cubes to the pot, mix well and reseal. Cook the goulash on setting 3 (cooking indicator: 2nd ring) for 5 minutes or so until fully done. Remove the pressure cooker from the heat and release the steam.

TO FINISH: rinse the parsley, shake dry, pluck off the leaves and finely chop. Season the goulash with the cinnamon and smoked paprika to taste.

Divide between four deep plates, topping each portion with sour cream and a sprinkling of chopped parsley, then serve.

TIP: goulash can easily be prepared in advance or in larger quantities (in a large 6–10 L pressure cooker) and then frozen in portions (before the potatoes are added). For those who prefer a more soup-like goulash, simply add a little more water or stock.

COOKING LEVEL VITAVIT® | COOKING LEVEL VITAQUICK® | COOKING TIME

International favorites
with beef & sucuk

MAKES: 4 PORTIONS **PREP TIME:** APPROX. 25 MIN.

Asian beef stew
with soy potatoes (1)

2 lbs (1 kg) boneless beef chuck (blade) roast | 1.5 lbs (750 g) round (waxy) potatoes | 4 green onions | 2 dried chile peppers | 2 tsp Szechuan or black peppercorns | 2 bay leaves | 2 star anise pods | 1 cinnamon stick | 1 tsp ground cumin | 6 tbsp (80 g) packed brown sugar | 2 tbsp + 2 tsp (50 g) chu hou paste (alternatively hoisin sauce) | 5 tsp dark soy sauce | 2 tbsp light soy sauce | 1 tbsp salt

1. Pat the meat dry and cut into approx. 1-inch (2.5 cm) cubes. Peel and wash the potatoes, then chop into large pieces. Trim and wash the green onions, then chop them into rings.

2. Put the meat, potatoes and half the green onion rings into the pressure cooker together with the other ingredients and 4 cups (1 L) water, then mix well. Close the pressure cooker, set the pressure regulator to setting 3 and heat the pot on the highest setting. As soon as the yellow ring appears (cooking indicator: 1st ring), reduce the heat. When the green ring becomes visible (cooking indicator: 2nd ring), the approx. 20-minute cooking time begins.

3. Remove the pot from the heat, release the steam and open the lid. Simmer down slightly, uncovered. Remove the bay leaves. Season the beef stew to taste, spoon onto deep plates and serve with a sprinkling of remaining green onion rings.

Bean stew with sucuk (2)

8 oz (250 g) sucuk (kangal sucuk – Turkish ring or other spicy cured sausage) | 3 onions | 5 Turkish green peppers (or other long hot green chile peppers) | 4 garlic cloves | 1 beef marrow bone | 3 tbsp (45 ml) olive oil | 2 cups (500 ml) tomato juice (or tomato passata) | 2 cups (400 g) dried cannellini (white kidney) beans | 1 tsp ground cumin | 1 tsp ground pepper | $1\frac{1}{2}$ tsp salt | chili powder | 1 tbsp butter | basil

1. Skin the sucuk, cut into $\frac{1}{2}$-inch (1 cm) slices and quarter each slice. Peel the onions and wash and trim the peppers, then cut both into approx. $\frac{1}{2}$-inch (1 cm) pieces. Peel the garlic and crush into a paste in a mortar.

2. Sear the sausage in a pressure cooker (at least 4.5 L, ideally 6 L) for approx. 2 minutes, until the fat seeps out, then remove and set aside. Sear the marrow bone in the remaining fat until browned. Add the olive oil and sear the onions. Add the peppers and continue to fry briefly, then stir in the garlic paste.

3. Pour in the tomato juice, add the dried beans and season with cumin, black pepper, salt and 1–2 pinches of chili powder. Put the sucuk, butter and $\frac{2}{3}$ cup (150 ml) water into the pressure cooker and mix well.

4. Seal the pot, turn the pressure regulator to setting 2 and cook (cooking indicator: 1st ring) for 20–25 minutes.

5. Release the steam from the pot and open the lid. Season the bean stew to taste, divide between four deep plates, garnish with a few small basil leaves and serve.

(1)

RECIPES >> SOUPS & ONE-POT DISHES   195

COOKING LEVEL VITAVIT®

COOKING LEVEL VITAQUICK®

COOKING TIME

Turkish
kofta & potato stew

MAKES: 4 PORTIONS   **PREP TIME:** APPROX. 35 MIN.

FOR THE BEEF MIXTURE
3 handfuls of walnuts
1 onion
1.4 lbs (700 g) ground beef
6 tbsp (43 g) dry breadcrumbs
1 bunch of parsley
3 tsp salt
2–3 tsp freshly ground pepper
½–1 tsp chili powder
2 tsp paprika
1 tsp ground cumin
2 tsp kofta spice mix
3 tbsp (45 ml) olive oil

FOR THE POTATOES AND SAUCE
4 large, round (waxy) potatoes
1 onion
1 tbsp olive oil
1 tbsp butter
3 Turkish green peppers (or other long hot green chile peppers)
4 small tomatoes
6–7 garlic cloves
1 large tomato, peeled (or 2 peeled canned tomatoes)
1 tbsp tomato paste
1 tsp salt
1 tsp freshly ground pepper
1 tsp granulated sugar
½ tsp chili powder, as desired

TO FINISH
⅔ cup (150 g) plain yogurt (10% fat)

FOR THE BEEF MIXTURE: briefly toast the walnuts in the pressure cooker without fat, set aside, let cool and then chop coarsely. Peel and finely dice the onion. Put the ground beef in a bowl and add the breadcrumbs and diced onion. Wash, shake dry, finely chop and add the parsley. Add the salt, pepper, remaining spices and oil, mix well and work into a malleable meat mixture.

Divide the meat mixture into 1.5-oz (45 g) portions. Shape each portion into a ball **(1)**, then press flat and briefly set the meat patties (koftas) aside.

FOR THE POTATOES AND SAUCE: peel and wash the potatoes and cut into approx. ½-inch (1 cm) thick slices. Peel and finely dice the onion. Heat the oil and butter in a pressure cooker, sauté the onion until slightly browned, then remove the pot from the heat and leave it to cool slightly.

Place potato slices and koftas in an alternating pattern upright (note the maximum fill level) next to each other in a circle around the pot. Wash and trim the green pepper, then quarter it lengthwise. Wash the tomatoes and also cut into quarters or wide wedges. Spoon the vegetables onto the potatoes and koftas **(2)**. Peel and add the garlic.

Finely blend the peeled tomato with the tomato paste. Put the blended mixture into a measuring jug and top up with water to 1 cup + 6 tbsp (350 ml). Season the sauce with salt, black pepper, sugar and 1 pinch of chili powder if desired.

Pour the sauce over the potatoes, koftas and vegetables **(3)** and seal the pressure cooker with the lid. Set the pressure regulator to setting 2 and heat the pot on the highest setting. As soon as the yellow ring appears (cooking indicator: 1st ring), reduce the heat. When the green ring becomes visible (cooking indicator: 1st ring), the 10-to-11-minute cooking time begins.

TO FINISH: stir the yogurt in a small bowl until smooth. Remove the pressure cooker from the heat, release the steam and open the lid. Carefully remove the potato and kofta mixture, plate up with vegetables from the pot and serve. Serve the yogurt separately.

TIP: this dish goes wonderfully with boiled rice or naan. The kofta spice mix for seasoning the mince mixture can be found in Turkish food stores or online.

Clever combinations

For plenty of flavor, we recommend adding roasting juices to vegetables, meat or fish. You can either do this before pressure cooking (for the stuffed calamari), or afterwards in the oven (for the braised duck legs) or under the grill (for the holy BBQ trinity: spare ribs, pulled pork and brisket). For certain recipes you'll need an unperforated insert (e.g., to cook meatloaf and terrines), which is available as an optional accessory.

COOKING LEVEL VITAVIT®: 3

COOKING LEVEL VITAQUICK®: 2

COOKING TIME: 10

Stuffed mushrooms with lentils and broccoli

MAKES: 4 PORTIONS **PREP TIME:** APPROX. 30 MIN.

FOR THE LENTILS
1 cup (200 g) dried green or brown lentils
1 onion
2 garlic cloves
2 tbsp olive oil
1 2/3 cups (400 ml) vegetable stock
1 bay leaf

FOR THE DRESSING
1 garlic clove
2 1/2 tsp (10 g) finely diced peeled gingerroot
2 tbsp apple cider vinegar
1 tbsp lemon juice
1 tbsp soy sauce
1 1/2 tsp hot mustard
1 tsp liquid honey, or according to taste
3 tbsp (45 ml) olive oil
2 tbsp sesame oil
salt
freshly ground pepper

FOR THE STUFFED MUSHROOMS
8 large button mushrooms (or 4 portobello mushrooms)
3 tbsp (45 ml) olive oil
salt
1 small beet, diced
1 2/3 cups (200 g) diced peeled sweet potatoes

TO FINISH:
4 1/2 cups (400 g) broccoli florets
chili flakes, for sprinkling
salt

FOR THE LENTILS: rinse the lentils and strain. Peel and finely dice the onion and garlic. Heat the oil in a pressure cooker, add the onion and sauté until translucent. Add the garlic and continue frying for approx. 1 minute. Stir in the lentils and continue frying briefly, then deglaze with the stock. Add the bay leaf, close the pressure cooker with the lid and set the pressure regulator to setting 3. Heat the pot on the highest setting. As soon as the yellow ring appears (cooking indicator: 1st ring), reduce the heat. When the green ring becomes visible (cooking indicator: 2nd ring), the 10-minute cooking time begins.

Remove the pressure cooker from the heat, release the steam and open the lid. Strain the lentils and remove the bay leaf. Rinse out and dry the pressure cooker.

FOR THE DRESSING: peel and finely dice the garlic. Put the ginger and garlic in a bowl together with the vinegar, lemon juice, soy sauce, mustard, honey and both types of oil and whisk together. Season the dressing lightly with salt and pepper.

Put the lentils in a bowl, pour the dressing on top and marinate briefly.

FOR THE STUFFED MUSHROOMS: trim the mushrooms and remove the stems. Brush the caps with 1 tbsp olive oil and season lightly with salt. Heat 1 tbsp olive oil in the pressure cooker, add the mushrooms and brown them on both sides for 2–3 minutes, then remove them from the pot. Grease a perforated insert with the remaining oil. Put the mushrooms (curved-side-down) in the insert and fill them with the marinated lentils. Add the beet and diced sweet potato on top or mix with the lentils.

Fill the pressure cooker with the minimum amount of water. Put the insert on the tripod and seal the pot. Set the pressure regulator to setting 2 and heat the pot on the highest setting. As soon as the yellow ring appears (cooking indicator: 1st ring), reduce the heat. When the green ring becomes visible (cooking indicator: 1st ring), cook the mushrooms for 6 minutes. Remove the stuffed mushrooms and keep them warm.

TO FINISH: put the broccoli florets in the insert on the tripod. Seal the pot, set the pressure regulator to setting 1 and heat the pot on the highest setting. As soon as the yellow ring appears (cooking indicator: 1st ring), reduce the heat. When the green ring becomes visible (cooking indicator: 1st ring), the 2-minute cooking time begins. Remove the pressure cooker from the heat, release the steam and open the lid.

Arrange the stuffed mushrooms on plates with some broccoli florets on the side. Sprinkle with 1–2 pinches of chilli flakes, season lightly with salt and serve.

Calamari ripieni (stuffed squid)

COOKING LEVEL VITAVIT®   **COOKING LEVEL VITAQUICK®**   **COOKING TIME**

MAKES: 4 PORTIONS   **PREP TIME:** APPROX. 40 MIN.   **SOAKING TIME:** 10 MIN.

FOR THE POTATOES
salt
7.3 oz (220 g) russet potatoes

FOR THE CALAMARI
2 garlic cloves
8 medium-sized calamari (with fins and tentacles, prepared by fishmonger, ready to cook)
2 tbsp olive oil
½ cup (125 ml) dry white wine
2 tbsp capers (in brine)
2 small zucchini
2 tbsp grated Parmesan
1 egg white
1–2 tbsp breadcrumbs
2 tbsp chopped flat-leaf parsley
¼ cup (30 g) black olives, pitted
salt
freshly ground pepper
1 cup (250 ml) poultry stock

TO FINISH
1⅓ cups (200 g) baby plum tomatoes (or grape tomatoes)
salt
freshly ground pepper
small basil leaves, to garnish

FOR THE POTATOES: put the minimum amount of water and some salt in a pressure cooker. Wash the potatoes, put them in the perforated insert on the tripod or directly in the pressure cooker. Seal the pot and set the pressure regulator to setting 3. Heat the pot on the highest setting. When the yellow ring appears (cooking indicator: 1st ring), reduce the heat. When the green ring becomes visible (cooking indicator: 2nd ring), the 10-to-12-minute cooking time begins. Remove the pot from the heat, release the steam and open the lid. Leave the steam from the potatoes to evaporate briefly, then clean the pressure cooker.

FOR THE CALAMARI: peel the garlic. Wash and strain the calamari, then remove the fins and tentacles. Heat 1 tbsp oil in the pressure cooker, add 1 garlic clove and fry briefly. Add the fins and tentacles and continue frying briefly, while stirring, then deglaze with half of the white wine and simmer briefly. Remove the garlic. Set the pressure cooker aside, remove the fins and tentacles, leave them to cool briefly, then finely dice them and transfer to a bowl. Strain the cooking juices through a sieve and clean the pot.

Rinse the capers, then soak them in cold water for approx. 10 minutes. Wash, trim and finely dice the zucchini. Peel the potatoes and pass them through a potato ricer into a bowl while still warm. Finely dice the remaining garlic clove and add it to the fried calamari offcuts along with the diced zucchini. Strain the capers and add them to the stuffing together with the Parmesan, egg white, breadcrumbs and chopped parsley. Finely dice the olives, then stir them into the mixture. Season the stuffing with salt and pepper and mix well. Fill the calamari tubes with the stuffing (without overstuffing them) and close the openings crosswise with a cocktail stick.

Heat the remaining oil (1 tbsp) in the pressure cooker and briefly sear the stuffed calamari tubes all over, adding some more oil if necessary. Deglaze with the rest of the white wine (¼ cup/60 ml) and the stock. Seal the pot, set the pressure regulator to setting 2 and heat on the highest setting. As soon as the yellow ring appears (cooking indicator: 1st ring), reduce the heat. When the green ring becomes visible (cooking indicator: 1st ring), the 10-minute cooking time begins.

TO FINISH: wash the tomatoes, pat them dry and cut them in half lengthwise. Set the pot aside, release the steam and open the lid. Add the tomatoes and leave everything to simmer slightly in the open pot.

Season the sauce to taste with salt and pepper. Garnish the stuffed calamari with basil leaves. If desired, cut them in half at an angle and serve them on plates with some sauce and tomatoes.

TIP: if your fishmonger doesn't have any fresh calamari, you can always use frozen squid tubes. In this case, simply thaw one extra tube, finely dice it and fry it instead of the tentacles and fins.

Cooked in the insert
and briefly browned afterwards

204　RECIPES　»　CLEVER COMBINATIONS

| COOKING LEVEL VITAVIT® | COOKING LEVEL VITAQUICK® | COOKING TIME |

Swabian potato salad
with meatloaf (1)

MAKES: 4 PORTIONS   **PREP TIME:** APPROX. 30 MIN.

1½ day-old bread rolls | 1 large onion | ½ bunch of parsley | 2 tbsp butter | 1 lb (500 g) mixed ground beef, veal and/or pork | 1 egg (large) | salt | freshly ground pepper | dried marjoram | dried thyme | breadcrumbs, as required | **For the salad:** 2 lbs (1 kg) yellow flesh or round (waxy) potatoes | 1¼ cups (300 ml) vegetable stock | 1 tsp granulated sugar | salt | freshly ground pepper | 2 tsp mustard | ⅓ cup (75 ml) white wine vinegar | 1 diced onion | 2 tbsp vegetable oil | 2 tbsp minced chives

1. Soak the bread rolls in lukewarm water. Peel and finely dice the onion. Rinse the parsley, shake it dry and finely chop.
2. Melt 4 tsp (20 g) butter in a small frying pan, add the diced onion and parsley and sauté briefly, then set aside and let cool slightly.
3. Grease an unperforated insert thoroughly with the remaining butter. Put the ground meat in a bowl. Add the egg, the well-squeezed bread rolls and the onion mixture. Season with 1½ tsp salt, pepper, some marjoram and thyme, then mix together into a malleable meat mixture. If the mixture is too soft, add some breadcrumbs. Put the meat mixture in the prepared insert.
4. Fill the pressure cooker with the minimum amount of water. Put the insert with the meatloaf on the tripod and cook on setting 3 (cooking indicator: 2nd ring) for 30 minutes.
5. Preheat broiler. To make the salad, peel the potatoes and cut them into ⅛-inch (3 mm) thick slices.
6. Remove the pressure cooker from the heat, release the steam and open the lid. Remove the meatloaf, put it on a baking sheet lined with parchment paper and brown it under the broiler for 5–8 minutes.
7. Clean the pot. Put the potatoes, stock, sugar, salt, pepper, mustard and vinegar in the pressure cooker and cook on setting 2 (cooking indicator: 1st ring) for 5–7 minutes.
8. Remove the pressure cooker from the heat, release the steam and open the lid. Stir in the diced onion and oil and leave everything to infuse in the pot for another 5 minutes or so.
9. Season the potato salad to taste and sprinkle with chives. Remove the meatloaf from the oven, cut it into slices and serve it on a platter or on plates with the potato salad.

| COOKING LEVEL VITAVIT® | COOKING LEVEL VITAQUICK® | COOKING TIME |

Farmhouse terrine with mâche
& caramelized apples (2)

MAKES: 4 PORTIONS   **PREP TIME:** APPROX. 40 MIN. + 14 HRS

1 tbsp dried marjoram | 2 tbsp brandy | 3 tbsp (45 g) butter | 8 oz (250 g) each lean ground pork and poultry | 1 large onion | salt | pepper | ¼ tsp ground coriander | 1 pinch of ground allspice | 7 oz (200 g) poultry liver | 3.3 oz (100 g) smoked bacon slices | **For the dressing:** 3 tbsp (45 ml) apple cider vinegar | 1 tsp mustard | 1–2 tbsp pure maple syrup | salt | pepper | ¼ cup (60 ml) olive oil | 2 tbsp walnut oil | **Other ingredients:** 2 small apples | 2 tbsp butter | 2 tbsp granulated sugar | 7 oz (200 g) mâche | ⅔ cup (75 g) chopped walnuts | ¼ cup (68 g) cranberry sauce (canned)

1. Mix together the marjoram and brandy and marinate for 2 hours. Generously grease an unperforated insert with 1 tbsp butter. Place the ground pork and poultry meat into a bowl.
2. Peel and finely dice the onion, then sauté it in the rest of the butter, let cool slightly, then add to the meat together with the strained marinated marjoram. Season the mixture with salt, pepper, coriander and allspice and mix well. Pat the poultry liver dry, chop it into small pieces and stir it into the mixture.
3. Arrange the bacon slices in a square lattice shape, make a round loaf out of the meat mixture and put it in the middle of the lattice. Fold over the overhanging bacon and place the terrine seam-side-down in the prepared insert.
4. Fill the pressure cooker with the minimum amount of water, put the insert on the tripod and seal the pot. Set the pressure regulator to setting 2 (cooking indicator: 1st ring), heat the pot on the highest setting and cook the terrine for 35 minutes.
5. Remove the pot from the heat and let stand for around 5 minutes, then release the steam and open the lid. Remove the terrine, leave it to cool in the insert, then wrap it in plastic wrap and leave it to rest in the fridge overnight.
6. To make the dressing, mix together the vinegar and the other ingredients in a salad bowl and season to taste.
7. Wash, halve and core the apples, then slice them into wedges. Heat the butter and sugar in a frying pan, add the apple wedges and caramelize briefly.
8. Toss the greens and walnuts in the dressing. Slice the terrine, arrange the slices on plates together with some salad, apple wedges and cranberry sauce, and serve.

Braised duck legs
with fried potatoes

COOKING LEVEL VITAVIT®

COOKING LEVEL VITAQUICK®

COOKING TIME

MAKES: 4 PORTIONS   **PREP TIME:** APPROX. 40 MIN.

FOR THE DUCK LEGS
2 shallots
2 carrots
4 small(ish) duck legs
salt
freshly ground pepper
1 cup + 2 tbsp (150 g) cubed (½ inch/1 cm) peeled celeriac (celery root)

FOR THE FRIED POTATOES
2 lbs (1 kg) firm potatoes
6 tbsp + 2 tsp (100 g) duck fat (or goose fat)
salt
freshly ground pepper
3 garlic cloves
½ handful of flat-leaf parsley
fleur de sel

FOR THE DUCK LEGS: peel the shallots and carrots and chop them into approx. ½-inch (1 cm) cubes. Pat dry the duck, then season them with salt and pepper. Fill the pressure cooker with the minimum amount of water, add the vegetables and place the duck legs on top.

Close the lid of the pressure cooker, set the pressure regulator to setting 3 and heat the pot on the highest setting. As soon as the yellow ring appears (cooking indicator: 1st ring), reduce the heat. When the green ring becomes visible (cooking indicator: 2nd ring), the 30-minute cooking time begins.

FOR THE FRIED POTATOES: peel and wash the potatoes, cut them into approx. ⅛-inch (3 mm) thick slices, then pat them dry with paper towels. Heat half of the duck fat in a large frying pan (or 2 smaller pans). Add the potatoes, fry them over a high heat for approx. 10 minutes, turning them over from time to time, then season with salt and pepper. Reduce the heat, add the remaining duck fat and continue frying and browning the potatoes over a low heat for another 10 minutes or so.

In the meantime, peel and finely dice the garlic. Wash the parsley, shake it dry, finely chop it and mix it with the garlic. Add the mixture to the pan and cook the potatoes for another 4–5 minutes until done.

TO FINISH: preheat the oven broiler. Remove the pressure cooker from the heat, release the steam and open the lid.

Put a wire rack over a rimmed baking sheet (drip pan). Remove the duck legs from the pot, place them on the rack skin-side-down and broil them for approx. 4 minutes. Remove them, turn them over, season lightly with salt, then broil them skin-side-up for another 5 minutes or so until crispy.

Season the potatoes to taste with fleur de sel. Remove the duck legs from the oven, arrange them on plates with the fried potatoes and serve.

TIPS: if you're in a hurry or you're having guests and you want to prepare other courses of a menu, you can also precook the potatoes in advance in your pressure cooker. To do so, simply wash the potatoes and put them in the perforated insert. Fill the pot with the minimum amount of water and add the tripod. Put the insert on the tripod and pressure cook the potatoes on setting 3 (cooking indicator: 2nd ring) for 8–12 minutes, depending on their size. Then peel them, leave them to cool, cut them into slices and fry them in ¼ cup (60 g) duck fat, turning occasionally, until golden brown.

Strain the cooking juices from the pressure cooker through a sieve, let cool, skim off the fat and freeze. This makes a great basis for a delicious sauce.

COOKING LEVEL VITAVIT®: 3 | COOKING LEVEL VITAQUICK®: 2 | COOKING TIME: 15

Braised & glazed pork belly

MAKES: 4 PORTIONS **PREP TIME:** 20–30 MIN. **STEAMING TIME:** 6 MIN. (PAK CHOI)

Pork belly
braised in rice wine (1)

1.6 lbs (800 g) pork belly | ¾-inch (2 cm) piece gingerroot | 1 green onion | ⅔ cup + 1 tbsp (150 g) packed brown sugar | 1 cinnamon stick | 2 star anise pods | 2 cups (500 ml) Shaoxing rice wine | 3 tbsp + 1 tsp (50 ml) dark soy sauce | ⅓ cup (75 ml) light soy sauce | 1 tbsp salt | 2 bay leaves | **To finish:** 1–2 tsp cornstarch | 2 green onions, cut into thin rings | 1–2 tsp sesame seeds

1. Pat the pork belly dry and cut it into approx. 1½-inch (4 cm) cubes. Peel and finely slice the ginger. Wash and trim the green onion, then cut into thin rings.
2. Melt the sugar in the pressure cooker, add the meat, sear it all over and let caramelize. Add the green onion, cinnamon, star anise and ginger and continue frying. Deglaze with the rice wine and both types of soy sauce, then add the salt and bay leaves. Seal the pot, set the pressure regulator to setting 3 and heat everything. When the yellow ring appears (cooking indicator: 1st ring), reduce the heat again. When the green ring becomes visible (cooking indicator: 2nd ring), cook everything for 15 minutes.
3. Release the steam from the pot, open the lid and continue cooking in the open pot for approx. 10 minutes, until the liquid has reduced substantially. Remove the bay leaves. Thicken the sauce with some cornstarch mixed with a little cold water. Remove the pork belly, arrange it on plates with some sauce, sprinkle with green onion rings and sesame seeds, and serve. Basmati rice makes the perfect side.

Char siu with pak choi (2)

2 lbs (1 kg) pork belly | ¼ cup (60 ml) soy sauce | 2 tbsp Shaoxing rice wine (or sherry) | 4 cups (1 L) poultry stock | ½ cup (125 ml) char siu sauce (jar) | 2 tbsp liquid honey | 2 tsp sesame oil | 1 tbsp peanut oil | salt | 4 baby pak choi (bok choy), trimmed, halved or quartered

1. Pat the meat dry. Put the soy sauce, rice wine, stock and ¼ cup (60 ml) of the char siu sauce in an open pressure cooker and reduce the liquid for approx. 5 minutes. Add the pork belly, seal the pot and cook the meat on setting 3 (cooking indicator: 2nd ring) for 15 minutes.
2. Remove the pot from the heat, release the steam and open the lid. Remove the meat, leave it to cool and measure out 1 cup (250 ml) of the cooking juices. Cut the pork belly into approx. 1¼-inch (3 cm) cubes.
3. Put the honey and sesame oil in a small bowl with the rest of the char siu sauce and mix well. Heat the peanut oil in a frying pan, sear and brown the meat all over for 5–10 minutes, brushing it repeatedly with the honey mixture.
4. Pour 1⅔ cups (400 ml) water into the pressure cooker and add some salt. Put the pak choi in a perforated insert, put the insert on the tripod and steam without pressure for approx. 6 minutes (or steam the conventional way). Leave the cooking liquid (1 cup/250 ml) to reduce over a high heat until it thickens. Serve the char siu with some sauce and pak choi. Basmati rice makes the perfect side.

(2)

RECIPES >> CLEVER COMBINATIONS 209

COOKING LEVEL VITAVIT® **COOKING LEVEL VITAQUICK®** **COOKING TIME**

Veal roast
with beet salad

MAKES: 4 PORTIONS **SOAKING TIME:** 12 HRS **PREP TIME:** APPROX. 25 MIN.

FOR THE VEAL
2 lbs (1 kg) beef soup bones
4 marrow bones
3 lbs (1.5 kg) veal outside (bottom) round
sea salt
1 carrot
1 small celeriac
1 celery stalk
1 leek
½ browned Spanish onion

FOR THE BEET SALAD
3 beets
salt
1 shallot
¼ bunch of chives
4 tsp red wine vinegar
salt
granulated sugar

TO FINISH
freshly ground black pepper
1–2 tbsp minced chives
freshly grated horseradish

FOR THE VEAL: rinse the bones, scoop out the marrow and let the bones soak for approx. 12 hours, changing the water from time to time.

FOR THE BEET SALAD: wash the beets and dab them dry, then put them in the perforated insert. Fill the pressure cooker with the minimum amount of water and season the beets with salt. Put the insert on the tripod (or cook the beets directly in the pressure cooker) and seal the pot. Set the pressure regulator to setting 2 and heat the pot on the highest setting. As soon as the yellow ring appears (cooking indicator: 1st ring), reduce the heat. When the green ring becomes visible (cooking indicator: 1st ring), the 20-to-25-minute cooking time begins (depending on the size of the beets). Remove the pot from the heat, release the steam and open the lid. Remove the beets and let cool.

COOK THE VEAL: rinse the bones and meat, put them in a saucepan, cover with salted water, bring to the boil and blanch for 3–4 minutes, repeatedly skimming off the foam. Remove the bones and meat and rinse again. Peel the carrot and celeriac, wash and trim the celery and leek and coarsely dice all of the vegetables.

Put the bones in a pressure cooker, cover with cold water and bring to the boil. Add the veal to the boiling water, then add the diced vegetables and the browned onion and close the pressure cooker. Set the pressure regulator to setting 3 and heat the pot on the highest setting. As soon as the yellow ring appears (cooking indicator: 1st ring), reduce the heat. When the green ring becomes visible (cooking indicator: 2nd ring), the 45-minute cooking time begins. Afterwards, remove the pressure cooker from the heat, release the steam and open the lid. Remove the meat, cover and let rest for approx. 10 minutes. Strain the stock through a sieve and season with salt to taste.

FINISH THE SALAD: peel the beets, cut into wedges and put in a bowl. Peel and very finely dice the shallot. Wash the chives, shake them dry and cut them into fine rings. Take ¼ cup (60 ml) of the stock and mix it together with the vinegar, salt, sugar, diced shallot and half of the chives. Pour the dressing over the warm beet wedges and leave the salad to marinate briefly.

TO FINISH: cut the veal roast across the grain into thin slices, arrange on plates and drizzle with some stock. Season lightly with pepper and serve with a sprinkling of chives and freshly grated horseradish. Sprinkle the remaining chives over the beet salad and serve separately.

TIP: if desired, cut the marrow into approx. ½-inch (1 cm) slices and marinate briefly in the stock. Then serve it first with some toasted bread and fleur de sel.

COOKING LEVEL VITAVIT® 3 | COOKING LEVEL VITAQUICK® 2 | COOKING TIME 20–30

Succulent and crispy: grilled spare ribs

MAKES: 4 PORTIONS **PREP TIME:** APPROX. 20 MIN. **GRILL TIME:** 7–10 MIN.

BBQ-style spare ribs (1)

1.6 lbs (800 g) pork back ribs | salt | 2 tbsp brown sugar | 3 tbsp (18 g) paprika | ½ tsp chili powder | salt | 2 onions | 2 garlic cloves | 3 tbsp (45 ml) vegetable oil | ¾ cup + 1 tbsp (200 g) ketchup | 1¼ cups (300 ml) vegetable stock | ⅓ cup (80 g) peach jam | 2 tbsp apple cider vinegar | 2 tbsp medium-hot mustard | smoked salt

1. Pat the ribs dry and cut them into pieces (2 ribs per piece). Mix together the sugar, paprika, chili powder and 2 tsp of salt.
2. Peel and finely dice the onions and garlic. Heat 2 tbsp oil in a pressure cooker, add the diced onion and sauté for around 5 minutes until browned. Add the garlic and continue frying for about 30 seconds, while stirring. Add the ketchup, vegetable stock, peach jam, cider vinegar and mustard and mix well. Pour the spicy sauce into a bowl and let cool briefly.
3. Brush the ribs all over with the spicy sauce and stand them upright (with the meat side facing out) in the pressure cooker. Drizzle 1¼ cups (300 ml) of the spicy sauce over the ribs. Seal the pot, set the pressure regulator to setting 3 and heat on the highest setting. When the yellow ring appears (cooking indicator: 1st ring), reduce the heat. When the green ring becomes visible (cooking indicator: 1st ring), cook everything for 15–20 minutes.
4. Preheat the broiler (or convection oven to 410°F/210°C). Brush a wire roasting rack with the remaining oil and place it over a rimmed baking sheet. Release the steam from the pressure cooker and open the lid. Remove the ribs and place them on the rack with the meat part facing upwards. Strain the fat from the sauce (pp. 98–99), simmer with the remaining spicy sauce in the open pot for approx. 10 minutes, then season to taste with smoked salt.
5. Brush the ribs with the sauce and broil for approx. 7 minutes, turning occasionally and generously brushing the ribs with the sauce on a regular basis. Serve the spare ribs with the remaining sauce. Creamy sweet potato mash makes a wonderful side dish.

Asian-style spare ribs (2)

2 lbs (1 kg) pork back ribs | 1 tsp salt | 1 tsp freshly ground pepper | 1 tsp garlic powder | 2 tsp ground ginger | 1 tsp rice vinegar | ¾ cup + 2 tbsp (200 ml) soy sauce | 3 tbsp (40 g) packed brown sugar | 1 tsp sesame oil | 2 tsp chili sauce | 2 tsp cornstarch | 2 garlic cloves | 1 green onion, green part, cut into strips

1. Pat the pork ribs dry. Mix together the salt, pepper, garlic powder and 1 tsp ground ginger in a small bowl, then rub the mixture onto the ribs.
2. Fill the pressure cooker with the minimum amount of water. Stand the ribs upright in an insert (p. 79) on the tripod. Seal the pot and cook the ribs on setting 3 (cooking indicator: 2nd ring) for 20–30 minutes, remove the pot from the heat, let stand for 10 minutes, then open the lid.
3. Mix together the remaining ground ginger with the vinegar, soy sauce, sugar, oil, chili sauce and cornstarch. Peel and crush the garlic and add it to the marinade. Mix well, heat the marinade in a frying pan, then simmer over a medium heat for approx. 5 minutes.
4. Preheat the broiler (or convection oven to 410°F/210°C). Put an oven-proof rack on a rimmed baking sheet, place the ribs with the meat side upwards on the rack and broil them in the oven for approx. 7 minutes, regularly brushing them with the marinade. Remove the spare ribs, garnish with strips of green onion and serve.

TIP: before cooking, remove the silver skin from the underside of the ribs with a spoon. Finish cooking the ribs on a lightly oiled cooking grate on a charcoal or gas BBQ.

COOKING LEVEL VITAVIT®

COOKING LEVEL VITAQUICK®

COOKING TIME

Tex-Mex street food
tortillas and tacos

MAKES: 4 PORTIONS   **PREP TIME:** APPROX. 30 MIN.

Beef fajitas (1)

1 lb (500 g) boneless beef steak (e.g., sirloin) | salt | ½–1 tsp ground cumin | ½ tsp chili powder | ½ tsp pepper flakes | 1 garlic clove | 2 tbsp vegetable oil | 2 tbsp lemon juice | 1 large red bell pepper | 1 large onion | 1 avocado | 2 tbsp lime juice | 8 flour tortillas (approx. 8 inches/20 cm) | 1 jalapeño chile pepper, in rings | 2 small tomatoes, diced | ¾ cup (80 g) shredded cheddar cheese | fresh cilantro

1. Pat the meat dry, cut it into strips and mix with ½ tsp salt and the spices. Peel and finely dice the garlic.
2. Heat the oil in a pressure cooker, sear the meat all over in portions, then remove it. Add the lemon juice, top up to 1¼ cups (300 ml) with water and loosen the cooking juices with the liquid. Add the garlic and return the meat to the pot. Seal the pot, set the pressure regulator to setting 3 (cooking indicator: 2nd ring) and cook for 20 minutes. Wash and trim the red pepper, peel the onion and cut both into strips.
3. Remove the pot from the heat and let stand for around 10 minutes, then release the steam. Remove the meat and keep it warm. Cook the red pepper and onion in the cooking juices in the pressure cooker on setting 3 (cooking indicator: 2nd ring) for 5 minutes, then release the steam.
4. Cut the avocado in half, remove the stone and the skin, cut it crosswise into slices and drizzle with lime juice. Season the meat to taste. Heat up the tortillas, fill them with steak strips, red pepper and the remaining ingredients and serve garnished with cilantro.

Pulled pork carnitas (2)

3 lbs (1.5 kg) pork tenderloin | 2 tbsp olive oil | salt | pepper | 1 large onion | 3 garlic cloves | 2 jalapeño chile peppers | 2¼ cups (400 g) chopped tomatoes | 1 tbsp dried oregano | ½–1 tsp chili powder | 2 tsp ground cumin | juice of 2 oranges | 1 small onion | 6 tbsp (90 ml) lime juice | 4 finely diced tomatoes | 8 taco shells | 2–3 handfuls of romaine lettuce, in strips | cilantro leaves

1. Pat the pork dry, drizzle with 1 tbsp oil and season with salt and pepper. Peel and coarsely dice the large onion and garlic. Wash, trim and finely chop the chile peppers. Heat the remaining oil (1 tbsp) in the pressure cooker and sear the meat all over. Add the diced large onion and garlic and let caramelize slightly. Stir in the chopped tomatoes, half of the diced chile, and the oregano and spices. Measure orange juice and top up with water to 1¼ cups (300 ml), then pour into pot.
2. Seal the pot, heat on the highest setting and cook on setting 3 (cooking indicator: 2nd ring) for 30 minutes.
3. Peel and finely dice the small onion and put it in a bowl with the rest of the diced chile, ¼ cup (60 ml) lime juice, ¾ tsp salt and the finely diced tomato. Leave the salsa to marinate briefly.
4. Remove the pot from the heat, release the steam, remove the meat, pull it into strips, then put it back into the pot. Season with salt, pepper and the remaining lime juice. Warm up the tacos, fill them with lettuce and meat, top with salsa and serve with some cilantro leaves.

COOKING LEVEL VITAVIT®

COOKING LEVEL VITAQUICK®

COOKING TIME

Brisket
with coleslaw

MAKES: 4 PORTIONS **MARINATING TIME:** 12 HRS **PREP TIME:** 30 MIN. **COOLING TIME:** 4 HRS

FOR THE RUB
2 tbsp brown sugar
1 tsp chili powder
1½ tsp freshly ground pepper
1 tsp onion powder
1 tsp garlic powder
1 pinch of ground cinnamon
1 tsp coarse sea salt
½ tsp smoked salt
½ tsp ground cumin
½ tsp ground fennel seeds
¼ tsp cayenne pepper

FOR THE MEAT
2 lbs (1 kg) beef brisket, flat cut (approx. 2 inches/5 cm thick)
2 onions
3 garlic cloves
1 tbsp pure maple syrup
1 tbsp liquid honey
2 tbsp apple cider vinegar
¾ cup + 2 tbsp (200 ml) poultry stock
¾ cup + 2 tbsp (200 ml) ketchup
3 tbsp + 1 tsp (50 ml) BBQ sauce (with smoky flavor if desired)
2 tbsp Dijon mustard
1 tbsp brown sugar
salt
freshly ground pepper
fleur de sel

FOR THE COLESLAW
1 shallot
1 tbsp apple cider vinegar
3 tbsp (45 ml) lemon juice
salt
freshly ground pepper
¼ cup (60 g) mayonnaise
¼ cup (60 g) sour cream
1 tbsp pure maple syrup
15 oz (450 g) green cabbage
10 oz (300 g) red cabbage
1 large carrot

FOR THE RUB: put the brown sugar, chili powder, pepper and the other ingredients in a bowl and mix well.

FOR THE MEAT: pat the brisket dry, put it on a chopping board, sprinkle it with the rub (1) and rub it into the meat. Wrap the meat in plastic wrap and marinate overnight in the fridge.

The next day, peel the onions and garlic. Cut the onions into rings and finely dice the garlic. Put both in a large pressure cooker. Add the maple syrup, honey and vinegar. Pour in the poultry stock and top up with as much water as needed to reach the pressure cooker's minimum volume mark. Remove the brisket from the plastic wrap and put it in the pot (2).

Seal the pot with the lid. Set the pressure regulator to setting 3 and heat the pot on the highest setting. As soon as the yellow ring appears (cooking indicator: 1st ring), reduce the heat. When the green ring becomes visible (cooking indicator: 2nd ring), the 40-to-60-minute cooking time begins.

FOR THE COLESLAW: peel and finely dice the shallot and put it in a bowl. Add the cider vinegar, lemon juice, salt, pepper, mayonnaise, sour cream and maple syrup. Mix well and season the dressing to taste.

Remove the outer leaves from the green and red cabbage, remove the thick ribs and chop the rest into thin slices. Peel and finely grate the carrot. Put everything in a bowl with the dressing, mix well, cover with plastic wrap and refrigerate for approx. 4 hours.

TO FINISH: preheat the broiler. Remove the pressure cooker from the heat, release the steam and open the lid. Remove the brisket, cover and let rest. Strain the fat from the cooking juices if necessary, then reduce slightly in the open pot. Stir in the ketchup, BBQ sauce, mustard and sugar and reduce for approx. 10 minutes until it thickens, then season with salt and pepper to taste.

Put a wire roasting rack on a rimmed baking sheet. Place the cooked brisket on the rack, brush generously with the sauce (3) and broil briefly in the oven until it starts to caramelize.

Remove the meat, cut it across the grain into slices and arrange the slices on a serving platter or plates. Sprinkle the brisket with a little fleur de sel and serve with the coleslaw. Serve the remaining sauce separately.

TIP: the cooking time may vary depending on the quality of the meat and how long it has been hung. If the meat is not tender enough after 1 hour, simply close the pressure cooker again and cook the brisket on setting 3 (cooking indicator: 2nd ring), for another 15 minutes.

Curries & braised dishes

Pressure cookers are ideal for preparing Thai curry with green vegetables or spicy Indian curries with lentils, potatoes, chicken or pork. They are also perfect for making Mediterranean dishes such as couscous and chickpeas, which taste as if they were prepared in a tajine but are much faster to cook. But pressure cookers really come into their own with braising dishes, such as melt-in-your-mouth US- and Asian-style short ribs, various takes on goulash, braised beef cheeks and tender shoulder of venison.

COOKING LEVEL VITAVIT® | **COOKING LEVEL VITAQUICK®** | **COOKING TIME**

Thai green vegetable curry

MAKES: 4 PORTIONS **PREP TIME:** APPROX. 35 MIN.

FOR THE CURRY PASTE
3 shallots
4 garlic cloves
1¼-inch (3 cm) piece galangal (or gingerroot)
2–3 green chile peppers
1 lemongrass stalk
½ bunch of cilantro, with roots
1 tsp coriander seeds
1 tsp cumin (whole)
½ tsp ground turmeric
½ tsp freshly ground pepper
2–3 tbsp vegetable oil
1 organic lime
1–2 tsp salt

FOR THE VEGETABLE CURRY
1 onion
¾-inch (2 cm) piece gingerroot
8 oz (250 g) broccolini (or broccoli)
1¼ cups (80 g) sugar snap peas
5 oz (150 g) green beans
½ cup (80 g) green peas (fresh or frozen)
11.6 oz (350 g) green asparagus
2 tbsp coconut oil
1¼ cups (300 ml) vegetable stock
1¼ cups (300 ml) coconut milk

TO FINISH
½ handful of Thai basil (or ¼ handful each of mint and basil)
2 tbsp vegan fish sauce
1 tbsp palm sugar
salt
freshly ground pepper
2 tbsp toasted coconut chips

FOR THE CURRY PASTE: peel and coarsely chop the shallots, garlic and galangal. Trim or peel, wash and chop the chile peppers, lemongrass and cilantro roots. Pluck the cilantro leaves and set them aside.

Toast the coriander seeds and cumin for around 1 minute in the pressure cooker or a frying pan without any fat, stirring constantly, until they become fragrant. Put the spices, the other prepared ingredients and the oil in a food chopper or a mortar and grind into a fine paste. Wash the lime in hot water, then dab it dry, finely zest the peel and squeeze the juice. Add the lime zest and juice and the salt to the curry paste and mix.

FOR THE VEGETABLE CURRY: peel the onion, cut it in half, then into thin strips. Peel and finely grate the ginger. Wash and strain the vegetables. Trim the broccolini and beans and cut them both into 2- to 2½-inch (5 to 6 cm) pieces. Remove the bottom third of the asparagus and chop the rest at an angle into 2- to 2½-inch (5 to 6 cm) pieces. Wash and trim the sugar snap peas, then cut them in half at an angle.

Heat the coconut oil in a pressure cooker, add the onion and ginger and sauté lightly for 2–3 minutes, while stirring. Add the curry paste and continue frying for about another 2 minutes, still stirring constantly. Deglaze with the stock, pour in the coconut milk, then add the broccolini, asparagus pieces (except the tips) and green beans.

Close the pressure cooker, set the pressure regulator to setting 2 and heat the pot on the highest setting. As soon as the yellow ring appears (cooking indicator: 1st ring), reduce the heat again. When the green ring becomes visible (cooking indicator: 1st ring), the 2-minute cooking time begins.

TO FINISH: in the meantime, rinse the Thai basil, shake it dry, then pluck the leaves and tips. Remove the pressure cooker from the heat, release the steam and open the lid.

Stir in the vegan fish sauce and palm sugar, then add the asparagus tips, sugar snap peas, peas and cilantro leaves to the open pot and cook for another 3 minutes or so.

Season the curry with salt and pepper and divide between four plates. Garnish with Thai basil and toasted coconut chips and serve.

TIP: basmati or long-grain brown rice tastes great with this vegan green curry. You can vary the vegetables you use according to the season, depending on what is growing in your garden or balcony, or what is freshly available at the market. Pak choi (bok choy) and romanesco also taste great – but if you use these vegetables, reduce the pressure cooking time slightly.

Vegetarian curries
with lentils, cabbage and potatoes

COOKING LEVEL VITAVIT® | COOKING LEVEL VITAQUICK® | COOKING TIME

COOKING LEVEL VITAVIT® | COOKING LEVEL VITAQUICK® | COOKING TIME

Coconut & lentil curry
with vegetables (1)

MAKES: 4 PORTIONS **PREP TIME:** APPROX. 20 MIN.

1 cup (200 g) dried brown lentils | 2 onions | 3 garlic cloves | ¾-inch (2 cm) piece gingerroot | 1 chile pepper | 1 tbsp coconut oil | 2 cups (500 ml) vegetable stock | 3 carrots | 2 bell peppers | 1 pak choi (bok choy) | 1 cup (250 ml) coconut milk | 1 tbsp red curry paste | 1 tsp ground turmeric | 1 tsp curry powder | 1 tbsp soy sauce | salt | toasted sesame oil | chile rings, pistachios, lime wedges

1. Rinse the lentils and leave them to strain. Peel and finely dice the onions, garlic and ginger. Wash, trim and finely dice the chile pepper.
2. Heat the oil in the pressure cooker, add the prepared ingredients and sauté briefly, while stirring. Add the lentils and continue frying briefly, then deglaze with the stock. Close the pressure cooker, set the pressure regulator to setting 3 and heat the pot on the highest setting. When the yellow ring appears (cooking indicator: 1st ring), reduce the heat. When the green ring becomes visible (cooking indicator: 2nd ring), cook for 10 minutes.
3. In the meantime, peel the carrots, wash and trim the peppers and cut both into small pieces. Trim and wash the pak choi and cut it into bite-size pieces.
4. Remove the pot from the heat, release the steam and open the lid. Stir in the coconut milk and curry paste and cook briefly in the open pot. Add the vegetables, turmeric, curry powder and soy sauce. Close the pressure cooker again and finish cooking on the lowest pressure setting for another 3 minutes or so.
5. Release the steam from the pot and open the lid. Season to taste lightly with salt. Divide the curry between four deep plates, drizzle with sesame oil, garnish with chile rings, pistachios and lime wedges and serve.

Green cabbage curry
with potatoes (2)

MAKES: 4 PORTIONS **PREP TIME:** APPROX. 25 MIN.

1 small green cabbage (approx. 1 lb/500 g) | 1 lb (500 g) round (waxy) potatoes | 2 tomatoes | 1–2 garlic cloves | 1 red chile pepper | 1 lemongrass stalk | 1⅔ cups (100 g) sugar snap peas | 3 tbsp (45 g) ghee (or clarified butter) | 2 bay leaves | ½ tsp cumin seeds | 1 tsp ground turmeric | ½ tsp chili powder | 1½ tsp ground cumin | 2 tbsp finely chopped peeled gingerroot | 1 tsp ground coriander | 1 tsp salt | ½ tsp brown sugar | 1¼ cups (300 ml) vegetable stock

1. Cut the cabbage into quarters, remove the outer leaves and core and chop crosswise into approx. ½-inch (1 cm) strips. Peel the potatoes and cut them into approx. ½-inch (1 cm) cubes. Wash, quarter, seed and finely dice the tomatoes. Peel and finely chop the garlic. Wash, trim and finely dice the chile pepper. Remove the outer leaves from the lemongrass and finely chop the light part into thin rings. Wash and trim the sugar snap peas, then cut them in half at an angle.
2. Heat the ghee in a large pressure cooker, add the bay leaves, cumin seeds and lemongrass and fry for approx. 1 minute until they become fragrant. Add the garlic, ginger and chile and continue to fry briefly. Add the cabbage, potatoes, tomatoes, sugar snap peas, remaining spices, salt and sugar and continue frying for 2 minutes, while stirring. Deglaze with the stock.
3. Seal the pot, set the pressure regulator to setting 2 and heat the pot on the highest setting. As soon as the yellow ring appears (cooking indicator: 1st ring), reduce the heat. When the green ring becomes visible (cooking indicator: 1st ring), cook everything for 7 minutes. Release the steam from the pot and open the lid. Remove the bay leaves. Season the cabbage curry to taste, divide between four plates and serve.

Curry variations
with chicken and lamb

MAKES: 4 PORTIONS   **MARINATING TIME:** 30 MIN. (CHICKEN)   **PREP TIME:** 25–30 MIN.

COOKING LEVEL VITAVIT®   **COOKING LEVEL VITAQUICK®**   **COOKING TIME**

COOKING LEVEL VITAVIT®   **COOKING LEVEL VITAQUICK®**   **COOKING TIME**

Chicken and vegetable curry (1)

1 lb (500 g) boneless skinless chicken breasts | ¾ cup + 2 tbsp (200 ml) milk | 3 small red onions | 3 garlic cloves | 12 cherry tomatoes | salt | pepper | 2 tbsp cornstarch | 1 tbsp peanut oil | 2 tbsp butter | 2¾ cups (250 g) broccoli florets | 2¼ cups (250 g) cauliflower florets | 1½ cups (200 g) cubed (¾ inch/2 cm) butternut squash | 1 tbsp finely diced peeled gingerroot | 2 tbsp curry powder | 1 tsp sweet paprika | 1 tsp brown sugar | ¾ cup + 2 tbsp (200 ml) poultry stock | ½ cup (125 ml) coconut milk | ⅔ cup (150 ml) tomato passata | 1 organic lime | 2 tbsp fresh cilantro

1. Pat the chicken dry, then soak it in the milk for 30 minutes, turning it once after 15 minutes.
2. Peel the onions and cut them into wedges. Peel and finely dice the garlic. Wash the tomatoes and, depending on their size, either leave them whole or cut them in half.
3. Strain the chicken and discard the milk. Cut chicken into 1¼- to 1½-inch (3 to 4 cm) pieces, season with salt and pepper, then coat in cornstarch.
4. Heat the oil and butter in the pressure cooker, then sear the chicken in portions until golden brown, turning occasionally. Add the onions, vegetables, garlic, ginger, spices and brown sugar and stir. Deglaze with the stock and coconut milk, then stir in the tomato passata.
5. Close the pressure cooker with the lid and set the pressure regulator to setting 2. Heat the pot on the highest setting. As soon as the yellow ring appears (cooking indicator: 1st ring), reduce the heat. When the green ring becomes visible (cooking indicator: 2nd ring), the 8-minute cooking time begins.
6. Wash the lime in hot water, dab it dry and cut it into wedges. Remove the pot from the heat, release the steam and open the lid. Season the curry to taste, divide between four plates and serve garnished with lime wedges and cilantro.

Ground lamb curry (2)

2 garlic cloves | 2 tbsp coconut oil | 10 oz (300 g) ground lamb | ¾ cup (100 g) diced onion | 1 tbsp curry powder | 1½ cup (125 g) finely diced eggplant | 2 tbsp tomato paste | 2¼ cups (550 ml) vegetable stock | 1 can (14 oz/400 ml) coconut milk | 2 tsp medium-hot mustard | 1 cup + 6 tbsp (250 g) long-grain white rice | ½ mild red chile pepper | 1¾ cup (300 g) chopped green bell pepper | 1 tsp salt | cayenne pepper | juice of ½ lemon | 1 tbsp honey | ½ handful of cilantro | ½ tsp nigella seeds

1. Peel and finely dice 1 garlic clove. Heat the coconut oil in the pressure cooker and sear the lamb in the oil. Stir in the onion and the curry powder and continue frying for another 3 minutes or so. Add the eggplant and continue to fry briefly. Stir in the tomato paste and cook for another minute or so. Deglaze with the stock and the coconut milk, stir in the mustard and add the rice.
2. Close the pressure cooker, set the pressure regulator to setting 3 and heat the pot on the highest setting. When the yellow ring appears, reduce the heat. When the green ring becomes visible (cooking indicator: 2nd ring), the 7-minute cooking time begins.
3. In the meantime, wash and trim the mild chile pepper and peel the remaining garlic clove. Finely dice the garlic and mild chile pepper. Remove the pot from the heat and release the steam. Add the green pepper, mild chile pepper and garlic to the pot, then season with salt, cayenne pepper, lemon juice and honey.
4. Leave the curried rice to simmer in the open pressure cooker for a little longer, then season to taste, divide between four plates and serve with a sprinkling of cilantro and nigella seeds.

TIP: to make a vegan version, simply fry 10 oz (300 g) tofu-based ground meat replacement in the pressure cooker and round off the curry with 1 tbsp brown sugar or pure maple syrup instead of honey.

RECIPES » CURRIES & BRAISED DISHES   225

Tender and aromatic
Indian butter chicken

COOKING LEVEL VITAVIT®

COOKING LEVEL VITAQUICK®

COOKING TIME

MAKES: 4 PORTIONS **MARINATING TIME:** 12 HRS **PREP TIME:** 20–30 MIN.

FOR THE MARINADE
1 tbsp ginger & garlic paste
1–2 tsp ground cumin
1–2 tsp ground coriander
1 tsp garam masala
1 tsp paprika
1 tbsp lemon juice
¾ cup + 1 tbsp (200 g) plain yogurt (10% fat)
salt

FOR THE CHICKEN
1.6 lbs (800 g) boneless skinless chicken breasts
2 onions
⅓ cup (80 g) butter
1 tsp granulated sugar
½ tsp ground cardamom
½ tsp ground cinnamon
2 cloves
1 tbsp ginger & garlic paste
1½ tsp garam masala
¾ cup + 2 tbsp (200 ml) poultry stock
2¼ cups (400 g) chopped tomatoes
1½ tsp paprika
6 tbsp + 2 tsp (100 ml) heavy or whipping (35%) cream
salt
freshly ground pepper
cayenne pepper

FOR THE MARINADE: put the ginger and garlic paste in a shallow dish with the ground cumin and mix together with the remaining spices. Add the lemon juice, yogurt and some salt and stir well.

FOR THE CHICKEN: pat them dry. Cut the chicken into ¾- to 1¼-inch (2 to 3 cm) pieces, put it in the marinade, mix well, cover with plastic wrap and marinate in the fridge overnight.

The next day, peel and finely dice the onions. Remove the chicken pieces from the marinade, strain or pat dry. Discard marinade. Heat half of the butter in a pressure cooker, sear the chicken all over in portions until browned, then remove it.

Lightly sauté the onions in the fat remaining in the pan, sprinkle the sugar on top and let caramelize slightly and turn golden brown. Add the cardamom, cinnamon and cloves and cook for approx. 1 minute. Add the remaining butter, stir in the ginger and garlic paste and the garam masala and continue frying for another 1–2 minutes, stirring occasionally.

Deglaze with the stock, then stir in the chopped tomatoes and paprika and simmer in the open pot for another 5–10 minutes.

Finally, stir in the cream and add the chicken. Close the pressure cooker with the lid and set the pressure regulator to setting 2. Heat the pot on the highest setting. As soon as the yellow ring appears (cooking indicator: 1st ring), reduce the heat. When the green ring becomes visible (cooking indicator: 1st ring), the 10-minute cooking time begins.

Remove the pressure cooker from the heat, release the steam and open the lid. Season with salt, pepper and 1 pinch of cayenne pepper.

TO SERVE: season the butter chicken to taste, divide it between four deep plates or bowls and serve with basmati rice and naan, as desired.

TIP: you can also cook the rice with the curry. To do so, simply put the rinsed basmati rice and water (at a ratio of 1:1.2) and some salt in an unperforated insert. Place the insert above the chicken in the pressure cooker – without exceeding the maximum fill level – and cook as described in the recipe. Alternatively, you can pressure cook the basmati rice separately for approx. 5 minutes on setting 3.

COOKING LEVEL VITAVIT® 3
COOKING LEVEL VITAQUICK® 2
COOKING TIME 15

Pork vindaloo

MAKES: 4 PORTIONS **MARINATING TIME:** 4–5 HRS **PREP TIME:** APPROX. 25 MIN.

FOR THE SPICE PASTE
1 tbsp coriander seeds
4 cloves
1 tbsp cumin seeds
1 cinnamon stick (approx. 2 inches/5 cm)
1 tsp peppercorns
1½ tsp fenugreek seeds
½ tsp black mustard seeds
1 tsp fennel seeds
½ tsp palm sugar (or brown sugar)
¼ cup (60 ml) coconut vinegar (or rice vinegar)

FOR THE CURRY
1.6 lbs (800 g) boneless pork roast (e.g., leg)
2 onions
5 garlic cloves
2–5 red chile peppers
3 tbsp (45 g) ghee (or clarified butter)
1½ tbsp finely chopped peeled gingerroot
1 bay leaf
¾ cup + 2 tbsp (200 ml) vegetable stock
1 cup + 6 tbsp (250 g) chopped tomatoes
salt

TO SERVE
2 tbsp fresh cilantro

FOR THE SPICE PASTE: toast the coriander seeds, cloves, cumin and remaining spices in the pressure cooker or a frying pan without any fat for 3–4 minutes, stirring from time to time, until they become fragrant. Set the pot aside and leave the spices to cool slightly, then finely grind the palm sugar in a food chopper (or mortar) and stir it into the coconut vinegar.

FOR THE CURRY: pat the pork dry, remove any visible fat and skin and cut into approx. 1¼-inch (3 cm) cubes. Put the meat in a bowl, mix together with the spice paste, cover with plastic wrap and marinate in the fridge for 4–5 hours.

In the meantime, peel and finely dice the onions and garlic. Wash, trim and finely dice the chile peppers.

Heat the ghee in the pressure cooker and sear the marinated meat in portions until slightly browned, then remove it. Fry the onions, ginger and chile in the fat remaining in the pan for about 3 minutes, while stirring. Add the garlic and continue frying for about another minute, still stirring.

Put the meat back in the pot, add the bay leaf and pour in the stock. Stir in the chopped tomatoes and season lightly with salt. Close the pressure cooker with the lid and set the pressure regulator to setting 3. Heat the pot on the highest setting and as soon as the yellow ring appears (cooking indicator: 1st ring), reduce the heat again. When the green ring becomes visible (cooking indicator: 2nd ring), the 15-minute cooking time begins.

TO SERVE: wash the cilantro, shake it dry and pluck the leaves. Remove the pressure cooker from the heat, release the steam and open the lid.

Remove the bay leaf. Season the curry to taste, divide it between four plates, garnish with a couple of cilantro leaves and serve. This dish goes wonderfully with basmati rice (p. 86–87) or naan.

TIP: the spiciness of chile peppers can vary greatly, so it's best to dose them carefully starting with 1–2 peppers. If you don't like your food to be too spicy, remove the small white seeds from the chile peppers before chopping them up. If you prefer more of a kick, use the seeds as well.

COOKING LEVEL VITAVIT® 3
COOKING LEVEL VITAQUICK® 2
COOKING TIME 6–30

Arabian-inspired

MAKES: 4 PORTIONS   **SOAKING TIME:** 12 HRS (ETLI NOHUT)   **PREP TIME:** 25 MIN.

Braised butternut squash with date couscous (1)

1.9 lbs (900 g) butternut squash | 1 red onion | 2 garlic cloves | 1–2 mild red chile peppers | 2 tbsp olive oil | ½ tsp ground turmeric | 1½ tsp ground cumin | 1 tsp ground ginger | 2 tsp sweet paprika | 2 pinches of cayenne pepper | ½–1 tsp ground coriander | ⅔ cup (150 ml) vegetable stock | 2¼ cups (400 g) chopped tomatoes | 6 tbsp + 2 tsp (100 ml) tomato passata | 1 tbsp brown sugar | 1 cinnamon stick (approx. 2 inches/5 cm) | salt | pepper | **For the couscous:** 6 Medjool dates (or other dates) | 1 mild green chile pepper | 2¼ cups (400 g) instant couscous | 2 tbsp butter | grated zest of 1 organic lemon | 1⅔ cups (400 ml) vegetable stock, boiling hot | 3 tbsp (24 g) toasted pine nuts | salt | freshly ground white pepper | 2–3 tbsp chopped cilantro

1. Peel the squash, remove the seeds and dice the flesh into approx. ¾-inch (2 cm) cubes. Peel and finely dice the onion and garlic. Wash, trim and finely dice the mild chile peppers.
2. Heat the oil in the pressure cooker, add the onion and sauté until translucent, then add the garlic and continue frying for about 1 minute. Sprinkle in the spices, continue frying for 1–2 minutes, stirring occasionally, until they become fragrant. Deglaze with the stock, add the chopped tomatoes, passata, mild chile peppers, sugar and cinnamon, and season lightly with salt and pepper. Seal the pot and cook the squash on setting 3 (cooking indicator: 2nd ring) for 6–7 minutes.
3. For the couscous: cut the dates in half, remove the pits, then cut each half crosswise into thin strips. Wash, trim and finely dice the mild chile pepper. Put the couscous, butter, lemon zest and mild chile pepper in a heatproof bowl, add boiling-hot vegetable stock, cover, let sit for approx. 3 minutes, then loosen the grains with a fork. Stir in the dates, toasted pine nuts, a pinch of salt and pepper and some fresh cilantro and season to taste.
4. Remove the pressure cooker from the heat and release the steam. Season the squash, divide between four deep plates with the couscous and serve garnished with the remaining fresh cilantro.

Etli nohut – chickpea stew with beef (2)

1½ cups (300 g) dried chickpeas | 2 onions | 4 garlic cloves | 1 large red bell pepper | 1 lb (500 g) stewing beef (or shoulder of lamb) | 2 tbsp olive oil | 1 tbsp tomato paste | sea salt | pepper | 1 tbsp sweet paprika | 1–2 pinches of chili powder | 2¼ cups (400 g) chopped tomatoes | 1 cup (250 ml) vegetable stock | 2 tbsp fresh cilantro

1. Soak the chickpeas in cold water overnight. The next day, put them in a colander and strain.
2. Peel and finely dice the onions and garlic. Wash and trim the pepper, then slice into thick rings. Pat the meat dry and chop into 1¼-inch (3 cm) cubes if necessary.
3. Heat the oil in a pressure cooker, add the onions and pepper rings and fry for 3–5 minutes. Briefly sear the meat in the oil, turning occasionally. Stir in the tomato paste and continue frying for 1–2 minutes. Season with salt, pepper, paprika and chili powder. Add the chopped tomatoes and stock, briefly bring to the boil, then stir in the strained chickpeas.
4. Seal the pot and cook on setting 3 (cooking indicator: 2nd ring) for 30 minutes. Remove the pot from the heat and release the steam. Season the stew, divide it between four plates, sprinkle with pepper and serve garnished with fresh cilantro.

COOKING LEVEL VITAVIT® COOKING LEVEL VITAQUICK® COOKING TIME

Rabbit and lamb
braised to perfection

MAKES: 4 PORTIONS   **MARINATING TIME:** 12 HRS (LAMB)   **PREP TIME:** 30–35 MIN.

Rabbit stifado (1)

1 rabbit, ready to cook (approx. 3 lbs/1.5 kg, or 4 rabbit legs) | 14 oz (400 g) pearl onions (or small shallots) | 3 garlic cloves | salt | freshly ground pepper | 1 tbsp all-purpose flour | 3 tbsp (45 ml) olive oil | 2 tbsp Greek balsamic vinegar with honey | 1 cup (250 ml) red wine | 1 cup (250 ml) poultry stock | 1 2/3 cups (250 g) chopped tomatoes | 2 bay leaves | 1 cinnamon stick (approx. 2 inches/5 cm) | 4 allspice berries | 3–4 sprigs of thyme

1. Cut the rabbit into 10–12 pieces and pat them dry. Peel and halve the pearl onions and garlic. Season the meat with salt and pepper and dust it with flour.
2. Heat the oil in the pressure cooker, sear the rabbit pieces all over until browned, then remove them. Loosen the cooking juices with the vinegar and simmer until syrupy. Pour in the red wine and simmer in the open pot for approx. 5 minutes.
3. Add the pearl onions and garlic to the pot and pour in the poultry stock. Add the rabbit pieces, chopped tomatoes, bay leaves, cinnamon, allspice berries and thyme. Close the pressure cooker with the lid and set the pressure regulator to setting 3. Heat the pot on the highest setting. As soon as the yellow ring appears (cooking indicator: 1st ring), reduce the heat. When the green ring becomes visible (cooking indicator: 2nd ring), the approx. 15-to-20-minute cooking time begins.
4. Remove the pressure cooker from the heat, release the steam and open the lid. Remove the bay leaves. Season the stifado to taste, divide it between four plates, and serve with a sprinkling of ground pepper. Cooked orzo pasta makes a great side dish.

Braised lamb shanks (2)

4 medium-sized lamb shanks | 1 sprig of rosemary | 2 sprigs of thyme | 4 garlic cloves | 10 peppercorns | 1/3 cup (75 ml) olive oil | sea salt | 3/4 cup + 2 tbsp (200 ml) dry white wine | 3 tbsp + 1 tsp (50 ml) sherry | 1/2–1 tsp smoked paprika (e.g., pimentón de la Vera dulce) | 1 2/3 cups (400 ml) lamb (or poultry) stock | 1 bay leaf | freshly ground pepper

1. Rinse the lamb shanks and pat them dry. Wash the herbs and shake them dry. Peel the garlic and finely chop with the herbs. Coarsely grind the peppercorns and mix them with 2 tbsp oil, the herbs and the garlic. Rub the mixture over the shanks, cover with plastic wrap and marinate in the fridge overnight.
2. The next day, season the meat with salt. Heat the remaining oil in the pressure cooker, add the shanks and brown them all over. Deglaze with the wine and sherry, then leave the liquid to reduce. Sprinkle the shanks with paprika, pour in the stock and add the bay leaf.
3. Seal the pot, set the pressure regulator to setting 3 and cook the meat on setting 3 (cooking indicator: 2nd ring) for approx. 25 minutes.
4. Remove the pot from the heat, release the steam and open the lid. Remove the shanks and keep them warm. Remove the bay leaf. Reduce the sauce in the open pot to the desired consistency and season with pepper. Arrange the lamb shanks on four plates, drizzle with sauce and serve. Boiled potatoes complement this dish perfectly.

RECIPES >> CURRIES & BRAISED DISHES   233

234　RECIPES ≫ CURRIES & BRAISED DISHES

Braised beef short ribs
Korean and classic

COOKING LEVEL VITAVIT® | COOKING LEVEL VITAQUICK® | COOKING TIME

COOKING LEVEL VITAVIT® | COOKING LEVEL VITAQUICK® | COOKING TIME

Braised beef with radish & shiitake (1)

MAKES: 4 PORTIONS **PREP TIME:** 25 MIN. + 30 MIN.
2 lbs (1 kg) bone-in chuck short ribs (English cut) | 3 garlic cloves | ½ onion | 1 leek | 5 oz (150 g) daikon radish | 1 medium carrot | 3.3 oz (100 g) shiitake mushrooms | 1 tbsp molasses | **For the marinade:** ½ very ripe, soft pear, cored | ½ small onion | 2½ tsp finely diced peeled gingerroot | 4 tsp soy sauce | 3 tsp diced leek | 1 tsp diced garlic | 2 tsp granulated sugar | 1 tsp toasted sesame oil | 1¼ cups (300 ml) poultry stock

1. Remove any visible fat from the ribs. Soak them in cold water for 30 minutes, then rinse. Fill the pressure cooker with the minimum amount of water and add the meat. Peel the garlic and onion. Finely dice them, add them to the pot and close the lid. Set the pressure regulator to setting 1 and heat the pot on the highest setting. When the yellow ring appears (cooking indicator: 1st ring), remove the pot from the heat and release the steam. Rinse the ribs and strain. Clean the pot.
2. Wash and trim the leek. Peel the radish and carrot and chop all three vegetables into large chunks. Trim and halve the mushrooms.
3. To make the marinade, peel the pear and onion and finely blend them. Put the blended mixture in a dish with the remaining ingredients, add the meat, mushrooms and vegetables and marinate for 30 minutes. Strain out vegetables and set aside.
4. Cook the meat and marinade in the pressure cooker on the highest pressure cooking setting for 40 minutes. Remove the pot from the heat and release the steam. Add the mushrooms, radish and carrots and cook on the lowest pressure cooking setting for another 10 minutes. Remove the pot from the heat, release the steam, open the lid and stir in the molasses. Arrange the ribs on a platter with the vegetables and mushrooms and serve.

Short ribs with carrots (2)

MAKES: 4 PORTIONS **PREP TIME:** APPROX. 25 MIN.
3 lbs (1.5 kg) bone-in chuck short ribs (English cut) | ½ tsp salt | ½ tsp freshly ground pepper | 2 large onions | 5 garlic cloves | 3 sprigs of thyme | 1–2 tbsp vegetable oil | 1 tbsp tomato purée | 1 cup (250 ml) dry red wine (or beef stock) | 1 bay leaf | 2 cups (500 ml) beef stock | 4 medium-sized carrots | 1–2 tbsp cornstarch

1. Pat the ribs dry, separate them between the bones and season with salt and pepper. Peel and halve the onions and chop them into wedges (approx. ½-inch/1 cm thick). Peel and finely dice the garlic. Wash the thyme and shake it dry.
2. Heat the oil in the pressure cooker, sear the ribs all over in portions until browned, then remove them. Sauté the onions in the remaining fat, then cook for 8–9 minutes while stirring. Add the garlic and tomato purée and continue cooking for 1 more minute. Deglaze with the red wine and reduce slightly. Add the bay leaf and thyme, pour in the stock and reduce by around a half in the open pot for 8–10 minutes.
3. Return the ribs to the pot, close the lid and cook them at the highest pressure cooking setting for 45 minutes.
4. Peel the carrots and cut them at an angle into 1-inch (2.5 cm) long pieces. Remove the pot from the heat and release the steam. Add the carrots and cook on the highest setting for another 7 minutes.
5. Release the steam from the pressure cooker, remove the short ribs, vegetables, thyme and bay leaf. Strain the fat from the cooking juices (pp. 98–99), reduce slightly in the open pot, then thicken the sauce with a corn starch/cold water mixture. Season the sauce to taste and serve together with the short ribs and vegetables.

COOKING LEVEL VITAVIT®

COOKING LEVEL VITAQUICK®

COOKING TIME

Two takes on goulash
vegetarian & game

MAKES: 4 PORTIONS **MARINATING TIME:** 48 HRS (VENISON) **PREP TIME:** 25 MIN.

Potato goulash (1)

1.2 lbs (600 g) round (waxy) potatoes | 10 oz (300 g) sweet potatoes | 3 onions | 1 tbsp vegetable oil | 3 tbsp tomato paste | 1 tsp ground caraway | 1 tbsp dried marjoram | 2 tbsp sweet paprika | 2 cups (500 ml) vegetable stock | salt | freshly ground pepper | ¾ cup + 2 tbsp (200 ml) tomato passata | 2 young garlic cloves | zest of ½ organic lemon | 6 tbsp (90 g) sour cream | 1 tbsp chopped parsley

1. Wash and peel the potatoes and sweet potatoes and chop them into approx. ¾-inch (2 cm) cubes. Peel and finely dice the onions.
2. Heat the oil in the pressure cooker, add the diced onion and sauté until golden brown. Add the tomato paste, the caraway and marjoram and continue frying for around 2 minutes, stirring from time to time. Add the paprika and continue frying for 1 more minute or so. Deglaze with stock, season with salt and pepper, add the passata and top up with enough stock or water so that the potato and sweet potato cubes are just covered.
3. Close the pressure cooker, set the pressure regulator to setting 2 and heat the pot on the highest setting. When the yellow ring appears (cooking indicator: 1ˢᵗ ring), reduce the heat. When the green ring becomes visible (cooking indicator: 1ˢᵗ ring), cook the goulash for 10 minutes. Peel and finely dice the garlic. Remove the pot from the heat and release the steam. Add the garlic and lemon zest to the goulash, season to taste, divide between four deep plates, top with sour cream, sprinkle with parsley and serve.

Venison goulash (2)

2 lbs (1 kg) boneless venison shoulder | 2⅓ cups (300 g) coarsely diced red onions | 1 cup (128 g) coarsely diced peeled carrots | 1 cup (120 g) coarsely diced peeled celery root (celeriac) | 2 cups (500 ml) full-bodied red wine | 5 garlic cloves | 1 bay leaf | ⅓ cup (10 g) dried porcini mushroom slices | 10 peppercorns | salt | pepper | 2 tbsp + 2 tsp (40 ml) vegetable oil | 3.3 oz (100 g) diced smoked bacon | 1–2 tbsp all-purpose flour | 1 cup (250 ml) game or beef stock | ¼ cup (60 ml) red currant jelly | 2 tbsp medium-hot mustard | 1 tbsp chopped flat-leaf parsley

1. Pat the meat dry, chop it into 1¼- to 1½-inch (3 to 4 cm) cubes, put them in a dish with the diced vegetables and pour the wine on top. Peel the garlic and add it to the dish together with the bay leaf, mushrooms and peppercorns, cover with plastic wrap and marinate in the fridge for 48 hours.
2. Remove the meat and vegetables from the marinade, dab dry and season with salt and pepper. Reserve marinade. Heat the oil in the pressure cooker, sear the meat in portions, then remove them. Briefly fry the bacon and the vegetables, dust with the flour and deglaze with the marinade and stock. Bring the liquid to the boil, then return the meat to the pot.
3. Close the pressure cooker and cook the goulash on the highest pressure cooking setting for 25 minutes. Remove the pot from the heat, release the steam, open the lid and simmer for a while as desired. Add the red currant jelly and mustard to the goulash, season to taste, sprinkle with parsley and serve with bread dumplings (p. 247).

(1)

COOKING LEVEL VITAVIT® | **COOKING LEVEL VITAQUICK®** | **COOKING TIME**

Braised beef cheeks

MAKES: 4 PORTIONS **MARINATING TIME:** 48 HRS **PREP TIME:** APPROX. 45 MIN.

FOR THE BEEF CHEEKS
2 lbs (1 kg) beef cheeks
2.6 oz (80 g) smoked bacon slices
salt
freshly ground pepper
2 tbsp clarified butter
2 tbsp butter
2/3 cup (85 g) peeled diced carrot
1/4 cup (30 g) diced peeled celery root (celeriac)
1/4 cup (30 g) diced peeled parsnip
1 3/4 cups (225 g) coarsely diced red onions
2 tbsp tomato paste
1 cup + 6 tbsp (350 ml) veal stock
2/3 cup (150 ml) veal jus (or beef stock)
1 tbsp Dijon mustard

FOR THE MARINADE
1 tomato
6 garlic cloves
1 bunch of thyme
1 1/3 cups (100 g) sliced mushrooms
1 bay leaf
1 tbsp white peppercorns
2 cups + 6 tbsp (600 ml) full-bodied red wine (e.g., Merlot)

FOR THE BEEF CHEEKS: remove any thick sinews from the outside of the beef cheeks, but leave any on the inside of the meat. Refrigerate the offcuts and sinews until ready to use.

FOR THE MARINADE: wash, quarter and deseed the tomato, then finely dice the flesh. Peel and quarter the garlic. Wash the thyme and shake it dry. Put those in a bowl, add the mushrooms, the bay leaf and peppercorns and pour in the red wine. Add the beef cheeks, cover with plastic wrap and marinate in the fridge for 48 hours.

PREPARING THE BEEF CHEEKS: two days later, coarsely dice the smoked bacon.

Remove the meat from the marinade and strain. Strain the marinade liquid through a sieve and set aside. Dab the meat dry with paper towel, then season it with salt and pepper.

Heat the clarified butter in a pressure cooker, add the beef cheeks and sear them all over, then add the offcuts, sinews and bacon and fry everything briefly. Remove everything from the pot and pour off the fat.

Heat the butter in the pot until foamy, add the carrots, celery root and parsnip and brown them. Add the onions and continue to fry briefly. Stir in the tomato paste and cook for another 2 minutes or so. Deglaze with 6 tbsp + 2 tsp (100 ml) of the marinade liquid and reduce almost entirely.

Pour in the rest of the marinade, the veal stock and the jus. Bring to the boil, add the herbs and spices from the marinade, stir in the mustard and return the beef cheeks to the pot.

Close the pressure cooker with the lid and set the pressure regulator to setting 3. Heat the pot on the highest setting. As soon as the yellow ring appears (cooking indicator: 1st ring), reduce the heat. When the green ring becomes visible (cooking indicator: 2nd ring), the 40-45-minute cooking time begins.

Remove the pressure cooker from the heat, release the steam and open the lid. Remove the beef cheeks and keep them warm. Strain the sauce through a sieve, reduce to the desired consistency and season to taste.

Slice the beef cheeks, divide the slices between four preheated plates, pour some sauce on top and serve.

TIP: pappardelle pasta, spaetzle or savoy cabbage go wonderfully with these melt-in-your-mouth beef cheeks.

Roulades with
and without meat

MAKES: 4 PORTIONS **PREP TIME:** APPROX. 45 MIN.

COOKING LEVEL VITAVIT® | COOKING LEVEL VITAQUICK® | COOKING TIME

Beef roulades with olives (1)

4 beef roulade slices (e.g., thinly sliced top round, approx. 5 oz/150 g each) | salt | pepper | 2 tbsp Dijon mustard | 2 tbsp all-purpose flour | 1 tbsp each of vegetable oil and butter | 2⅓ cups (300 g) finely diced root vegetables (e.g., onions, carrots, celery root/celeriac, leeks) | 2 tbsp tomato paste | ½ cup (125 ml) red wine | 2 cups (500 ml) beef stock | **For the filling:** 1 red onion | 2 apples | 7 oz (200 g) porcini or other exotic mushrooms (or 1 cup/32 g dried porcini mushroom slices, soaked) | 10 black olives, pitted | 3 dry-packed sun-dried tomatoes | 2 tbsp vegetable oil | salt | pepper | 1 pinch of granulated sugar | 2 tbsp cream cheese

1. Pat the beef roulade slices dry and tenderize them a little with a meat mallet.
2. To make the filling, peel or trim the onion, apples and mushrooms and finely dice them. Finely dice the olives and tomatoes. Heat the oil in the pressure cooker, add the onion and sauté in the oil. Add the mushrooms, olives and tomatoes and continue frying for 3–4 minutes, then add the apples and fry for another 1–2 minutes. Season the filling with salt and pepper, and the sugar then remove from the pot, let cool slightly, then stir in the cream cheese.
3. Clean the pot. Season the meat slices with salt and pepper, spread with mustard, and place around a quarter of the filling in each one and roll them up. Tie up the roulades with kitchen twine, dust them with flour and sear them all over in oil and butter in the pressure cooker, then remove them from the pot. Lightly brown the root vegetables in the remaining fat. Add the tomato paste and continue frying for 1 minute, then deglaze with red wine and reduce slightly. Pour in the stock, add the roulades and cook at the highest pressure cooking setting for 25–30 minutes.
4. Remove the pot from the heat and release the steam. Remove the roulades and keep them warm. Reduce the sauce slightly in the open pot, season to taste and serve with the roulades. This dish tastes great with mashed potato.

COOKING LEVEL VITAVIT® | COOKING LEVEL VITAQUICK® | COOKING TIME

Vegetarian cabbage roulades (2)

1 onion | 1 garlic clove | 1 red and 1 yellow bell pepper | 1 Italian eggplant | 7 tbsp (105 ml) olive oil | ¾ cup + 2 tbsp (200 g) cooked rice | salt | pepper | 2 tbsp chopped herbs (parsley, oregano, thyme) | ⅔ cup (100 g) crumbled feta cheese (or ¾ cup + 2 tbsp/100 g shredded Gouda) | **For the sauce:** 3 shallots | 1 carrot | 2 tbsp olive oil | ¾ cup + 2 tbsp (80 g) finely diced leeks | ⅓ cup (75 ml) white wine | ¾ cup + 2 tbsp (200 ml) vegetable stock | 2 tbsp lemon juice | 1 bay leaf | 5 sprigs of parsley | ½ tsp each of coriander seeds and peppercorns | salt | **Other ingredients:** 16 green cabbage leaves, blanched | ¼ cup (28 g) dry breadcrumbs | 3 tbsp (45 g) butter

1. Peel and finely dice the onion and garlic. Wash, trim and finely dice the peppers and eggplant, brown them in 5 tbsp (75 mL) oil in the pressure cooker, remove them and strain off the fat.
2. Clean the pot. Heat up the rest of the oil, add the onion and sauté lightly for approx. 5 minutes. Add the garlic and continue frying for 1 minute. Let cool briefly, mix together with the rice and eggplant, season with salt and pepper and fold in the herbs and cheese.
3. Peel or trim the shallots and carrot for the sauce and finely dice them. Heat the oil in the pressure cooker, add the shallots, carrot and leeks and sauté them for 4–5 minutes, then deglaze with the wine, stock and lemon juice. Add the herbs and spices, simmer for 10 minutes in the open pot, then season with salt. Remove the bay leaf.
4. Prepare 2 overlapping cabbage leaves per roulade. Add one-eighth of the filling to each pair of leaves, fold the leaves over the filling and roll them up. Tie up the cabbage roulades with kitchen twine and cook on setting 2 (cooking indicator: 1st ring) for approx. 10 minutes.
5. Toast the breadcrumbs in the butter in a frying pan until golden brown. Remove the pressure cooker from the heat and release the steam. Serve the roulades with some sauce and breadcrumbs.

Shoulder of venison with glazed chestnuts

COOKING LEVEL VITAVIT®

COOKING LEVEL VITAQUICK®

COOKING TIME

MAKES: 4 PORTIONS **MARINATING TIME:** 12 HRS **PREP TIME:** APPROX. 45 MIN.

FOR THE SHOULDER OF VENISON
- 1 boneless shoulder of venison (approx. 2.4 lbs/1.2 kg)
- 2–3 sprigs of thyme
- 2–3 sprigs of rosemary
- 3–4 bay leaves
- 12 juniper berries
- 1 tsp peppercorns
- 1 tsp coriander seeds
- 3–4 cloves
- 2–3 small onions, peeled and halved
- 2 cups (250 g) coarsely diced root vegetables (carrots, celery root/celeriac, parsnips, leeks)
- 2 cups (500 ml) full-bodied red wine
- 2 tbsp clarified butter
- salt
- freshly ground pepper
- 1 tbsp tomato paste
- $1^{2}/_{3}$ cups (400 ml) game or beef stock

FOR THE CHESTNUTS
- ¼ cup (50 g) granulated sugar
- 1 cup (143 g) peeled chestnuts (cooked)
- ¾ cup + 2 tbsp (200 ml) orange juice
- ⅓ cup (75 g) cold butter

FOR THE POTATO & CREAM CABBAGE
- 1 lb (500 g) savoy cabbage
- 2 tbsp butter
- $2^{1}/_{3}$ cups (300 g) diced peeled round (waxy) potatoes
- 2 tbsp all-purpose flour
- ¾ cup + 2 tbsp (200 ml) vegetable stock
- 6 tbsp + 2 tsp (100 ml) heavy or whipping (35%) cream
- 6 tbsp (90 g) sour cream
- salt
- freshly ground pepper
- freshly grated nutmeg

TO FINISH
- 1–2 tbsp cornstarch mixed with some cold water

FOR THE SHOULDER OF VENISON: rinse the shoulder of venison, pat it dry and put it in a roaster with the herbs, spices and vegetables. Pour the red wine on top (1), cover with plastic wrap and marinate overnight in the fridge.

The following day, remove the venison from the marinade. Strain the marinade through a sieve and catch the liquid. Set aside the vegetables, herbs and spices from the sieve. Spread out the venison on a work surface, roll it up and tie it into shape with kitchen twine like a rolled roast.

Heat the clarified butter in a pressure cooker, add the venison shoulder, season with salt and pepper and sear all over until browned. Remove the meat and set it aside. Put the vegetables, herbs and spices from the sieve in the pot and roast them in the cooking juices for 4–6 minutes. Stir in the tomato paste and briefly cook together. Deglaze with the red-wine marinade, pour in the game stock and return the venison to the pot (2).

Close the pressure cooker with the lid and set the pressure regulator to setting 3. Heat the pot on the highest setting. As soon as the yellow ring appears (cooking indicator: 1st ring), reduce the heat. When the green ring becomes visible (cooking indicator: 2nd ring), the 45-minute cooking time begins.

FOR THE CHESTNUTS: in the meantime, caramelize the sugar in a frying pan until golden brown. Add the chestnuts and coat them in the caramelized sugar. Deglaze with the orange juice (3), reduce until syrupy for approx. 8 minutes, then set aside.

FOR THE POTATO & CREAM CABBAGE: trim and rinse the savoy cabbage, then chop it into small pieces. Melt the butter in a pot, add the cabbage and potatoes and sauté lightly for 1–2 minutes. Dust the vegetables with flour and add them to the pot. Deglaze with the stock and cream, then simmer in the open pot for approx. 10 minutes, stirring occasionally. Afterwards, stir in the sour cream and season to taste with salt, pepper and nutmeg.

TO FINISH: remove the pot from the heat, release the steam and open the lid. Remove the meat from the braising stock using a meat fork, and keep it warm. Strain the stock through a sieve, then reduce slightly in a pot. Season the sauce, then thicken it slightly with the cornstarch mixture.

Reheat the chestnuts, then remove the pan from the stove and add the cold butter, chopped into pieces. Remove the kitchen twine from the venison and cut it into slices. Season the potato and cream cabbage and put a portion on one side of each warmed plate. Arrange a few venison slices next to the cabbage and pour some sauce on top. Top with glazed chestnuts and serve.

Side dishes & baby food

With a pressure cooker, you can prepare peeled potatoes, unpeeled potatoes and purées in next to no time. Pressure cooking is also ideal for dumplings of all shapes and colors, whether filled or not, and Chinese dumplings and gyoza can be cooked gently in steam without pressure. You can select this function directly on the Vitavit®, or if you own a Vitaquick®, you can use an optional additional lid made of glass or metal.

COOKING LEVEL VITAVIT® 2

COOKING LEVEL VITAQUICK® 1

COOKING TIME 12–15

Colorful dumplings

MAKES: 4 PORTIONS **WAITING TIME:** 20–30 MIN. **PREP TIME:** APPROX. 30 MIN.

Bread dumplings

8 oz (250 g) bread rolls, from previous day | approx. 1/2 cup (125 ml) warm milk | 1 small onion | 4 tsp butter | 2 tbsp finely chopped parsley | salt | freshly ground pepper | freshly grated nutmeg | 3 eggs

1. Cut the rolls into 1/8-inch (3 mm) thick slices using a serrated knife, put them in a large bowl, pour the milk on top, cover and let steep for 20–30 minutes.
2. Peel and finely dice the onion. Melt the butter in a frying pan, add the onion and sauté until translucent. Add the parsley and continue frying briefly, then season with salt, pepper and nutmeg and let cool slightly. Add the eggs and the cooled onion mixture to the soaked bread and mix well.
3. With damp hands, shape 8–10 small dumplings out of the mixture and place them in the perforated insert. Fill the pressure cooker with the minimum amount of water, put the insert on the tripod and seal the pot. Set the pressure regulator to setting 2 and heat the pot on the highest setting. When the yellow ring appears (cooking indicator: 1st ring), reduce the heat. When the green ring becomes visible (cooking indicator: 1st ring), cook the dumplings for 12–15 minutes.
4. Remove the pressure cooker from the heat, release the steam and open the lid. Remove the dumplings and serve.

Bacon dumplings

14 oz (400 g) bread rolls, from previous day | 1 1/2 cups (375 ml) warm milk | 3.3 oz (100 g) smoked bacon slices | 1/2 cup (65 g) diced onion | 2 tbsp chopped parsley | 3 eggs | salt | pepper

1. Cut and soak the bread rolls as described in step 1 of the bread dumplings recipe.
2. Finely dice the bacon, fry in a pan, then sauté the onion with the bacon. Add the parsley and fry briefly, then leave everything to cool.
3. Add the bacon mixture to the other ingredients, shape into small dumplings and cook them (as per steps 3 and 4 of the bread dumplings recipe).

Beet dumplings

2 medium beets (7 oz/200 g) | 6 tbsp + 2 tsp (100 ml) heavy or whipping (35%) cream | 1–2 tbsp cornstarch | 3 eggs | salt | 8 oz (250 g) white bread, from previous day, in slices | 1 tbsp liquid honey | 1 small onion, diced | 1/4 cup (60 g) butter | 3 tbsp (9 g) chopped parsley | 1 tsp chopped thyme | 7 tbsp (40 g) grated Parmesan | 7 tbsp (50 g) shredded Alpine-style cheese | 2 tbsp all-purpose flour | pepper | 1/2 cup (125 ml) beet juice

1. Peel and grate the beets and blend them with the cream. Stir in the cornstarch, eggs and 1 tsp salt. Put the bread in a bowl and pour the mixture on top, add the honey, mix lightly, cover and let rest for around 20 minutes.
2. Sauté the onion in 2 tbsp butter, then add to the bread mixture with the rest of the ingredients (except the juice). Mix well, shape into small dumplings and cook in the pressure cooker as described in the bread dumplings recipe.
3. In a pan, heat up the remaining butter and the beet juice. Toss the cooked dumplings in the juice and serve.

Stuffed mushroom dumplings

7 oz (200 g) white bread, from previous day | 6 tbsp + 2 tsp (100 ml) milk | 3 tbsp + 1 tsp (50 g) heavy or whipping (35%) cream | 3 tbsp (50 g) melted butter | 3 eggs | 1/2 tsp salt | pepper | nutmeg | 4 tsp butter | 10 oz (300 g) fresh porcini or other exotic mushrooms, trimmed and finely diced | 2 1/2 tbsp (20 g) diced shallot | 1 garlic clove, peeled and finely diced | 1 tbsp each of chopped parsley and oregano | 3 1/2 tbsp (35 g) diced air-cured ham, as desired | 1/3 cup (40 g) all-purpose flour

1. Finely dice the white bread, put it in a bowl and pour the milk, cream and melted butter on top. Add the eggs, season with salt, pepper and nutmeg and let sit for at least 30 minutes.
2. Melt the butter in a frying pan, add the mushrooms and sauté briefly. Add the diced shallot, garlic, herbs and ham (as desired), continue to fry briefly, then let cool slightly. Mix one-third of the mushroom mixture and the flour into the soaked bread.
3. Divide the mixture into approx. 1.6-oz (50 g) portions and shape into small dumplings. Press a well into the middle of each dumpling, fill with 1 tbsp of the remaining mushroom mixture, then cover with the dumpling mixture. Shape the dumplings into balls again, cook them in the pressure cooker (as described in the bread dumplings recipe) and serve.

Spinach dumplings

7 cups (200 g) packed baby spinach | 1 small onion | 1 garlic clove | 4 tsp butter | 8 oz (250 g) white bread, from previous day, in slices | 2 eggs | 1/2 cup (125 ml) warm milk | 3/4 cup (40 g) chopped parsley | salt | pepper | freshly grated nutmeg | 3/4 cup (100 g) all-purpose flour

1. Wash the spinach, shake dry and finely chop. Peel and finely dice the onion and garlic. Sauté them lightly in a pan in the butter. Put the bread in a bowl. Whisk the eggs and milk, add the spinach and parsley and then mix together with all of the remaining ingredients.
2. Shape the mixture into small dumplings and cook in the pressure cooker as described in the bread dumplings recipe.

Alpine dumpling specialties

MAKES: 4 PORTIONS   **WAITING TIME:** 20–30 MIN.   **PREP TIME:** APPROX. 30 MIN.

COOKING LEVEL VITAVIT®   COOKING LEVEL VITAQUICK®   COOKING TIME

COOKING LEVEL VITAVIT®   COOKING LEVEL VITAQUICK®   COOKING TIME

Pretzel dumplings (1)

5 soft pretzels, from previous day (approx. 14 oz/400 g) | 1 cup (250 ml) warm milk | 2–3 green onions | 1 tbsp butter | 1 cup (50 g) chopped leafy herbs (e.g., chives or parsley) | 2 eggs | salt | freshly ground pepper | 1 pinch ground allspice

1. Cut the pretzels into small cubes or slices, put them in a bowl, pour the warm milk on top and soak for 30 minutes.
2. In the meantime, wash, trim and finely dice the green onions. Melt the butter in a frying pan, add the onions and sauté lightly. Add the chopped herbs and continue frying briefly, then set the mixture aside and let cool slightly.
3. Add the onion and herb mixture, the eggs and the spices to the soaked pretzels and mix well. Shape small dumplings out of the mixture. Put the pretzel dumplings in the perforated insert. Fill the pressure cooker with the minimum amount of water. Put the insert on the tripod and seal the pot. Set the pressure regulator to setting 2 and heat the pot on the highest setting. When the yellow ring appears (cooking indicator: 1st ring), reduce the heat. As soon as the green ring becomes visible (cooking indicator: 1st ring), cook the dumplings for 10–12 minutes.
4. Remove the pressure cooker from the heat, release the steam and open the lid. Remove the dumplings and serve.

Buckwheat dumplings (2)

3.3 oz (100 g) bread rolls, from previous day | 2.6 oz (80 g) dry 'Schüttelbrot' bread or wasa crackers | ⅔ cup (150 ml) lukewarm milk | 1 garlic clove | ½ cup (45 g) thin strips leek | 4 tsp butter | 2 tbsp chopped herbs (e.g., parsley, chives, lovage) | ½ tsp salt | white pepper | 1 pinch of nutmeg | 2 eggs | 7 tbsp (60 g) whole-grain buckwheat flour | 1¾ cups (200 g) coarsely shredded Alpine-style cheese

1. Cut the bread rolls into thin slices, crumble the Schüttelbrot into fine breadcrumbs, put them together in a bowl, pour the milk on top and soak for around 15 minutes.
2. Peel and finely dice the garlic. Sauté the leek and garlic in a frying pan in the butter, let cool briefly and add to the bread mixture. Add the herbs, spices, eggs and buckwheat flour, mix lightly, leave the dough to steep for around 15 minutes, then stir in the cheese.
3. Shape small dumplings out of the mixture, put them in the perforated insert and fill the pressure cooker with the minimum amount of water. Put the insert on the tripod and seal the pot. Set the pressure regulator to setting 2 and heat the pot on the highest setting. When the yellow ring appears (cooking indicator: 1st ring), reduce the heat. As soon as the green ring becomes visible (cooking indicator: 1st ring), cook the dumplings for 8–10 minutes.
4. Remove the pressure cooker from the heat, release the steam and open the lid. Remove the dumplings and serve.

Two potato dumpling versions

MAKES: 4 PORTIONS   **RESTING TIME:** 1 HR (COOKED DUMPLINGS)   **PREP TIME:** 30 MIN.

FOR THE COOKED-POTATO DUMPLINGS
1 lb (500 g) medium-size yellow flesh or russet potatoes
salt
3 tbsp + 1 tsp (50 g) butter
½ cup (100 g) potato starch
3 egg yolks
freshly ground pepper
freshly grated nutmeg

TO FINISH
⅓ cup (75 g) butter
½ bunch of flat-leaf parsley

FOR THE HALF-AND-HALF POTATO DUMPLINGS
4 lbs (2 kg) medium-size yellow flesh or russet potatoes
1 tbsp white vinegar
6 tbsp + 2 tsp (100 ml) milk
salt

COOKING LEVEL VITAVIT® — COOKING LEVEL VITAQUICK® — COOKING TIME

FOR THE COOKED-POTATO DUMPLINGS: wash the potatoes and put them in the perforated insert. Fill the pressure cooker with the minimum amount of water, add some salt and put the tripod in the pot. Put the insert on the tripod (1) and close the pressure cooker with the lid. Set the pressure regulator to setting 3 and heat the pot on the highest setting. When the yellow ring appears (cooking indicator: 1st ring), reduce the heat. As soon as the green ring (cooking indicator: 2nd ring) becomes visible, the 12-minute cooking time begins.

Remove the pressure cooker from the heat, slowly release the steam and open the lid. Leave the steam to evaporate briefly from the potatoes, then peel them and pass them through a ricer or food mill into a bowl while still warm. Brown the butter in a frying pan, let cool briefly, then add to the potato mixture together with the potato starch, egg yolks, salt, pepper and nutmeg. Mix until smooth, then let rest for around 1 hour. Afterwards, divide the potato mixture into portions, shape 1½- to 2-inch (4 to 5 cm) dumplings out of them and put them in the perforated insert (2). Fill the pressure cooker with the minimum amount of water and put the insert on the tripod. Set the pressure regulator to the steam cooking symbol and steam the dumplings without pressure for 12–15 minutes.

TO FINISH: in the meantime, melt the butter in a frying pan until it turns frothy. Rinse the parsley, shake it dry, pluck off the leaves and finely chop them. Remove the insert from the pot (3) and put the cooked dumplings in a bowl. Drizzle the potato dumplings with the melted butter, sprinkle with parsley and serve.

COOKING LEVEL VITAVIT® — COOKING LEVEL VITAQUICK® — COOKING TIME

FOR THE HALF-AND-HALF POTATO DUMPLINGS: wash the potatoes, weigh out 1 lb (500 g) and cook them on setting 3 (cooking indicator: 2nd ring) in the pressure cooker. Peel the remaining potatoes and put them in some water mixed with 1 tbsp vinegar until ready to use, so that they don't turn brown. Finely grate the raw potatoes. Firmly squeeze the grated raw potatoes in a cloth to extract the liquid, then put them in a bowl. Bring the milk to the boil in a saucepan, then pour it over the grated raw potatoes. Peel the cooked potatoes and pass them through a press while still hot. Season with salt and work into a soft dough. Shape small dumplings out of the mixture. Fill the pressure cooker with the minimum amount of water, put the insert on the tripod and cook the dumplings on setting 3 (cooking indicator: 2nd ring) for approx. 5 minutes.

TIP: potato dumplings are ideal for stuffing, for example with butter-toasted croutons or finely diced ham and herbs.

Exquisitely filled dim sum

MAKES: 4 PORTIONS   **WAITING TIME:** 20–30 MIN.   **PREP TIME:** APPROX. 45 MIN.

COOKING LEVEL VITAVIT® | COOKING LEVEL VITAQUICK® | COOKING TIME 12–14

Fish dim sum (1)

3 cups (400 g) all-purpose flour | 1 tsp granulated sugar | salt | ½ oz (15 g) fresh compressed yeast (or 2¼ tsp/8 g quick-rising/instant yeast) | 2–3 green onions | 1 tbsp sesame oil | 1–2 tsp toasted sesame seeds | **For the filling:** ⅓ cup (10 g) dried wood-ear mushrooms | 10 oz (300 g) salmon fillet | 6 tbsp (55 g) diced papaya flesh | 1 garlic clove | 1 tsp pickled ginger (sushi ginger) | salt | pepper | 3 tbsp (9 g) chopped cilantro

1. Put the flour in a bowl with the sugar and 1 pinch of salt and mix together. Crumble the yeast into ¾ cup (175 ml) lukewarm water, mix together, pour over the flour mixture and knead into a smooth dough. Cover the dough with a damp cloth and let rise for around 30 minutes.
2. To make the filling, soak the wood-ear mushrooms for around 20 minutes, then strain and chop them. Rinse the salmon fillet, pat it dry and finely dice it and mix together with papaya. Peel the garlic, strain the ginger and finely dice both ingredients. Put the prepared ingredients together in a bowl and season with salt, pepper and cilantro.
3. Divide the dough into small portions, shape them into balls, then roll them out. Put around 1 tbsp of the filling in the middle of each dough circle, then fold over the dough and press together.
4. Put the dumplings in the perforated insert. Fill the pressure cooker with the minimum amount of water, put the insert on the tripod, seal the pot and cook the dim sum on setting 1 (cooking indicator: 1st ring) for 12–14 minutes.
5. Wash and trim the green onions, cut them into rings and sauté them in sesame oil in a frying pan. Remove the pressure cooker from the heat, release the steam and open the lid. Remove the dim sum, top with the green onion rings and sesame seeds and serve.

COOKING LEVEL VITAVIT® | COOKING TIME 13–16

Vegetable dim sum (2)

⅓ cup (10 g) dried wood-ear mushrooms | 1 carrot | ¾ cup (50 g) sugar snap peas | 1 green onion | 1 red chile pepper | 1 garlic clove | 2 tbsp vegetable oil | 6 tbsp (50 g) corn kernels (frozen or fresh) | ½ cup (40 g) diced shiitake mushroom caps | 2 tbsp soy sauce | 1 tbsp vegetarian oyster sauce | salt | ½ tsp ground wasabi | 2 tsp agave syrup | approx. 12 wonton wrappers

1. Soak the wood-ear mushrooms in lukewarm water for around 20 minutes. Peel the carrot, trim and wash the sugar snap peas and finely dice both vegetables. Wash and trim the green onion and chile pepper, cut the green onion into very thin rings and finely dice the chile pepper. Strain and finely chop the wood-ear mushrooms.
2. Heat the oil in a pressure cooker, add the garlic and chile and fry briefly. Add the carrot and continue cooking for 2–3 minutes, stirring from time to time. Stir in the sugar snap peas, green onion and corn and continue frying for 1–2 minutes. Add all of the mushrooms and fry for about another minute. Season the filling to taste with soy sauce, vegetarian oyster sauce, salt, ground wasabi and agave syrup.
3. Put some filling in the middle of each wonton wrapper and fold up each one into open baskets. Put the dim sum in the perforated insert. Pour 1⅔ cups (400 ml) water in the pressure cooker (Vitavit®), put the insert on the tripod and seal the pot. Set the pressure regulator to the steam cooking symbol and steam the dim sum without pressure for 13–16 minutes.
4. Open the pot, remove the dim sum from the insert and serve. Hoisin or soy sauce go wonderfully with this dish.

(2)

COOKING LEVEL VITAVIT®

COOKING TIME 12–20

Asian dumplings
gyoza and baozi

MAKES: 4 PORTIONS   **WAITING TIME:** 1–2 HRS   **PREP TIME:** APPROX. 1 HR

Vegetarian gyoza (1)

1 (14 oz / 400 g) package wonton wrappers | 10 oz (300 g) Chinese (napa) cabbage | salt | 3 green onions | 1 red chile pepper | 2 garlic cloves | 1½-inch (4 cm) piece gingerroot | 2 cups (150 g) finely diced shiitake mushroom caps | 1 tbsp ponzu sauce | 4 tsp cornstarch

1. If necessary, let wonton wrappers thaw at room temperature for 1–2 hours. Wash and trim the Chinese cabbage, cut it into very thin strips, season with salt, knead vigorously with your hands, then let sit briefly in a sieve.
2. Wash and trim the green onions and chile pepper, peel the garlic and ginger and finely dice all four ingredients. Firmly squeeze the Chinese cabbage, then mix it together with the mushrooms, green onion, chile, garlic, ginger, ponzu sauce and cornstarch.
3. Moisten the edges of each wrapper with water, then place 1 heaped tsp of filling in the middle of each one. Fold each wrapper into a semicircle, then hold it in your hand. Using your thumb and index finger, make small pleats along the top part of the wrapper. Put the gyoza on a baking sheet lined with parchment paper and cover.
4. Then put the gyoza in the perforated insert. Pour 1⅔ cups (400 ml) water in the pressure cooker (Vitavit®), put the insert on the tripod and seal the pot. Set the pressure regulator to the steam cooking symbol and steam the gyoza without pressure for 12–15 minutes. Remove and serve. Chili sauce makes a great dip.

Beef baozi (2)

1 cup + 3 tbsp (160 g) all-purpose flour | ½ oz (15 g) fresh compressed yeast (or 2¼ tsp/8 g quick-rising/instant yeast) | 3 tbsp (40 g) granulated sugar | ½ tsp salt | ¼ cup (60 ml) sesame oil | 1 bunch of green onions | ¾-inch (2 cm) piece gingerroot | 1 garlic clove | 14 oz (400 g) ground beef | 2 tbsp soy sauce | 1 tbsp each of oyster sauce & hoisin sauce | 1 tbsp cornstarch | 1 tsp granulated sugar | 1 egg white | 1 tsp nigella seeds | 3 tbsp (9 g) chopped cilantro | 2 tbsp toasted sesame seeds

1. Sift the flour into a bowl and make a well in the middle. Dissolve the crumbled yeast in 3 tbsp + 1 tsp (50 ml) warm water, add the 3 tbsp (40 g) sugar, pour into the well and mix with some of the flour from the edge of the bowl. Cover the dough and let rest for around 15 minutes. Add the salt, 1 tbsp oil and ⅔ cup (150 ml) warm water, knead for 5–10 minutes into a smooth dough, cover again and let rise for around 1 hour.
2. Wash and trim the green onions, peel the garlic and ginger. Finely chop them, sauté them in 1 tbsp sesame oil for approx. 3 minutes, let cool slightly, then mix with the ground meat and the soy sauce, oyster sauce, hoison sauce, cornstarch, sugar, egg white, nigella and cilantro.
3. Knead the dough once more, divide it into eight portions, shape into balls, cover and let rise for around 15 minutes.
4. Press each dough ball flat, put around one-eighth of the filling on each one, fold the dough over the top and shape into round dumplings again. Grease the perforated insert with 1 tbsp oil, put 4 baozi in it at a time, steam them without pressure for 15–20 minutes, remove them and keep them warm. Repeat with the remaining baozi. Sprinkle with sesame seeds and serve.

(1)

RECIPES » SIDE DISHES & BABY FOOD   255

Rice, couscous & beans
Spicy sides cooked quickly

MAKES: 4 PORTIONS PER RECIPE **PREP TIME:** 20–25 MIN. PER RECIPE

COOKING LEVEL VITAVIT® | COOKING LEVEL VITAQUICK® | COOKING TIME (5–6)

Biryani rice
with eggplant (1)

1 shallot | 1¼-inch (3 cm) piece gingerroot | 3 garlic cloves | ¼ cup (60 g) ghee (or clarified butter) | 1 cinnamon stick | 8 cardamom pods | 5 cloves | 2 cups (350 g) basmati rice | salt | 2 tbsp + 2 tsp (40 ml) rose water | 1 pinch of saffron threads | **For the eggplant topping (optional):** 1 Italian eggplant | salt | 3 tbsp (45 ml) vegetable oil | 1–2 tsp sesame seeds

1. Peel the shallot, cut it in half, then chop it into thin strips. Peel and finely dice the ginger and garlic.

2. Heat the ghee in the pressure cooker, add the spices and toast them for about 1 minute or until they become fragrant. Add the shallot, ginger and garlic and continue frying for 2 minutes. Pour in the rice and 1⅔ to 1¾ cups (400 to 425 ml) water and season with salt.

3. Close the pressure cooker with the lid, set the pressure regulator to setting 3 and heat the pot on the highest setting. When the yellow ring appears (cooking indicator: 1st ring), reduce the heat. As soon as the green ring becomes visible (cooking indicator: 2nd ring), the 5-to-6-minute cooking time begins.

4. Remove the pressure cooker from the heat, release the steam and open the lid. Heat the rose water and saffron threads in a small saucepan, simmer for about 1 minute, then pour the mixture over the cooked rice.

5. To make the (optional) eggplant topping, wash and trim the eggplant. Cut it into ½-inch (1 cm) cubes, season with salt, let sit for 10 minutes, then dry with paper towels. Heat the oil in the pressure cooker, fry the eggplant cubes all over, then sprinkle with sesame seeds. Brown slightly and season with salt.

6. Divide the rice between four bowls or deep plates and serve. Top with the browned eggplant as desired.

COOKING LEVEL VITAVIT® | COOKING TIME 8

Couscous with cashew nuts (2)

4 baby pak choi (bok choy) | 1¼ cups (300 ml) poultry stock | 2–3 young garlic cloves | 1 cup + 2 tbsp (200 g) couscous | salt | pepper | ½ tsp ground cumin | ½ cup (60 g) toasted cashew nuts

1. Wash and trim the pak choi, cut them in half lengthwise, then put them in the perforated insert and set aside. Pour the stock into the pressure cooker (Vitavit®). Peel and add the garlic.
2. Seal the pot with the lid, set the pressure regulator to the steam cooking symbol and bring the stock to the boil. Open the pot, add the couscous and insert the tripod. Put the insert with the pak choi on the tripod, seal the pot and steam without pressure for approx. 8 minutes.
3. Open the pot and remove the pak choi. Loosen up the couscous with a fork, season to taste with salt, pepper and cumin and divide between four plates. Top with the pak choi and cashew nuts and serve.

COOKING LEVEL VITAVIT® 2 | COOKING LEVEL VITAQUICK® 1 | COOKING TIME 30–40

Baked beans with bacon (3)

1¾ cups (350 g) white pea (navy) beans | 3.3 oz (100 g) bacon rind or smoked ham | 2 cups (500 g) chopped canned tomatoes | 1 onion, studded with 2 cloves and 1 bay leaf | 6 tbsp + 2 tsp (100 ml) pure maple syrup | 3 tbsp (40 g) packed brown sugar | 1 tsp hot mustard | salt | pepper | 1 tbsp vegetable oil | 12 smoked bacon slices | green Tabasco

1. Rinse the beans and put them in a large pressure cooker with the bacon rind, tomatoes and the studded onion. Add the maple syrup, sugar, mustard, 1 pinch of salt, pepper and 1 L water. Only fill the pot to ⅓, close the lid and cook on setting 2 (cooking indicator: 1st ring) for 30–40 minutes.
2. Heat the oil in a frying pan, add the bacon slices and fry until crispy, then remove it and place on some paper towels to strain the fat.
3. Remove the pot from the heat, release the steam and open the lid. Season the beans with salt and a couple of drops of Tabasco, divide between four plates, top with bacon and serve.

(2)

(3)

COOKING LEVEL VITAVIT® | **COOKING LEVEL VITAQUICK®** | **COOKING TIME**

Glazed carrots

MAKES: 4 PORTIONS   **PREP TIME:** APPROX. 30 MIN.
1 lb (500 g) carrots, with greens | 1 shallot | 2 tbsp butter | 1–2 tbsp honey | 1 cup (250 ml) vegetable stock | juice of 1 orange (approx. $\frac{1}{3}$ cup/75 mL) | sea salt | 1 pinch of ground cardamom

1. Peel or wash and trim the carrots, leaving $\frac{3}{4}$ to $1\frac{1}{4}$ inches (2 to 3 cm) of their greens. Shake some of the carrot greens dry and coarsely chop them. Peel and finely dice the shallot.
2. Sauté the shallot in the butter in the pressure cooker, then add the carrots, honey, stock, orange juice and 1 pinch of salt.
3. Seal the pot and steam the carrots on setting 3 (cooking indicator: 2nd ring) for 4–5 minutes, then release the steam. Remove the carrots and leave the cooking juices to boil down until syrupy. Glaze the carrots in the syrupy mixture, season to taste with salt and cardamom and serve with a sprinkling of carrot greens.

Green beans with tomatoes

MAKES: 4 PORTIONS   **PREP TIME:** APPROX. 25 MIN.
2 lbs (1 kg) Romano beans (Italian green beans) | 2 onions | 4 garlic cloves | 6 tbsp (90 ml) olive oil | 1–2 tsp chopped herbs (e.g., thyme, oregano, rosemary) | salt | granulated sugar | 4 large tomatoes | 1 organic lemon, in wedges

1. Wash and trim the beans, chop them in half crosswise, then cut them into strips lengthwise. Peel the onions and garlic, finely dice the onions and cut the garlic into thin slices.
2. Heat the oil in the pressure cooker, add the diced onion and sauté until golden brown. Add the beans, garlic, herbs and 1–2 tsp each of salt and sugar. Pour the minimum amount of water into the pressure cooker, wash and chop the tomatoes, then add them to the pot. Seal the pot, cook the bean mixture at setting 2 (cooking indicator: 1st ring) for 3–5 minutes, then release the steam. Season the bean mixture to taste and top with lemon wedges.

COOKING LEVEL VITAVIT®	COOKING LEVEL VITAQUICK®	COOKING TIME
3	2	4–6

COOKING LEVEL VITAVIT®	COOKING LEVEL VITAQUICK®	COOKING TIME
3	2	3–5

Red cabbage with cinnamon

MAKES: 4 PORTIONS **PREP TIME:** APPROX. 25 MIN. + 1 HR
2.4 lbs (1.2 kg) red cabbage | 1 apple | salt | 2 tbsp red wine vinegar | 2.6 oz (80 g) goose or duck fat | 1 cup + 6 tbsp (180 g) diced onion | 1 cup + 6 tbsp (350 ml) red wine | 1 small russet potato, diced | ½ tsp ground coriander | 1 cinnamon stick | 1–2 tbsp honey | juice and zest of 1 organic orange

1. Trim, quarter and finely slice the red cabbage. Peel, quarter, core and dice the apple. Put the cabbage and apple in a bowl with the salt and vinegar, press down slightly and let sit for about 1 hour.
2. Heat the fat in the pressure cooker, add the diced onion and sauté lightly. Add the red cabbage mixture and sauté briefly, then add the other ingredients (except the orange zest).
3. Seal the pot and cook on setting 3 (cooking indicator: 2nd ring) for 4–6 minutes, then release the steam. Season to taste and top with the orange zest.

Bavarian cabbage

MAKES: 4 PORTIONS **PREP TIME:** APPROX. 20 MIN.
2.4 lbs (1.2 kg) green cabbage | 1 large onion | 1 tbsp granulated sugar | ½ tsp ground caraway | 6 tbsp + 2 tsp (100 ml) dry white wine | salt | 1¼ cups (300 ml) vegetable stock | pepper | 1–2 tbsp sweet mustard | 3 tbsp to ¼ cup (9 to 12 g) flat-leaf parsley, coarsely chopped

1. Trim and quarter the cabbage, then cut it into approx. ¾-inch (2 cm) diamonds. Peel and finely dice the onion.
2. Lightly caramelize the sugar in the pressure cooker, add the onion and sauté briefly. Add the cabbage and caraway and continue frying for about 1 minute, stirring occasionally, then deglaze with the wine. Season lightly with salt, then pour in the stock.
3. Seal the pot and cook the cabbage on setting 3 (cooking indicator: 2nd ring) for 3–5 minutes, then release the steam from the pot and open the lid. Season the Bavarian cabbage to taste with pepper and mustard, then stir in the coarsely chopped parsley.

COOKING LEVEL VITAVIT® 3 | COOKING LEVEL VITAQUICK® 2 | COOKING TIME 15

COOKING LEVEL VITAVIT® 2 | COOKING LEVEL VITAQUICK® 1 | COOKING TIME 15

Creamy mashed potato (1)

MAKES: 4 PORTIONS **PREP TIME:** APPROX. 10 MIN.
2 lbs (1 kg) yellow flesh or russet potatoes | salt | ½ cup (125 g) butter | 6 tbsp + 2 tsp (100 ml) heavy or whipping (35%) cream | sea salt | freshly grated nutmeg

1. Peel, wash and coarsely dice the potatoes, then put them in the perforated insert. Fill the pressure cooker with the minimum amount of water and season the potatoes with salt. Put the insert on the tripod and seal the pot.
2. Set the pressure regulator to setting 3 and heat the pot on the highest setting. When the yellow ring appears (cooking indicator: 1st ring), reduce the heat. When the green ring becomes visible (cooking indicator: 2nd ring), cook the potatoes for approx. 15 minutes.
3. In the meantime, melt the butter in a saucepan until it turns slightly brown. Remove the pressure cooker from the heat, release the steam and open the lid. Mash the potatoes, then fold in the browned butter and the cream. Season the mash to taste with salt and nutmeg.

Potato and pepper purée (3)

MAKES: 4 PORTIONS **PREP TIME:** APPROX. 20 MIN.
1 lb (500 g) russet potatoes | salt | 1 shallot | 1 red bell pepper | 3 tbsp + 1 tsp (50 g) butter | sugar | 3 tbsp + 1 tsp (50 ml) heavy or whipping (35%) cream | 2 tbsp olive oil | pepper | smoked paprika | Espelette pepper

1. Peel, wash and coarsely dice the potatoes, then cook them in the pressure cooker on setting 2 (cooking indicator: 1st ring) for approx. 15 minutes, as described in the mashed potato recipe.
2. In the meantime, peel and finely dice the shallot. Wash, trim and finely dice the pepper. Melt the butter in a pan, add the shallot and pepper and sauté lightly, then season with salt and sugar.
3. Leave the steam to evaporate from the potatoes, add them to the pepper mixture with the remaining ingredients and mash everything together. Season to taste and serve. As a topping, you could use 2–3 tbsp finely diced pepper and 1 tbsp thinly sliced chives.

COOKING LEVEL VITAVIT® 3 | COOKING LEVEL VITAQUICK® 2 | COOKING TIME 6–8

COOKING LEVEL VITAVIT® 3 | COOKING LEVEL VITAQUICK® 2 | COOKING TIME 25

Pumpkin purée with amaretti (2)

MAKES: 4 PORTIONS **PREP TIME:** APPROX. 15 MIN.
1.4 lbs (700 g) pumpkin or winter squash | 1 cinnamon stick | 2 cloves | 2 tbsp white port | 1.6 oz (50 g) amaretti cookies | salt | pepper | 2 tbsp + 2 tsp butter | ⅔ cup (60 g) grated Parmesan | 1–2 tbsp lime juice | 1 pinch of cayenne pepper

1. Peel the pumpkin, remove the seeds, cut the flesh into approx. ½-inch (1 cm) cubes and put them in the unperforated insert with the spices and port. Fill the pressure cooker with the minimum amount of water, put the insert on the tripod and seal the pot. Cook the pumpkin on setting 3 (cooking indicator: 2nd ring) for 6–8 minutes.
2. Remove the pot from the heat and release the steam. Remove the pumpkin and puree in a blender with the amaretti. Season with salt and pepper. Melt the butter and stir it into purée with the Parmesan. Season with lime juice and cayenne pepper.

Spicy bean purée (4)

MAKES: 4 PORTIONS **PREP TIME:** APPROX. 20 MIN.
1½ cups (300 g) white pea (navy) beans, | 2 garlic cloves, peeled | 1 bay leaf | 2 sprigs of thyme | 7 tbsp (60 g) diced shallot | 3 tbsp (45 g) butter | 6 tbsp + 2 tsp (100 ml) white wine | salt | pepper | 1 pinch of granulated sugar | juice of 1 lemon | ½ tsp each of chopped thyme and rosemary | 1 tbsp olive oil

1. Put the beans in the pressure cooker with 2 cups + 6 tbsp (600 ml) water, the garlic, bay leaf and thyme (only fill the pot to ⅓) and cook on setting 3 (cooking indicator: 2nd ring) for 20–25 minutes.
2. Release the steam from the pot, then strain the beans, catching 6 tbsp + 2 tsp (100 ml) of the cooking liquid. Clean the pot and lightly sauté the shallots in the butter. Add the wine, the cooking liquid and the beans and cook on setting 3 for another 5–6 minutes. Strain through a sieve and season the purée with the remaining ingredients.

COOKING LEVEL VITAVIT®

COOKING LEVEL VITAQUICK®

COOKING TIME

Homemade
baby food

MAKES: 2 PORTIONS PER RECIPE (FOR 5–7 MONTHS) **PREP TIME:** APPROX. 10 MIN.

Carrot and potato mash with beef

2.3 oz (70 g) boneless beef chuck (blade) | 1½ cups (200 g) sliced peeled carrots | ¾ cup (100 g) cubed (½ inch/1 cm) peeled potatoes | 4 tsp canola oil | 3 tbsp (45 ml) orange juice

1. Cut the beef into small cubes.
2. Put the diced vegetables and meat in the perforated insert and mix together. Fill the pressure cooker with the minimum amount of water, put the insert on the tripod and seal the pot.
3. Set the pressure regulator to setting 2 and heat the pot on the highest setting. When the yellow ring appears (cooking indicator: 1st ring), reduce the heat. As soon as the green ring becomes visible (cooking indicator: 1st ring), the 6-to-8-minute cooking time begins.
4. Remove the pressure cooker from the heat, release the steam and open the lid. Put the vegetable and meat mixture into a tall cup with the canola oil and orange juice, purée with an immersion blender and add some of the cooking liquid, until very smooth.
5. You can keep the purée for 1 day in the fridge.

Colorful vegetable mash with salmon

2 oz (60 g) salmon fillet (fresh or frozen) | ¾ cup (130 g) chopped red bell pepper | ½ cup (60 g) sliced peeled carrot | ¾ cup (100 g) cubed (½ inch/1 cm) peeled potatoes | 4 tsp canola oil | 3 tbsp (45 ml) orange juice

1. Rinse the fish, pat it dry and cut it into approx. ½-inch (1 cm) cubes.
2. Put the vegetables and fish in the perforated insert. Fill the pressure cooker with the minimum amount of water and put the insert on the tripod.
3. Close the pressure cooker with the lid, set the pressure regulator to setting 2 and heat the pot on the highest setting. When the yellow ring appears (cooking indicator: 1st ring), reduce the heat. As soon as the green ring becomes visible (cooking indicator: 1st ring), the approx. 4-minute cooking time begins.
4. Remove the pressure cooker from the heat, release the steam and open the lid. Put the vegetable and fish mixture into a tall cup with the canola oil and orange juice, purée with an immersion blender and add some of the cooking liquid if necessary, until very smooth.
5. You can keep the purée for 1 day in the fridge.

Spinach with pasta and chicken

3⅓ cups (100 g) packed baby spinach | 2.6 oz (80 g) boneless skinless chicken breast | ½ cup (100 g) cooked whole wheat pasta (e.g., fusilli or penne) | 4 tsp canola oil | 3 tbsp (45 ml) orange juice

1. Sort, wash and spin-dry the spinach. Pat dry the chicken and cut it into small cubes.
2. Put the chicken and spinach in the perforated insert. Fill the pressure cooker with the minimum amount of water and put the insert on the tripod. Position the tripod inside the pot and place the insert on top.
3. Close the pressure cooker with the lid, set the pressure regulator to setting 2 and heat the pot on the highest setting. When the yellow ring appears (cooking indicator: 1st ring), reduce the heat. As soon as the green ring becomes visible (cooking indicator: 2nd ring), the approx. 3-minute cooking time begins.
4. Remove the pressure cooker from the heat, release the steam and open the lid. Briefly heat up the cooked pasta in the steam, then put into a tall cup with the spinach and chicken mixture, canola oil and orange juice, purée with an immersion blender, adding some of the cooking liquid if necessary, until very smooth.
5. You can keep the mixture for 1 day in the fridge.

Colorful vegetable rice

¾ cup (100 g) corn kernels (frozen or drained canned) | 1 cup + 2 tbsp (100 g) small broccoli florets (or frozen broccoli) | ⅓ cup (80 g) cooked brown rice | 3 tbsp (18 g) quick-cooking rolled oats | 4 tsp canola oil | ¼ cup (60 ml) orange juice

1. Rinse corn in a colander with the broccoli and let strain. Put both vegetables in the perforated insert. Fill the pressure cooker with the minimum amount of water, put the insert on the tripod, seal the pot and cook on setting 2 (cooking indicator: 1st ring) for 3–4 minutes.
2. Remove the pot from the heat, release the steam and open the lid. Briefly heat up the cooked rice in the steam, then put it in a tall cup with the vegetables, rolled oats, canola oil and orange juice, purée with an immersion blender, adding some of the cooking liquid if necessary, until very smooth.
3. You can keep the mixture for 1 day in the fridge.

Sweets & desserts

This chapter reveals the sweet side of pressure cookers: dishes such as rice pudding, Thai sticky rice, porridge or fruit in syrup lend themselves perfectly to pressure cooking. For many of the sweet treats featured in this chapter, such as the Austrian pastry delicacies, you'll need a perforated insert, but for certain fine creams and cakes, you'll need an unperforated insert, which is available as an optional original accessory.

COOKING LEVEL VITAVIT® | COOKING LEVEL VITAQUICK® | COOKING TIME

COOKING LEVEL VITAVIT® | COOKING LEVEL VITAQUICK® | COOKING TIME

Caramel rice pudding

MAKES: 4 PORTIONS   **PREP TIME:** APPROX. 15 MIN.

¼ cup (50 g) granulated sugar | 1 tbsp heavy or whipping (35%) cream | ¾ cup (150 g) arborio rice (short grain) | 2½ cups (625 ml) milk | seeds from 1 vanilla pod | 1 cinnamon stick | 3–4 dates (e.g., Medjool dates) | ¼ cup (20 g) toasted sliced almonds

1. Melt the sugar in the pressure cooker, pour in the cream and caramelize until golden brown, while stirring. Add the rice, milk, 1¼ cups (300 ml) water, vanilla seeds and cinnamon.
2. Seal the pot, set the pressure regulator to setting 1 and heat on the highest setting. When the yellow ring appears (cooking indicator: 1st ring), reduce the heat. When the green ring becomes visible (cooking indicator: 1st ring), cook the rice for 15 minutes.
3. Meanwhile, pit the dates and chop them crosswise into small pieces. Release the steam from the pressure cooker, open the lid and remove the cinnamon. Adjust the seasoning, divide the rice pudding between four bowls and top with dates and almonds.

Rice pudding with blueberries

MAKES: 4 PORTIONS   **PREP TIME:** APPROX. 10 MIN.

1⅔ cups (250 g) blueberries | 1 cup (200 g) arborio rice (short grain) | 2 cups + 6 tbsp (600 ml) milk | 5 tbsp (65 g) granulated sugar | ½ tsp ground cinnamon | 2 to 3 tbsp heavy or whipping (35%) cream

1. Sort, wash and strain the blueberries. Put half of the berries in the pressure cooker with the rice, milk, sugar and ¼ tsp ground cinnamon. Pour in 1¼ cups (300 ml) water and seal the pot.
2. Set the pressure regulator to setting 1 and heat on the highest setting. When the yellow ring appears (cooking indicator: 1st ring), reduce the heat. As soon as the green ring becomes visible (cooking indicator: 1st ring), cook the rice for 15 minutes.
3. Release the steam from the pot, open the lid and fold the heavy cream into the rice. Adjust the seasoning to taste, then divide the rice pudding between four deep plates or bowls, top with the remaining blueberries, sprinkle lightly with cinnamon and serve.

 COOKING LEVEL VITAVIT®   COOKING LEVEL VITAQUICK® 15 COOKING TIME

 COOKING LEVEL VITAQUICK®   COOKING LEVEL VITAQUICK®   3 COOKING TIME

Sticky rice with mango

MAKES: 4 PORTIONS   **PREP TIME:** APPROX. 15 MIN.
1 cup (200 g) sticky rice | 1 cup (250 ml) coconut milk | salt | 5 tbsp (65 g) granulated sugar | 1 large ripe mango | juice of 1 lemon | 5 tbsp (30 g) toasted desiccated unsweetened coconut

1. Rinse the rice with cold water until the water runs clear, then strain. Put the rice in the pressure cooker with half of the coconut milk, salt and 1 cup (250 ml) water.
2. Seal the pot and cook the rice on the lowest setting (pressure regulator: setting 1, cooking indicator: 1st ring) for 15 minutes.
3. Mix together the remaining coconut milk and the sugar. Peel the mango, remove the flesh from the stone, chop it into large pieces and drizzle with lemon juice. Remove the pot from the heat and let stand for around 5 minutes, then release the steam and open the lid. Fold in the sweetened coconut milk. Season the sticky rice to taste, then divide it between four bowls, top with mango and desiccated coconut and serve.

Sweet porridge with berries

MAKES: 4 PORTIONS   **PREP TIME:** APPROX. 15 MIN.
2/3 cup (80 g) large-flaked rolled oats | 1/2 cinnamon stick | seeds from 1/2 vanilla pod | 1 cup (250 ml) coconut milk | 1 tbsp raisins | 1 cup (150 g) mixed berries | 3 tbsp (45 mL) agave syrup | 1–2 tbsp coarsely chopped walnuts

1. Put the rolled oats in a pressure cooker with the cinnamon, vanilla seeds, coconut milk and 1 3/4 cup + 3 tbsp (470 ml) water.
2. Seal the pot, set the pressure regulator to setting 2 and heat on the highest setting. When the yellow ring appears (cooking indicator: 1st ring), reduce the heat. When the green ring becomes visible (cooking indicator: 1st ring), cook for 3 minutes. Then remove the pot from the heat and let stand for around 10 minutes. Soak the raisins briefly in hot water. Sort, wash and strain the berries. Open the pot and fold in the strained berries, raisins and the agave syrup. Divide the porridge between four bowls, and serve with a sprinkling of berries and walnuts.

COOKING LEVEL VITAVIT®

COOKING LEVEL VITAQUICK®

COOKING TIME

Asian and red wine pears
poached in a spicy sauce

MAKES: 4 PORTIONS PER RECIPE **PREP TIME:** APPROX. 20 MIN. PER RECIPE

Asian pears in white wine & orange syrup (1)

2–3 Asian pears (or other firm pears, or peaches) | ½ tsp saffron threads | 4 cloves | 6 allspice berries | ¾ cup + 2 tbsp (200 ml) white wine | ¾ cup (150 g) granulated sugar | 2 juice oranges | 2 small oranges | 2–3 mint sprigs

1. Peel, quarter and core the Asian pears. Cut each quarter into 2–3 wedges. Put the saffron, cloves, allspice berries, white wine, 6 tbsp + 2 tsp (100 ml) water and ½ cup + 1 tbsp (120 g) sugar in a pressure cooker and mix well.
2. Add the pear wedges and close the pressure cooker. Set the pressure regulator to setting 1 and heat the pot on the highest setting. When the yellow ring appears (cooking indicator: 1st ring), reduce the heat. As soon as the green ring becomes visible (cooking indicator: 1st ring), cook the pears for 6 minutes.
3. In the meantime, squeeze the juice oranges. Peel the small oranges thoroughly and remove the fillets. Melt the rest of the sugar in a saucepan, deglaze with the orange juice and leave the sauce to simmer a little.
4. Release the steam from the pressure cooker, open the lid and remove the pear wedges. Reduce the cooking juices to a syrupy consistency, then set aside and let cool.
5. Arrange the pears on plates, put some orange fillets and sauce on top, drizzle with syrup and serve with mint.

Pears poached in red wine (2)

1 bottle (750 ml) full-bodied red wine | ⅔ cup (140 g) granulated sugar | 4–6 firm ripe pears (e.g., Bartlett or Bosc) | 1 cinnamon stick | 2–3 cloves | 3 star anise pods | 2 allspice berries | 1 sprig of rosemary | ½ organic lemon

1. Put the red wine and sugar in the open pressure cooker, reduce by half and set aside.
2. Peel the pears and cut them in half lengthwise without removing the seeds, stems or stalks. Put the pear halves in the reduced red wine and add the spices. Wash the rosemary and shake it dry. Wash the lemon in hot water and pat it dry. Cut 2 thick slices from the lemon and add them to the pears together with the rosemary.
3. Close the pressure cooker, set the pressure regulator to setting 1 and heat the pot on the highest setting. When the yellow ring appears (cooking indicator: 1st ring), reduce the heat. As soon as the green ring becomes visible (cooking indicator: 1st ring), the 6-minute cooking time begins.
4. Release the steam from the pot, open the lid and remove the pears. Reduce the cooking juices by about a half to a syrupy consistency, then set aside and let cool. Arrange the pears on plates, drizzle with the red wine sauce and serve.

TIP: if you leave the red wine pears to cool overnight in the spicy sauce, they turn a wonderful bright red color.

RECIPES >> SWEETS & DESSERTS

Sweet dumplings
cooked in the insert

MAKES: 4 PORTIONS   **RESTING TIME:** 30–60 MIN.   **PREP TIME:** 30–45 MIN.

Apricot dumplings
with potato dough (1)

1.2 lbs (600 g) russet potatoes | salt | ¼ cup (60 g) soft butter | 6 tbsp (60 g) semolina flour | 1 egg | ¾ cup + 2 tbsp (120 g) all-purpose flour + flour for dusting the work surface | 12 small apricots | 12 sugar cubes | 6 tbsp + 2 tsp (100 g) butter | 1 cup + 2 tbsp (120 g) dry breadcrumbs | ¾ cup + 2 tbsp (200 ml) vanilla sauce (as desired)

1. Wash the potatoes. Put the minimum amount of water and 1 pinch of salt in a pressure cooker. Put the potatoes in the perforated insert on the tripod, seal the pot and cook on setting 3 (cooking indicator: 2nd ring) for 12 minutes.
2. Release the steam from the pot, open the lid, remove the insert and drain off the water. Leave the steam to evaporate from the potatoes, then peel them, pass them through a ricer or food mill into a bowl while still warm and leave them to cool.
3. Make a well in the middle of the potatoes and add the soft butter, semolina, 1 pinch of salt and the egg. Mix together the ingredients, sieve the all-purpose flour over the top and knead everything into a smooth dough. Work some more flour into it, if necessary. Leave the dough to stand for around 15 minutes.
4. Then, on a floured work surface, roll it out to a thickness of ¼ inch (0.5 cm) and cut it into 2¾- to 3-inch (7 to 8 cm) squares.
5. Wash the apricots, dab them dry, cut them in half, remove the pit and fill each apricot with 1 sugar cube. Place 1 filled apricot on each dough square, fold over the edges and shape into small dumplings using your hands.
6. Put the dumplings in the perforated insert. Fill the pressure cooker with the minimum amount of water, put the insert on the tripod and seal the pot. Set the pressure regulator to setting 1 and heat the pot on the highest setting. When the yellow ring appears (cooking indicator: 1st ring), reduce the heat. As soon as the green ring becomes visible (cooking indicator: 1st ring), the 12-to-14-minute cooking time begins.
7. In the meantime, melt the butter in a pan and toast the breadcrumbs in the butter until golden brown. Remove the pressure cooker from the heat and release the steam. Remove the dumplings, coat them in the breadcrumbs and arrange on plates. Pour some vanilla sauce around them, as desired, and serve.

Curd cheese dumplings (2)

5 oz (50 g) bread rolls, from previous day | 5 oz (150 g) curd cheese (or cottage cheese) | ¼ cup (50 g) granulated sugar | ½ tsp salt | ¼ cup (60 g) melted butter | ¼ cup (60 g) sour cream | 2 eggs | 6 tbsp (50 g) all-purpose flour | 2 tbsp butter | confectioners' (icing) sugar

1. Make fine breadcrumbs out of the outer crusts of the rolls and set aside. Chop the insides into small cubes. Add to the cheese, granulated sugar, salt, melted butter, sour cream, eggs, flour and 1 tbsp of the breadcrumbs. Knead until smooth. Let rest for 30 minutes. Shape 8 small dumplings out of the dough.
2. Put the dumplings in the perforated insert. Fill the pressure cooker with the minimum amount of water, put the insert on the tripod and seal the pot. Cook on setting 1 (cooking indicator: 1st ring) for 12–14 minutes.
3. Melt the butter in a frying pan, toast the remaining breadcrumbs in the butter, then stir in 2 tbsp confectioners' sugar. Release the steam, remove the dumplings, coat in breadcrumbs and dust with confectioners' (icing) sugar before serving. Plum compote goes well with this dish.

Yeast dumplings (3)

1 cup + 2 tbsp (150 g) all-purpose flour | ¼ oz (7 g) fresh compressed yeast (or 1⅛ tsp/4 g quick-rising/instant yeast) | 1½ tbsp granulated sugar | ⅓ cup (75 ml) lukewarm milk | 1 egg yolk | 2 tbsp melted butter | ⅓ cup (85 g) plum jam | ½ tsp ground cinnamon | ⅓ cup (75 g) butter | ¼ cup (35 g) ground poppy seeds | 3 tbsp (24 g) confectioners' (icing) sugar

1. Sift the flour into a bowl and make a well in the middle. Mix the yeast with the granulated sugar and milk, pour into the well and stir in some flour from the edges. Cover the mother dough and leave in a warm place to rise for 15 minutes.
2. Add the egg yolk and 1 tbsp + 2 tsp (25 g) melted butter, knead until smooth and let rise for 15 minutes. Knead well again, divide into 8 portions, shape into balls and let rise for 15 minutes.
3. Mix together the plum jam and cinnamon. Press each ball flat, spread some plum jam on top, fold the dough over the filling, shape into balls again and let rest for 15 minutes.
4. Put the min. amount of water in a pressure cooker. Grease the perforated insert with the rest of the melted butter, add the dumplings, put the insert on the tripod (pay attention to the max. fill level). Seal the pot, cook on setting 1 (cooking indicator: 1st ring) for approx. 10 minutes (or steam without pressure for 20 minutes).
5. Melt the butter in a frying pan, add the poppy seeds, heat briefly, then stir in 2 tbsp confectioners' sugar. Release the steam, arrange the dumplings on plates, top with butter and poppy seeds and dust with confectioners' sugar before serving.

COOKING LEVEL VITAVIT®

COOKING LEVEL VITAQUICK®

COOKING TIME

Easy cakes: mocha/chocolate pudding

MAKES: 8 PORTIONS PER RECIPE **PREP TIME:** APPROX. 20 MIN. PER RECIPE

Mocha pudding (1)

3 cups (750 ml) milk | 7 tbsp (85 g) granulated sugar | 1 tbsp vanilla sugar | 3 tbsp (18 g) instant coffee | 8 soft lady fingers | butter for greasing the insert | 4 eggs | 4 tsp rum | 1 pinch of ground cardamom | $\frac{1}{2}$ tsp ground cinnamon

1. Put the milk, sugar and vanilla sugar in the open pressure cooker, bring to the boil, then dissolve the instant coffee in the liquid.
2. Halve the lady fingers, arrange them in a shallow dish, pour the hot coffee and milk mixture on top, then let sit and cool for 5 minutes. Clean the pressure cooker.
3. Generously grease an unperforated insert with butter. Beat the eggs with the rum, cardamom and cinnamon, fold into the lady finger mixture and pour the batter into the insert.
4. Fill the pressure cooker with the minimum amount of water, put the insert on the tripod and seal the pot. Set the pressure regulator to setting 1 and heat the pot on the highest setting. When the yellow ring appears (cooking indicator: 1st ring), reduce the heat. When the green ring becomes visible (cooking indicator: 1st ring), the 15-to-20-minute cooking time begins.
5. Remove the pot from the heat, release the steam and open the lid. Remove the mocha pudding from the pot, leave it to cool, then cut into slices and serve.

Chocolate pudding (2)

6 tbsp + 2 tsp (100 g) soft butter | $\frac{1}{4}$ cup (50 g) granulated sugar | $\frac{1}{4}$ cup (50 g) packed brown sugar | 2 eggs | seeds from 1 vanilla pod | 7 tbsp (60 g) all-purpose flour | 1–2 tsp baking powder | 1 tbsp unsweetened cocoa powder | 6 tbsp (40 g) ground almonds | 2–3 tbsp grated dark chocolate | 1 tbsp butter for greasing the insert

1. Beat the soft butter and both types of sugar in a bowl until light and creamy. Add the eggs one by one, working each one in well, then stir in the vanilla seeds. Mix together the flour, baking powder and cocoa powder, then sift the dry ingredients into the bowl. Fold in the almonds and chocolate and mix the batter until smooth.
2. Generously grease an unperforated insert with butter, then add the batter. Fill the pressure cooker with the minimum amount of water, put the insert on the tripod and seal the pot. Set the pressure regulator to setting 1 and heat the pot on the highest setting. As soon as the yellow ring appears (cooking indicator: 1st ring), reduce the heat. When the green ring becomes visible (cooking indicator: 1st ring), the approx. 20-minute cooking time begins.
3. Remove the pot from the heat, release the steam and open the lid. Remove the chocolate pudding from the pot, leave it to cool in the insert and then turn it out, turn it over, cut it into slices and serve.

TIP: both of these puddings go wonderfully with lightly whipped cream. If you steam the chocolate pudding without pressure for around 15 minutes before pressure cooking it, it will be particularly light and fluffy.

COOKING LEVEL VITAVIT®: 1
COOKING LEVEL VITAQUICK®: 1
COOKING TIME: 20

Caramelized custard desserts

(1)

Crème brûlée (1)

MAKES: 6–8 SLICES **PREP TIME:** 20–35 MIN.
RESTING TIME: 1 HR

1 cup + 6 tbsp (350 ml) heavy or whipping (35%) cream | 2 eggs | 2 egg yolks | ⅔ cup (80 g) confectioners' (icing) sugar | seeds from 1 vanilla pod | 1 heaped tsp agar-agar (3.5 g) | butter for greasing the insert | ¼ cup (50 g) brown sugar

1. In a bowl, mix together the cream, eggs and egg yolks. Add the confectioners' (icing) sugar and vanilla seeds. Dissolve the agar-agar in a little hot water, add to the bowl and mix everything well.
2. Generously grease an unperforated insert with butter, then add the cream mixture. Fill the pressure cooker with the minimum amount of water and put the insert on the tripod. Close the pressure cooker with the lid and set the pressure regulator to setting 1. Heat the pot on the highest setting. As soon as the yellow ring appears (cooking indicator: 1st ring), reduce the heat. When the green ring becomes visible (cooking indicator: 1st ring), the approx. 20-minute cooking time begins.
3. Remove the pressure cooker from the heat, release the steam and open the lid. Remove the cream from the pot and let cool in the insert for at least 1 hour (or until completely cool).
4. Carefully turn out the crème brûlée onto a plate or cake stand. Sprinkle the top with the brown sugar and caramelize with a flambé torch until golden brown. Cut the crème brûlée into slices (or cut it into slices before caramelizing it). Alternatively, serve the crème brûlée whole and make quenelles out of it.

Crème caramel (2)

MAKES: 6–8 SLICES **PREP TIME:** 20–35 MIN.
RESTING TIME: 1 HR

1–2 tbsp vegetable oil for greasing the insert | ½ cup (100 g) granulated sugar | ¼ vanilla pod | 2 cups (500 ml) milk | 3 eggs | 2 egg yolks | 7½ tbsp (90 g) granulated sugar | 1 heaped tsp agar-agar (3.5 g) | almond tuiles to serve, as desired

1. Grease an unperforated insert with oil. Heat ½ cup (100 g) sugar in a saucepan, pour in 4 tsp water while stirring and caramelize until golden brown. Pour the caramel into the insert and spread it evenly by tilting the insert.
2. Cut the vanilla pod lengthwise, put it in a pan with the milk and bring to the boil. Beat the eggs, egg yolks and 7½ tbsp (90 g) sugar well in a bowl, but not until frothy. Remove the vanilla pod from the pan, scoop out the seeds and add them to the hot milk. Dissolve the agar-agar in some of the hot milk and stir into the vanilla milk. Gradually stir the hot vanilla milk into the egg and sugar mixture, then leave the cream to rest for approx. 1 hour.
3. Strain the cream through a sieve and pour into the prepared insert. Fill the pressure cooker with the minimum amount of water and put the insert with the cream on the tripod.
4. Close the pressure cooker, set the pressure regulator to setting 1 and heat the pot on the highest setting. As soon as the yellow ring appears (cooking indicator: 1st ring), reduce the heat. When the green ring becomes visible (cooking indicator: 1st ring), the approx. 20-minute cooking time begins.
5. Remove the pot from the heat, release the steam and open the lid. Remove the insert and leave the crème caramel to cool completely. Then turn out the crème caramel onto a plate, cut it into slices and serve with almond tuiles (as desired).

TIP: you can easily make the crème caramel in advance, leave it to cool, cover it with plastic wrap and keep it refrigerated until ready to serve.

COOKING LEVEL VITAVIT®   **COOKING LEVEL VITAQUICK®**   **COOKING TIME**

Chocolate cheesecake with a biscuit base

MAKES: 8–10 SLICES   **PREP TIME:** APPROX. 40 MIN.   **COOLING TIME:** AT LEAST 5 HRS

FOR THE BASE
6 tbsp + 2 tsp (100 g) butter, or as needed
Butter for greasing the insert
3.3 oz (100 g) vanilla cookies
3.3 oz (100 g) plain digestive cookies

FOR THE TOPPING
8 oz (250 g) dark chocolate
15 oz (450 g) cream cheese
¼ cup + 2 tsp (60 g) granulated sugar
¼ cup + 2 tsp (60 g) brown sugar
1 egg
2 egg yolks
2 tbsp plain yogurt (10% fat)
¼–½ tsp ground cinnamon
1 pinch of ground cardamom

FOR THE BASE: melt the butter in a small saucepan and set aside. Generously grease an unperforated insert with butter. Place both types of cookies in a sealable bag and bash into fine crumbs using a rolling pin or other heavy object.

Add the melted butter and mix well. If necessary, add more butter and mix well until no dry crumbs remain. Transfer the cookie crumb mixture to the insert, spread out evenly and press down on the base and sides. Refrigerate the cookie base until ready to use.

FOR THE TOPPING: chop up the dark chocolate, place it in a metal bowl and melt it over a bain-marie, then set it aside and allow it to cool for about 10 minutes.

Beat the cream cheese with the granulated and brown sugar in a bowl until well combined, then beat in the egg. Mix in the egg yolks, yogurt, cinnamon and cardamom. Finally, fold in the slightly cooled (but still liquid) chocolate and mix everything well.

Pour the chocolate and cream cheese topping over the cookie base in the insert. Fill the pressure cooker with the minimum amount of water. Position the tripod inside the pot and place the insert on top. Seal the pressure cooker with the lid and set the pressure regulator to setting 2. Heat the pot on the highest setting until the yellow ring appears (cooking indicator: 1st ring), then reduce the heat. As soon as the green ring becomes visible (cooking indicator: 1st ring), the approx. 25-minute cooking time begins.

Afterwards, remove the pot from the heat, release the steam and open the lid. Remove the insert and leave the cheesecake inside it to cool for about 1 hour. Then cover the insert with plastic wrap and refrigerate the cheesecake for at least 4 hours or overnight.

Loosen the edge of the cheesecake with a knife, carefully remove it from the insert and turn it out on a plate. Turn the cheesecake over, put it on a cake stand, cut it into slices with a sharp knife and serve.

TIP: to ensure that the cheesecake slices retain their shape when being cut, dip the knife into hot water and clean it between each cut. If you wish to steam the cheesecake without pressure with other dishes on multiple levels, set the pressure regulator to the steam cooking symbol. In this case, you should steam the cake for 40 minutes, then release the steam, let cool and refrigerate as instructed.

COOKING LEVEL VITAVIT® 2 | COOKING LEVEL VITAQUICK® 1 | COOKING TIME 25

Cherry clafoutis & cheesecake

MAKES: 8–10 SLICES PER RECIPE   **PREP TIME:** 30–40 MIN.

Cherry clafoutis (2)

MAKES: 8–10 SLICES   **PREP TIME:** 30–40 MIN.

1 lb (500 g) cherries | 4 eggs | 6 tbsp + 1 tsp (80 g) granulated sugar | seeds from 1 vanilla pod | 1 pinch of salt | 1 tbsp dark rum | 1 cup (135 g) all-purpose flour | 1½ cups (375 ml) milk | butter and flour for the insert | confectioners' (icing) sugar for dusting

1. Wash, strain and pit the cherries. Beat the eggs and sugar until frothy. Stir in the vanilla seeds, salt and rum. Gradually sift and fold the flour into the mixture. Lastly, stir in the milk.

2. Grease and line an unperforated insert with butter and flour. Pour one-third of the mixture into the insert, put half of the cherries on top and cover with the rest of the mixture. Top with the remaining cherries and press slightly.

3. Fill the pressure cooker with the minimum amount of water, put the insert on the tripod and seal the pot. Set the pressure regulator to setting 2 and heat the pot on the highest setting. As soon as the yellow ring appears (cooking indicator: 1st ring), reduce the heat. When the green ring becomes visible (cooking indicator: 1st ring), the approx. 25-minute cooking time begins. Release the steam from the pot and open the lid.

4. Remove the clafoutis, let cool briefly, turn out from the insert and dust with a little confectioners' (icing) sugar. Cut the clafoutis into slices and serve.

Berry cheesecake (1)

MAKES: 8–10 SLICES   **PREP TIME:** 30–40 MIN.
COOLING TIME: 6 HRS

14 oz (400 g) cream cheese | ½ cup + 2 tbsp (125 g) granulated sugar | 2 eggs | ¼ cup (60 g) quark (or full-fat sour cream) | 1 heaped tbsp all-purpose flour | 1 tsp vanilla extract | **For the base:** 6 tbsp (90 g) butter + butter for greasing the insert | 3.3 oz (100 g) vanilla cookies | 3.3 oz (100 g) plain digestive cookies | cranberry compote (or canned cranberry sauce)

1. Beat the cream cheese and sugar in a bowl until smooth, then add the eggs, one by one, working each one into the mixture. Fold in the quark, flour and vanilla extract and mix everything until smooth.

2. For the base, generously grease an unperforated insert with butter. Melt the 6 tbsp (90 g) butter and set it aside. Place both types of cookies in a sealable bag and bash into fine crumbs using a rolling pin. Mix the cookie crumbs with the butter to form a moist mixture, adding more butter or crumbs as required. Transfer the mixture to the insert, spread it out and press down firmly on the base and sides.

3. Fill the pressure cooker with the minimum amount of water, put the insert on the tripod, seal the pot and cook on setting 2 (cooking indicator: 1st ring) for approx. 25 minutes.

4. Remove the pot from the heat, release the steam and open the lid. Remove the insert and leave the cheesecake to cool within it for about 1 hour, then cover the insert with plastic wrap and refrigerate for at least 5 hours or (even better) overnight.

5. Loosen the edge of the cheesecake with a knife, carefully turn it out onto a plate, turn it over and place it on a cake stand. Top the cheesecake with cranberry compote and cut into slices before serving.

(1)

Brownies and lemon cake

(1)

Glazed brownies (1)

MAKES: 8 SLICES   **PREP TIME:** APPROX. 45 MIN.
COOLING TIME: 12 HRS

3.3 oz (100 g) dark chocolate | ¼ cup (60 g) soft butter | 2 tbsp + 2 tsp (40 ml) brewed coffee | 3 eggs (large) | 6 tbsp (75 g) granulated sugar | seeds from 1 vanilla pod | ¾ cup (75 g) finely ground almonds | 1 tbsp unsweetened cocoa powder | 3 tbsp + 2 tsp (30 g) all-purpose flour | butter and flour for the insert | **For the glaze:** 3.3 oz (100 g) dark chocolate

1. Chop up the chocolate and melt it with the butter over a bain-marie. Stir in the coffee and leave the mixture to cool until lukewarm. In the meantime, beat the eggs and sugar until light and creamy, stir in the vanilla seeds, then fold in the chocolate mixture while still runny. Mix together the ground almonds, cocoa powder and flour and fold into the batter.
2. Generously grease and line an unperforated insert with butter and flour, then add the brownie batter. Fill the pressure cooker with the minimum amount of water, put the insert on the tripod and seal the pot.
3. Set the pressure regulator to setting 1 and heat the pot on the highest setting. When the yellow ring appears (cooking indicator: 1st ring), reduce the heat. When the green ring becomes visible (cooking indicator: 1st ring), the 20-to-30-minute cooking time begins.
4. Remove the pressure cooker from the heat, release the steam and open the lid. Remove the cake from the pot and leave it to cool in the insert overnight. To make the glaze, chop up the chocolate and melt it over a bain-marie. Let cool slightly, then reheat to 86°F (30°C).
5. Loosen the edge of the cake with a knife, carefully turn it out onto a plate, turn it over and place it on a cake stand. Cut into about 8 slices, cover with the glaze, let set, then serve.

Lemon cake with hazelnuts (2)

MAKES: 8 SLICES   **PREP TIME:** APPROX. 45 MIN.
COOLING TIME: 12 HRS

2 large eggs | ¾ cup + 2 tbsp (180 g) granulated sugar | 1 pinch of salt | 6 tbsp + 2 tsp (100 g) soft butter | grated zest of 2 organic lemons | 2 tbsp lemon juice | 1 tsp vanilla extract | ½ cup (120 g) plain yogurt | 1 cup (135 g) all-purpose flour | 2 tsp baking powder | 1 handful of toasted, coarsely chopped hazelnuts | flour and butter for the insert | **For the sauce:** 2 organic lemons, washed in hot water | 3 eggs | ¾ cup + 2 tbsp (180 g) granulated sugar | ¼ cup (60 g) soft butter, in pieces

1. Beat the eggs, sugar and salt in a bowl until light and creamy, then add the soft butter and mix well. Add the lemon zest and juice, the vanilla extract and the yogurt and mix again. Mix together the flour and baking powder, sift the mixture into the batter and fold in carefully.
2. Grease and line an unperforated insert with butter and flour, then add the batter. Fill the pressure cooker with the minimum amount of water, put the insert on the tripod and seal the pot. Cook the cake on setting 1 (cooking indicator: 1st ring) for 20–30 minutes. Then release the steam from the pot and open the lid. Remove the cake, leave it to cool in the insert, cover with plastic wrap and refrigerate for 12 hours.
3. The same day, to make the sauce, finely grate the zest of 1 lemon and squeeze the juice from both lemons. Beat the eggs, lemon juice and sugar over a bain-marie for around 10 minutes or until thick and creamy, then strain through a sieve and stir in the butter and lemon zest. Season the sauce to taste and refrigerate overnight.
4. The following day, remove the cake from the insert (as described in the brownies recipe), cut into slices, drizzle with the sauce, sprinkle with hazelnuts and serve.

Multilevel cooking

Pressure cooking is particularly effective when several dishes with the same cooking time are cooked on top of each other on different levels. You can cook many dishes together this way, such as starters, soups, stews and braised dishes, or even sweets and desserts. If the various items of your menu have different cooking times, you can simply cook them one after the other in the pressure cooker.

Teriyaki chicken with brown rice

COOKING LEVEL VITAVIT®

COOKING LEVEL VITAQUICK®

COOKING TIME

MAKES: 4 PORTIONS   **PREP TIME:** APPROX. 20 MIN.

FOR THE CHICKEN
¼ cup (60 ml) soy sauce
2 tbsp brown sugar
2 tbsp mirin (or sherry)
1 tbsp rice vinegar
1 tsp grated gingerroot
2 garlic cloves
4 boneless skinless chicken breasts (approx. 5 oz/150 g each)
2 tbsp vegetable oil
¾ cup + 2 tbsp (200 ml) poultry stock

FOR THE RICE
2 cups (360 g) long-grain brown rice
1 tsp salt

TO FINISH
2 tsp cornstarch
1 green onion
2 tsp toasted sesame seeds

FOR THE CHICKEN: mix together the soy sauce, brown sugar, mirin, rice vinegar, ginger and ¼ cup (60 ml) water in a small bowl. Peel and crush the garlic, add it to the mixture and set the spicy sauce aside.

Pat the chicken dry. Heat the oil in the pressure cooker, add the chicken fillets and briefly fry them until browned, turning occasionally, then deglaze with the spicy sauce and pour in the stock.

FOR THE RICE: prepare an appropriately sized unperforated insert and a tripod. Rinse the rice, leave it to strain, then put it in the insert with 2 cups (500 ml) of water (ratio 1:1). Season the rice with salt, then put the insert on the tripod above the chicken in the pressure cooker.

Close the pressure cooker with the lid and set the pressure regulator to setting 3. Heat the pot on the highest setting. As soon as the yellow ring appears (cooking indicator: 1st ring), reduce the heat again. When the green ring becomes visible (cooking indicator: 2nd ring), the 9-minute cooking time begins.

Remove the pot from the heat and continue cooking for another 2 minutes, then release the steam and open the lid.

TO FINISH: remove the insert with the rice, the tripod and the chicken breast fillets. Keep the rice and chicken warm. Mix the cornstarch with 1 tbsp water until smooth, pour into the pot and leave the sauce to simmer briefly in the open pot until it thickens slightly.

In the meantime, wash and trim the green onion, then slice it at an angle into thin rings. Season the teriyaki sauce to taste and coat the chicken breasts in it. Divide the brown rice between four deep plates or bowls. Cut each chicken breast fillet into diagonal slices, arrange the slices on top of the rice and pour over some sauce. Sprinkle with some toasted sesame seeds and green onion rings and serve.

TIP: mirin is a sweet rice wine brewed from fermented rice that is commonly used in Japanese cuisine. It goes well with many Japanese ingredients as it enhances their taste, and it perfectly rounds off sauces and marinades, such as this teriyaki sauce. You should be able to find mirin in any well-stocked supermarket or Asian supermarket. If you can't find it, you can also make this dish with a medium-dry or sweet sherry.

RECIPES » MULTILEVEL COOKING 285

COOKING LEVEL VITAVIT®

COOKING LEVEL VITAQUICK®

COOKING TIME

Veal paupiettes with ratatouille

MAKES: 4 PORTIONS **PREP TIME:** 45–50 MIN.

FOR THE RATATOUILLE
1 large onion
2 garlic cloves
1 small eggplant
1 small zucchini
1 red bell pepper
1 green bell pepper
1 yellow bell pepper
3 ripe tomatoes
2 tbsp olive oil
3 tbsp + 1 tsp to 1/3 cup (50 to 75 ml) vegetable stock
salt
freshly ground pepper
1 tsp chopped herbs (thyme, rosemary, oregano)

FOR THE PAUPIETTES
1 shallot
1 garlic clove
2 tbsp olive oil
2/3 cup (85 g) finely diced peeled carrots
2/3 cup (80 g) finely diced celery
7 oz (200 g) veal sausage (or sausage meat/ground veal)
Espelette pepper (or medium-hot paprika)
1/2 tsp chopped thyme
1–2 tbsp chopped flat-leaf parsley
fleur de sel (or sea salt)
4 slices veal scallopini
6 tbsp + 2 tsp (100 ml) dry white wine
3/4 cup + 2 tbsp (200 ml) veal or poultry stock
freshly ground pepper

FOR THE RATATOUILLE: peel and finely dice the onion and garlic. Wash and trim the vegetables and cut them into approx. 1/2-inch (1 cm) pieces. Heat the oil in the pressure cooker, add the onion and garlic and sauté lightly. Add the eggplant and fry briefly, turning occasionally, until slightly browned. Add the zucchini and bell peppers and continue cooking, while stirring, then deglaze with the stock. Season the vegetables with salt, pepper and herbs, remove them from the pot, put them in a perforated insert and set them aside. Clean the pressure cooker.

FOR THE PAUPIETTES: peel and finely dice the shallot and garlic. Heat 1 tbsp oil in the pressure cooker, add the shallot, garlic, carrots and celery and sauté them lightly, then leave them to cool slightly. Put the veal sausage in a bowl and add the vegetables. Season the stuffing to taste with Espelette pepper, thyme, parsley and some salt.

Pat the veal scallopini dry and tenderize them (see tip). Score the surface of the meat crosswise with a sharp knife and season lightly with salt. Divide the stuffing into quarters, shape it into balls and place one ball in the middle of each **(1)**. Wrap the escalopes around the stuffing, shape the paupiettes into round parcels, then secure each one in place by tying it crosswise three times **(2)**.

Heat the remaining oil (1 tbsp) in the pressure cooker, briefly fry the paupiettes all over until browned, then deglaze with white wine and pour in the veal stock. Seal the pot, set the pressure regulator to setting 3 and heat on the highest setting.

As soon as the yellow ring appears (cooking indicator: 1st ring), reduce the heat. When the green ring becomes visible (cooking indicator: 2nd ring), the 5-to-6-minute cooking time begins.

Remove the pot from the heat, release the steam and open the lid. Put the ratatouille in the insert on the tripod **(3)**. Seal the pot and set the pressure regulator to setting 2. Heat the pot on the highest setting. As soon as the yellow ring appears (cooking indicator: 1st ring), reduce the heat. When the green ring becomes visible (cooking indicator: 1st ring), the 4-to-5-minute cooking time begins.

TO FINISH: remove the pot from the heat, release the steam and open the lid. Remove the ratatouille and the paupiettes and keep warm briefly. Leave the braising stock to simmer slightly, then season with salt and pepper. Divide the ratatouille between four plates. Remove the twine from the paupiettes, put one on each plate, drizzle a little sauce over and around the paupiettes and serve.

TIP: to tenderize the meat, simply wrap it in plastic wrap or parchment paper and pound it with a large, heavy frying pan. If your butcher has only small escalopes, take two per paupiette and arrange them so that they overlap slightly.

Osso buco with gremolata and risotto Milanese

COOKING LEVEL VITAVIT®

COOKING LEVEL VITAQUICK®

COOKING TIME

MAKES: 4 PORTIONS **PREP TIME:** 35 MIN.

FOR THE OSSO BUCO
1 large onion
1 garlic clove
4 slices of veal shank (osso buco, approx. 8 oz/250 g each)
2 tbsp all-purpose flour
¼ cup (60 g) butter
salt
freshly ground pepper
⅔ cup (85 g) finely diced peeled carrots
⅔ cup (85 g) finely diced celery
6 tbsp + 2 tsp (100 ml) dry white wine
1 cup (250 ml) veal or poultry stock
1–2 tsp cornstarch mixed with some cold water

FOR THE RISOTTO MILANESE
2 shallots
2 tbsp olive oil
1½ cups (300 g) short-grain rice (e.g., arborio, carnaroli)
½ cup (120 ml) dry white wine
salt
freshly ground pepper
1 capsule saffron powder (0.1 g)
2 cups (500 ml) poultry stock
2 tbsp butter
⅓ cup (30 g) grated Parmesan

FOR THE GREMOLATA
1 organic lemon
½ handful of flat-leaf parsley
1 young garlic clove

FOR THE OSSO BUCO: peel and finely dice the onion and garlic. Pat the veal shank slices dry, coat them in flour and tap off any excess flour.

Heat the butter in a pressure cooker, add the osso buco slices and fry/brown them on both sides, then season them with salt and pepper and remove them. Sauté the onion, garlic and diced vegetables in the remaining fat, let brown slightly, then deglaze with white wine. Put the veal slices back in the pot and pour in the veal stock.

Close the pressure cooker with the lid and set the pressure regulator to setting 3. Heat the pot on the highest setting. As soon as the yellow ring appears (cooking indicator: 1st ring), reduce the heat. When the green ring becomes visible (cooking indicator: 2nd ring), the approx. 25-minute cooking time begins.

FOR THE RISOTTO MILANESE: peel and finely dice the shallots. Heat the oil in a pot, add the diced shallot and sauté until translucent. Add all of the rice and fry briefly, while stirring, until the tips of the rice grains become translucent. Deglaze with the wine and simmer briefly, while stirring. Season the rice with salt, pepper and saffron, put it in an unperforated insert and pour in the poultry stock.

Remove the pressure cooker from the heat, release the steam and open the lid. Put the insert on the tripod in the pot, above the meat. Close the pressure cooker again and finish cooking on setting 3 for approx. 5 minutes.

FOR THE GREMOLATA: wash the lemon in hot water, then dab it dry and finely zest it. Rinse the parsley, shake it dry, pluck off the leaves and finely chop them. Peel and finely dice the garlic.

TO FINISH: remove the pressure cooker from the heat, release the steam and open the lid. Fold the butter and half of the grated Parmesan into the risotto and add some more stock if necessary. Stir half of the gremolata into the braising stock, thicken the sauce slightly with the cornstarch mixture and season to taste.

Season the risotto Milanese to taste, divide it between four preheated plates and sprinkle with the remaining Parmesan. Add the osso buco slices with the diced vegetables and some sauce, sprinkle with the remaining gremolata and serve.

TIP: if you're in a hurry, you can also easily make the gremolata in a food chopper. To do so, thinly peel approx. ½-inch (1 cm) strips of lemon zest (without the white pith), add the parsley leaves and quartered garlic cloves and finely chop.

COOKING LEVEL VITAVIT®
COOKING LEVEL VITAQUICK®
COOKING TIME

Venison stew
with cranberry pears

MAKES: 4 PORTIONS **SOAKING TIME:** 20 MIN. **PREP TIME:** APPROX. 45 MIN.

FOR THE STEW
2/3 cup (20 g) dried porcini mushroom slices
1 1/2 lbs (750 g) boneless shoulder of venison
2 onions
1 carrot
2 tbsp vegetable oil
4 juniper berries
6 peppercorns
1–2 cloves
1 pinch of ground allspice
1 tsp tomato purée
1 tbsp all-purpose flour
3/4 cup + 2 tbsp (200 ml) red wine
1 2/3 cups (400 ml) game stock
1 bay leaf
4 tsp (20 ml) gin
1 tsp cornstarch, as desired

FOR THE PEARS
2 pears
2 tbsp lemon juice
3/4 cup + 2 tbsp (200 ml) white wine
1 tbsp granulated sugar

TO FINISH
10 oz (300 g) mixed mushrooms (e.g., chanterelles, porcini)
1/2 shallot
2 tsp butter
salt
freshly ground pepper
1/4 cup (68 g) cranberry sauce (canned)
1 tbsp chopped flat-leaf parsley

FOR THE STEW: soak the dried porcini in warm water for approx. 20 minutes. Pat the meat dry, remove any sinews and cut it into approx. 1 1/4-inch (3 cm) cubes. Peel and coarsely dice the onions and carrot.

Heat the oil in a pressure cooker. Add the juniper berries, peppercorns, cloves and allspice and fry in the oil until the spices become fragrant. Increase the temperature and sear the meat all over in portions until browned, then remove it. Add the diced onion and carrot to the pot, one after the other, and fry them together in the remaining fat. Stir in the tomato purée and cook for another minute or so. Dust everything with flour, deglaze with half of the red wine and then leave it to reduce completely. Pour in the remaining red wine and reduce it once again, but this time by half.

Coarsely chop the soaked porcini, if desired, drain, and add to the pot. Pour in the game stock, return the meat to the pot and add the bay leaf. Close the pressure cooker with the lid and set the pressure regulator to setting 3. Heat the pot on the highest setting. As soon as the yellow ring appears (cooking indicator: 1st ring), reduce the heat. When the green ring becomes visible (cooking indicator: 2nd ring), the 20-to-25-minute cooking time begins.

FOR THE PEARS: in the meantime, peel the pears, cut them in half and scrape out their cores with a melon scoop. Drizzle the pear halves with lemon juice, place them cut-side-up on the unperforated insert, then add the white wine and sugar. Remove the pressure cooker from the heat, release the steam and open the lid. Put the insert on the tripod above the stew, seal the pot again and cook everything on setting 1 for another 6–8 minutes.

TO FINISH: trim the mushrooms and, depending on their size, halve or slice them. Peel and finely dice the shallot. Melt 1 tsp butter in a frying pan, add the shallot and sauté until translucent. Add the mushrooms and fry them until the liquid running out of them has evaporated. Melt the remaining butter in the pan until it turns frothy, then fry and slightly brown the shallot and mushrooms for another 3–4 minutes. Season the mushrooms with salt and pepper to taste.

Remove the pressure cooker from the heat, release the steam and open the lid. Remove the meat and set it aside. Strain the sauce through a sieve. Stir in the gin and leave the sauce to simmer for a little longer. Alternatively, mix the cornstarch with 2–3 tsp cold water until smooth, pour into the sauce and simmer for another 1–2 minutes. Then put the meat back in the sauce. Remove the bay leaf.

Mix half of the fried mushrooms into the stew. Season to taste, then divide the stew between four preheated plates together with the remaining mushrooms. Fill each pear half with 1 tbsp cranberries and add to the plates. Sprinkle everything with some chopped parsley and serve. It goes well with fettuccine or another wide pasta.

COOKING LEVEL VITAVIT®   COOKING LEVEL VITAQUICK®   COOKING TIME

Essentials: stock

MAKES: 8–12 CUPS (2–3 L) PER RECIPE   **PREP TIME:** 20–25 MIN. PER RECIPE

Fish stock

2 lbs (1 kg) white fish carcasses (bones, fins, etc.) | 2 shallots | ½ fennel bulb | 1 parsnip | ⅔ cup (80 g) chopped celery | 3⅓ ounces (100 g) parsnip | 3 tbsp (45 g) butter | 1 cup (90 g) sliced trimmed leek | 1 cup (250 ml) dry white wine | 1 bay leaf | 2–3 sprigs thyme | ½ tsp white peppercorns

1. Chop up the fish carcasses, rinse them thoroughly with cold water or soak them for 20 minutes and strain.
2. Peel and finely dice the shallots. Wash and trim the fennel. Peel the parsnip and chop all of the vegetables into small pieces or slices.
3. Melt the butter in the pressure cooker, add the carcasses and sauté lightly for 3–4 minutes, turning occasionally. Add the shallots and vegetables and cook together briefly. Pour in the wine and 8 cups (2 L) cold water, then add the bay leaf, thyme and peppercorns.
4. Bring the stock to the boil, then skim off the foam. Seal the pot, set the pressure regulator to setting 3 (cooking indicator: 2nd ring) and cook for approx. 10 minutes. Release the steam from the pot and strain the stock through a sieve lined with a cloth.

Veal stock

2 lbs (1 kg) veal bones (rib bones with meat) and 1 lb (500 g) calf's foot, all chopped into roughly equal-sized pieces | 1 pinch of salt | 1½ cups (200 g) chopped onions | 1½ cups (180 g) chopped celery | 2¼ cups (200 g) chopped trimmed leeks (only the white and light green parts) | 1 bay leaf | ½ bunch of flat-leaf parsley

1. Rinse the veal bones and calf's foot in cold water, then blanch them in boiling water for 3–4 minutes. Rinse them in cold water once again.
2. Put the veal bones, calf's foot and salt in a large pressure cooker and add 12 cups (3 L) cold water. Seal the pot, set the pressure regulator to setting 3 and heat the pot on the highest setting. As soon as the yellow ring appears (cooking indicator: 1st ring), reduce the heat. When the green ring becomes visible (cooking indicator: 2nd ring), the approx. 25-minute cooking time begins.
3. Remove the pot from the heat and release the steam.
4. Add the vegetables, bay leaf and parsley, seal the pot and cook on setting 3 (cooking indicator: 2nd ring) for another 25 minutes or so.
5. Release the steam from the pot and open the lid. If desired, leave the stock to simmer for a little while in the open pot, then pass it through a sieve lined with a cloth and strain off the fat.

Lamb stock

2 onions | 2 stalks celery | 2 carrots | 3 tbsp (45 ml) vegetable oil | 2 lbs (1 kg) lamb breast with bones, in pieces | 2 lbs (1 kg) lamb bones, chopped | 2 garlic cloves | 1 bouquet garni made with carrot, leek and parsnip (1.6 oz/50 g each) and 1 sprig of parsley and 1 sprig of thyme

1. Preheat the oven to 400°F (200°C). Peel or trim the vegetables and coarsely dice them. Heat the oil in a roasting pan. briefly sear the lamb breast and bones and the vegetables in the oil, then spread them out.
2. Put the roaster in the oven and brown everything for around 20 minutes, turning repeatedly.
3. Put the contents of the roaster in a large pressure cooker (6 L or bigger), pour in 8 to 12 cups (2 to 3 L) cold water, bring to the boil and skim off the foam several times. Peel the garlic and add it to the pot together with the bouquet garni.
4. Close the pressure cooker, set the pressure regulator to setting 3 and heat the pot on the highest setting. As soon as the yellow ring appears (cooking indicator: 1st ring), reduce the heat. When the green ring becomes visible (cooking indicator: 2nd ring), the 25-to-30-minute cooking time begins.
5. Remove the pot from the heat, release the steam and open the lid. Reduce the stock by about a half over a low heat, then pass it through a sieve lined with a cloth to strain off the fat.

Game stock

1 lb (500 g) onions | 4 lbs (2 kg) game bones with meat, chopped | ½ cup (125 ml) vegetable oil | 1½ cups (200 g) coarsely diced peeled carrots | ¾ cup + 1 tbsp (100 g) coarsely diced celery | 1 tbsp tomato paste | 1 bottle (750 ml) full-bodied red wine | 1 sprig of thyme | 1 bay leaf | 3 allspice berries | 8–10 peppercorns | 2 cloves | 6–8 juniper berries | ½ star anise pod

1. Preheat the oven to 400°F (200°C). Peel and coarsely dice the onions. Put the bones and oil in a roaster and toast them in the oven for around 15 minutes. Add the vegetables and cook for another 10 minutes.
2. Remove the roaster, pour off the fat, stir in the tomato paste and fry briefly on the stove over a low heat. Deglaze with 1 cup (250 ml) red wine and leave it to reduce almost entirely. Repeat this process twice. Then add 8 cups (2 L) cold water and the herbs and seasonings and deglaze the cooking juices.
3. Put the contents of the roaster in a large pressure cooker, bring to the boil and skim off the foam again. Finish cooking the game stock on setting 3, as described in the lamb stock recipe (step 4 onward).

Pressure cooking time finder

As foods are natural products, cooking times vary greatly depending on various factors, such as the species, age and breed of animals, etc. It is therefore impossible to give exact times. The tables on the following pages provide guidance and recommendations on a wide range of products.

When pressure cooking, it takes about half the normal cooking time at the lowest pressure setting, and about a third of the usual time at the highest pressure setting. Meat and poultry are generally cooked on setting 3 (cooking indicator: setting 2). Very lean cuts, such as pork fillet, chicken breast or rabbit, remain tender and succulent when they are cooked with slightly less pressure (pressure regulator: setting 2, cooking indicator: setting 1). The size and thickness of the items also influences the cooking time: the heavier and more compact the food, the longer it takes to cook and vice versa. You can easily balance out different cooking times by dividing food into appropriate-sized portions. The letter 'I' in the tables means that we recommend pressure cooking this item in an insert, but all foods can of course be cooked directly in the pot with the minimum quantity of liquid. For further information on cooking times, please consult the relevant manufacturer's user instructions.

VEAL AND BEEF (1 LB/500 G)	COOKING TIME IN MINUTES	COOKED IN AN INSERT	VITAVIT® PREMIUM COOKING SETTING	VITAQUICK® PREMIUM COOKING SETTING[1]
Shank slices	20	*	3	2
Goulash	20–25	*	3	2
Veal (strips)	2–5	*	3	2
Veal roast	20–25	*	3	2
Veal goulash, fillet	3–5	*	3	2
Veal shank, breast	25–30	*	3	2
Veal roast with kidneys	20–30	*	3	2
Beef brisket	30–40	*	3	2
Beef meatballs	5–6	*	3	2
Roulades, fillet roasts	20–25	*	3	2
Marinated pot roasts, roast sirloin	30–40	*	3	2

* Can be cooked in an insert (e.g., for multilevel cooking) | [1] The cooking setting for Vitaquick® Premium also applies to other pressure cookers with two pressure cooking settings

PORK (1 LB/500 G)	COOKING TIME IN MINUTES	COOKED IN AN INSERT	VITAVIT® PREMIUM COOKING SETTING	VITAQUICK® PREMIUM COOKING SETTING[1]
Knuckle of pork	35–40	*	3	2
Meatballs	5–6	*	3	2
Smoked pork joint, in slices	10–12 3–5	*	3	2
Ham	25–30	*	3	2
Roast pork	30–35	*	3	2
Pork fillet (joint)	6–10	*	3 (2)	2 (1)
Braised pork, goulash	10–15	*	3	2

LAMB AND GAME (1 LB/500 G)	COOKING TIME IN MINUTES	COOKED IN AN INSERT	VITAVIT® PREMIUM COOKING SETTING	VITAQUICK® PREMIUM COOKING SETTING[1]
Roast lamb	20–25	*	3	2
Lamb shank	25	*	3	2
Lamb stew	10–15	*	3	2
Roast hare/ wild rabbit	15–25	*	3	2
Hare legs	10–15	*	3	2
Roast venison	25–30	*	3	2
Venison roulades, goulash	15–20	*	3	2
Roast venison	20–25	*	3	2
Venison leg/shoulder	40–50	*	3	2
Saddle of venison	20–25	*	3	2
Roast wild boar	25–30	*	3	2
Wild boar goulash	15–20	*	3	2

* Can be cooked in an insert (e.g., for multilevel cooking) | [1] The cooking setting for Vitaquick® Premium also applies to other pressure cookers with two pressure cooking settings

GAME/POULTRY AND RABBIT (1 LB/500 G)	COOKING TIME IN MINUTES	COOKED IN AN INSERT	VITAVIT® PREMIUM COOKING SETTING	VITAQUICK® PREMIUM COOKING SETTING[1]	STEAMING WITHOUT PRESSURE
Duck (breast/leg)	12–30	*	3	2	20–60
Pheasant	15–20	*	3	2	45–60
Goose (breast/leg)	25–30	*	3	2	75–90
Chicken (breast/leg)	5–20	*	3 (2)	2	20–40
Turkey (breast/leg)	18–20	*	3	2	30–50
Partridge/quail	12–15	*	3	2	25–35
Rabbit	12–20	*	3 (2)	2	40–60

FISH AND SEAFOOD (UP TO 2 LBS/1 KG)	COOKING TIME IN MINUTES	COOKED IN AN INSERT	VITAVIT® PREMIUM COOKING SETTING	VITAQUICK® PREMIUM COOKING SETTING[1]	STEAMING WITHOUT PRESSURE
Eel	6–7	I	1	1	20–30
Fish stew	3–4	*	3	1	15–25
Trout (blue)	3–5	I	3	1	10–15
Halibut	3–5	I	1	1	6–8
Cod/ haddock	7–8 6–7	I	1	1	8–9 7–8
Salmon (fillet)	6–8	I	1	1	6–10
Octopus/ calamari (stuffed squid)	5–6 10	*	2	1	35–40 20–25
King prawns/ venus clams/mussels	2–3	I	1	1	4–7 4–12
Redfish	3–6	I	1	1	8–10
Flounder (fillet)	3–4	I	1	1	4–5
Pollock (fillet)	3–6	I	1	1	5–8
Sole (fillet)	2–4	I	1	1	3–5

* Can be cooked in an insert (e.g., for multilevel cooking) | [1] The cooking setting for Vitaquick® Premium also applies to other pressure cookers with two pressure cooking settings

PULSES/LEGUMES (UP TO 14 OZ/400 G)	COOKING TIME IN MINUTES	COOKED IN AN INSERT	VITAVIT® PREMIUM COOKING SETTING	VITAQUICK® PREMIUM COOKING SETTING[1]	STEAMING WITHOUT PRESSURE
Beans, dried (soaked)	16	*	3	2	50–60
Beans, dried (not soaked)	20	*	3	2	80–90
Peas, dried	15–18	*	3	2	60–70
Chickpeas, dried	15	*	3	2	60–90
Black-eyed peas, dried	10–12	*	3	2	55–65
Lima/butter beans, dried	15–20	*	3	2	115–135
Lentils, dried (not soaked)	10–15	*	3	2	30–40
Red beans (adzuki beans), dried	15	*	3	2	95–105
Red kidney beans, dried	15–20	*	3	2	130–140
Soybeans, dried	15–20	*	3	2	60–90

CEREALS (UP TO 14 OZ/400 G)	COOKING TIME IN MINUTES	COOKED IN AN INSERT	VITAVIT® PREMIUM COOKING SETTING	VITAQUICK® PREMIUM COOKING SETTING[1]	STEAMING WITHOUT PRESSURE
Buckwheat (do not let swell)	4–5	*	3	2	15–20
Bulgur/ quinoa	4 / 5	*	2	1	9 / 15
Spelt	8	*	3	2	20–30
Barley	8–9	*	3	2	20–30
Green spelt	8	*	3	2	18–20
Oats	8	*	3	2	18–20
Millet (do not let swell)	2–3	*	3	2	10
Rye	8–9	*	3	2	20–30
Wheat	8–9	*	3	2	20–30

* Can be cooked in an insert (e.g., for multilevel cooking) | [1] The cooking setting for Vitaquick® Premium also applies to other pressure cookers with two pressure cooking settings

FRESH VEGETABLES (1 LB/500 G)	COOKING TIME IN MINUTES	COOKED IN AN INSERT	VITAVIT® PREMIUM COOKING SETTING	VITAQUICK® PREMIUM COOKING SETTING[1]	STEAMING WITHOUT PRESSURE
Artichokes (whole)	6–8	I	2	1	30–35
Eggplant (pieces)	3–4	I	1	1	10–15
Eggplant (stuffed)	8–10	I	2	1	20–30
Cauliflower (whole)	9–11	I	2	1	20–35
Cauliflower/broccoli (florets)	2–4	I	1	1	5–10
Chicory (halved)	2–3	I	1	1	5
Chestnuts (peeled)	2–3	*	2	1	15–20
Fennel (halved)	6–8	I	2	1	10–12
Green beans	6–8	I	2	1	7–10
Garden peas, fresh	2–3	I	2	1	5–10
Kohlrabi (½-inch/1 cm pieces)	2–3	I	2	1	5–10
Cabbage roulades	8–10	*	2	1	25–35
Pumpkin/squash	5–7	*	3	2	15–25
Leek (½-inch/1 cm rings)	2–3	*	2	1	4–6
Lotus root (whole)	15–18	*	2	1	20–30
Corn on the cob	5	*	2	1	30–35
Mixed vegetables	2–5	I	2	1	15–25
Carrots	4–6	I	3	2	15–20
Peppers	1–2	I	2	1	5–10
Peppers (stuffed)	8–10	I	2	1	25–30
Parsnips	3–6	I	3	2	15–20

* Can be cooked in an insert (e.g., for multilevel cooking) | [1] The cooking setting for Vitaquick® Premium also applies to other pressure cookers with two pressure cooking settings

APPENDIX » COOKING TIME FINDER

FRESH VEGETABLES (1 LB/500 G)	COOKING TIME IN MINUTES	COOKED IN AN INSERT	VITAVIT® PREMIUM COOKING SETTING	VITAQUICK® PREMIUM COOKING SETTING[1]	STEAMING WITHOUT PRESSURE
Parsnip	4–6	I	3	2	15–20
Brussels sprouts	2–3	I	2	1	10–12
Beets (whole)	20–25	I	2	1	40–55
Red cabbage	4–6	*	3	2	25
Sauerkraut	8–12	*	3	2	25–30
Black salsify (whole)	7	I	2	1	9–12
Celeriac (whole)	12–15	I	3	2	20–25
Celeriac (¾-inch/2 cm pieces)	1–2	I	2	1	5–6
Asparagus, white (whole)	3–6	I	2	1	9–15
Asparagus, green (whole)	2–5	I	2	1	7–10
Spinach/Swiss chard	1	*	1	1	2–5
Celery	1–2	*	2	1	4–5
Sweet potatoes	10–12	I	2	1	15–20
Tomatoes (whole)	1–2	I	2	1	10–12
Green cabbage	3–5	*	3	2	8–12
Winter squash	5	*	2	1	10–15
Savoy cabbage	2–3	I	2	1	8–12
Zucchini	1–2	I	1	1	5–10
Spiralized zucchini		I			5
Sugar snap peas	2–3	I	2	1	5–7
Onions	5	I	2	1	15–20

* Can be cooked in an insert (e.g., for multi-level cooking) | [1] The cooking setting for Vitaquick® Premium also applies to other pressure cookers with two pressure cooking settings

SOUPS AND STEWS (1 LB/500 G)	COOKING TIME IN MINUTES	COOKED IN AN INSERT	VITAVIT® PREMIUM COOKING SETTING	VITAQUICK® PREMIUM COOKING SETTING[1]	STEAMING WITHOUT PRESSURE
Pea soup	15–18	*	3	2	
Fish stock	10	*	3	2	
Fish soup/stew	8–15	*	3	2	
Meat stock	30–40	*	3	2	
Poultry stew	8–10	*	3	2	
Poultry stock	10–15	*	3	2	
Vegetable stew	4–6	*	3	2	
Vegetable & meat stew	10–15	*	3	2	
Vegetable soup	4–6	*	3	2	
Goulash soup	15–20	*	3	2	
Chicken soup	30–45	*	3	2	
Potato soup (1¼-inch/3 cm)	6–8	*	3	2	
Bone soup	30–35	*	3	2	
Lentil soup	10–15	*	3	2	
Oxtail soup	20–25	*	3	2	
Pot-au-feu	15–20	*	3	2	
Meat & rice stew	8–10	*	3	2	
Beef soup	25–30	*	3	2	
Tomato soup	5–6	*	3	2	
Game/lamb stock	25–30	*	3	2	
Game soup	20–25	*	3	2	

* Can be cooked in an insert (e.g., for multilevel cooking) | [1] The cooking setting for Vitaquick® Premium also applies to other pressure cookers with two pressure cooking settings

SIDE DISHES (4 CUPS/1 L)	COOKING TIME IN MINUTES	COOKING IN AN INSERT	VITAVIT® PREMIUM COOKING SETTING	VITAQUICK® PREMIUM COOKING SETTING[1]	STEAMING WITHOUT PRESSURE
Yeast dumplings	6–8	I	2	1	13–20
Steamed dumplings	12–14	I	1	1	15–20
Potato dumplings (2 inches/ 5 cm), dumplings	5–12 10–15	I	3 2	2 1	20–30
Polenta	6–10	*	3	2	15–25
Long-grain brown rice	7–9	*	3	2	30
Unpeeled potatoes	8–12	I	3	2	30
Risotto	5–6	*	3	2	20
Peeled potatoes, in wedges	6–8	I	3	2	15–20
Bread dumplings	10	I	1	1	25–35
White rice	5–7	*	3	2	15–20

SWEET TREATS (1 LB/500 G)	COOKING TIME IN MINUTES	COOKING IN AN INSERT	VITAVIT® PREMIUM COOKING SETTING	VITAQUICK® PREMIUM COOKING SETTING[1]	STEAMING WITHOUT PRESSURE
Creams/custard desserts	20–25	I	1	1	40
Fruit (in syrup)	6	I	1	1	15–40
Rice pudding	6–10	I	1	1	25–30
Cake	20–30	I	2	1	25–40
Sweet dumplings	10–15	I	1	1	20–30
Bain-marie/pudding (large)	15–25	I	2	1	40–45
Bain-marie/pudding (small)	6–7	I	2	1	25

* Can be cooked in an insert (e.g., for multilevel cooking) | [1] The cooking setting for Vitaquick® Premium also applies to other pressure cookers with two pressure cooking settings

Index

A
accessories and parts, 46–47
anniversary edition, Fissler 70th, 25

B
baby food pressure cooking, 92–93
beans pressure cooking, 76–77
beef pressure cooking, 78–79
blanching, browning and searing foods, 102–103
boiling temperature chart, pressure and, 13
braising and stewing meats, 78–79

C
cereals and grains pressure cooking, 90–91
chicken pressure cooking, 82–83
cleaning and care, 68–69
cooking methods versatility, 38–41, 44–45
cooking processes chart, 19
cooking valve
    Fissler "Comet," 7, 21
    Fissler design history, 22–25
    Fissler "Euromatic," 21
    Fissler innovation, 7, 21
    Fissler three-level safety system, 36–37
    spare parts, valves and handles, 47
    structure and function, 28–33
cooking with Fissler
    cooking times indicator, 61
    filling the pot, 58–59
    food preparation and cooking times, see specific foods, 70–107
    monitoring pressure level, 62–63
    preparation for initial use, 56–57
    right size cooker selection, 52–53
    sealing and building pressure, 60–61
    stovetop burner types, 61

D
defrosting frozen foods, 67
desserts pressure cooking, 94–95
dos & don'ts of pressure cooking, 48–49

E
energy savings of pressure cooking, 13, 17

F
FAQs, pressure cooking, 106–107
fish and seafood pressure cooking, 84–85
Fissler pressure cookers
    70 anniversary edition, 25
    accessories and parts, 46–47
    cooker size options, 52–53
    history of Fissler models, 7, 21, 22–25
    Hoppstadten-Weiersbach plant, Germany, 26–27
    models and processes, 8, 18–19, 28–33, 54–55
    patents and optimization, 7, 21
    production methods, 7, 18, 23, 26–27
    safety features, 7, 21, 34–35, 36–37
    sustainable materials, 7, 27
    Vitaquick® Premium structure and functions, 32–33, 55
    Vitavit® Premium structure and function, 28–31, 54
    warranties, 46
flavor enhancement, pre-cooking, 102–103
flavoring and seasoning tips, 104–105
food preparation and cooking overview
    defrosting frozen foods, 67
    food selections for pressure cooking, 42–43
    frequently asked questions, 106–107
    introduction and overview, 71
    pre-cooking flavor enhancement, 102–103
    quality ingredients, 71
    seasoning and flavoring tips, 104–105
food preparation and cooking times
    baby food, 92–93
    beans, 76–77
    beef, 78–79
    blanching, browning and searing, 102–103
    chicken, 82–83
    defrosting frozen foods, 67
    desserts and sweets, 94–95
    dumplings, 92–93
    fish and seafood, 84–85
    game meats, 80–81
    grains, 90–91
    lamb, 80–81
    legumes, 76–77
    meats, 78–81
    pasta and cereals, 90–91
    pork, 78–79
    poultry, 82–83
    pre-cooking flavor enhancement, 102–103
    rabbit, 82–83
    rice, 86–89
    sauces, 100–101
    seasoning and flavoring tips, 104–105
    side dishes, 92–93
    stocks, vegetable, poultry and beef, 96–99
    sweets and desserts, 94–95
    toasting spices, 102–103
    veal, 78–79
    vegetables, 72–75
frequently asked questions, pressure cooking, 106–107
frozen foods, defrosting, 67

G
game meats pressure cooking, 80–81
Germany, Hoppstadten-Weiersbach production plant, 26–27
grains and cereals pressure cooking, 90–91

H
history of pressure cooking
    early inventions, 20–21

Fissler "Comet," 7
Fissler "Euromatic," 21, 22
Fissler models, 7, 22–25
Fissler safety features, 21
Papin, Denis (1647-1713), 20
Hoppstadten-Weiersbach production plant, Germany, 26–27

L

lamb pressure cooking, 80–81
legumes pressure cooking, 76–77

M

meat pressure cooking, 78–81
multi-level cooking, 44–45, 46–47, 64–67

N

nutritional benefits of pressure cooking, 8, 13, 16–17, 71, 72–75

P

Papin, Denis (1647-1713), 20
parts and accessories, 46–47
pasta pressure cooking, 90–91
pork pressure cooking, 78–79
poultry pressure cooking, 82–83
pre-cooking flavor enhancement, 102–103
pressure and boiling temperature chart, 13
pressure cooker structure and function
 cleaning and care, 68–69
 cooker size options, 52–53
 Fissler three-level safety system, 36–37
 Vitaquick® Premium, 32–33, 55
 Vitavit® Premium, 28–31, 54
pressure cooking benefits
 energy savings, 13, 17
 inspiration, 7, 8
 nutritional benefits, 8, 13, 16, 71, 72–75
 pressure and boiling temperature chart, 13
 time efficiency, 16, 17, 18
pressure cooking methods
 cooking times indicator, 61

dos & don'ts, 48–49
filling the pot, foods and liquids, 58–59
food preparation and cooking times, see specific foods, 70–107
food selections for pressure cooking, 42–43
introduction, 8
monitoring pressure level, 62–63
multi-level cooking, 44–45, 64–67
pressure cooking with pressure, Vitavit® Premium, 15
sealing and building pressure, 60–61
steaming without pressure, Vitavit® Premium, 14
versatility of cooking methods, 38–41
pressure cooking, operating principles
 cooking processes chart, 19
 frequently asked questions, 106–107
 liquid and steam cooking, 13–15
 necessary cooking steps, 34–35
 preheating and boiling functions, 18–19
 pressure cooking, steps needed, 34
 pressure cooking, what happens inside the pot, 35
production plant, Hoppstadten-Weiersbach, Germany, 26–27

R

rabbit pressure cooking, 82–83
rice pressure cooking, 86–89

S

safety features
 cleaning and care, 68–69
 cooking valve innovation, 7, 21
 dos & don'ts of pressure cooking, 48–49
 Fissler technology, 36–37
 Fissler three-level safety system, 36–37
 necessary cooking steps, 34–35
 preparation for initial use, 56–57
sauces pressure cooking, 100–101
seafood and fish pressure cooking, 84–85

searing, blanching and browning foods, 102–103
seasoning and flavoring tips, 104–105
side dishes pressure cooking, 92–93
spare parts, 46–47
spices, toasting, 102–103
stacking foods. *see* **multi-level cooking**
stewing and braising meats, 78–79
stocks pressure cooking; vegetable, poultry and beef, 96–99
storage tips, multiple pots, 68–69
stovetop burner types, 61
sweets pressure cooking, 94–95

T

temperature chart, pressure and boiling, 13
time efficiency of pressure cooking, 16, 17, 18

V

valve, cooking. *see* **cooking valve**
veal pressure cooking, 78–79
vegetable pressure cooking, 72–75
vitamin and mineral preservation chart, 17
Vitaquick® Premium, Fissler
 70th anniversary special edition, 25
 features, 55
 history, 24–25
 introduction, 8
 pressure cooker settings, 19
 structure and function, 32–33
Vitavit® Premium, Fissler
 70th anniversary special edition, 25
 features, 54
 history, 22–25
 introduction, 8
 pressure cooker settings, 19
 pressure cooking with pressure, 15
 steaming without pressure, 14
 structure and function, 28–31

Recipe index

A

amaretti, Pumpkin purée with, 261
apples, Farmhouse terrine with mâche & caramelized, 205
Apricot dumplings with potato dough, 270
Asian beef stew with soy potatoes, 194
Asian chicken soup, 172
Asian pears in white wine & orange syrup, 268
Asian salad with succulent pork fillet & shrimp, 147
Asian squash stew, 115
Asian-style (Brussels) sprout salad, 140
Asian-style spare ribs, 213
asparagus, Risotto with green, 125
Asparagus ramen with udon noodles, 181

B

Baba ganoush, 149
baby food
    Carrot and potato mash with beef, 263
    Colorful vegetable mash with salmon, 263
    Colorful vegetable rice, 263
    Spinach with pasta and chicken, 263
bacon
    Bacon dumplings, 247
    Baked beans with bacon, 257
    Porcini mushroom soup with fried bacon, 163
    Thick oxtail soup, 178
Bavarian cabbage, 259
BBQ-style spare ribs, 213
Bean stew with sucuk, 194
beans. *see* legumes and pulses
beef
    cooking times, 294
    Asian beef stew with soy potatoes, 194
    Asian squash stew, 115
    Bean stew with sucuk, 194
    Beef baozi, 254
    Beef fajitas, 214
    Beef goulash with potatoes and sour cream, 192–193
    Beef roulades with olives, 241
    Bolognese sauce with beef, 128
    Braised beef cheeks, 239
    Braised beef with radish & shiitake, 235
    Brisket with coleslaw, 217
    Carrot and potato mash with beef (baby food), 263
    Chinese beef salad, 147
    Etli nohut - chickpea stew with beef, 231
    Five-bean chili with ground beef, 133
    Korean Gochujang, 177
    Pasta and polpette in tomato sauce, 189
    Pho bo with rice noodles, 183
    Short ribs with carrots, 235
    Stuffed peppers, 130
    Swabian potato salad with meatloaf, 205
    Thick oxtail soup, 178
    Turkish kofta & potato stew, 196
beets
    Beet dumplings, 247
    Beet hummus, 149
    Veal roast with beet salad, 210
Beluga lentil & pomegranate salad, 139
berries
    Berry cheesecake, 278
    Rice pudding with blueberries, 266
    Sweet porridge with berries, 267
    Venison stew with cranberry pears, 290
Biryani rice with eggplant, 256
Biscuit cake base, 276
Black-eyed pea salad with cherry tomatoes, 139
bok choy (pak choi), Char sui with, 208
Bolognese sauce with beef, 128
bowls, rice and quinoa
    Cucumber ribbon bowl with onions & egg, 153
    Thai Buddha Bowl with tofu, 153
    Thai sweet chili pork bowl, 155
Braised beef cheeks, 239
Braised beef with radish & shiitake, 235
Braised butternut squash with date couscous, 231
Braised duck legs with fried potatoes, 206–207
Braised lamb shanks, 232
Bread dumplings, 247
Brisket with coleslaw, 217
broccoli, Stuffed mushrooms with lentils and, 200
broccolini and enoki (mushroom), Tonkotsu ramen with, 181
Brussels sprout salad, Asian-style, 140
Buckwheat dumplings, 249
Bulgar pilaf with vegetables, 127

C

cabbage
    Bavarian cabbage, 259
    Brisket with coleslaw, 217
    Green cabbage curry with potatoes, 223
    Potato and cream cabbage, 243
    Red cabbage with cinnamon, 259
    Vegetarian cabbage roulades, 241
Calamari ripieni (stuffed squid), 202–203
Caldo verde, 167
Camembert quenelles, Chestnut soup with, 163
Caramel rice pudding, 266
carrots
    Carrot and potato mash with beef (baby food), 263
    Carrot soup with orange, 161
    Glazed carrots, 258
    Moroccan carrot salad, 141
    Short ribs with carrots, 235
cashew nuts, Couscous with, 257
Cauliflower salad, 141
cereals. *see* also rice
    cooking times, 297, 301

Braised butternut squash with date couscous, 231
Buckwheat dumplings (pseudo-cereal), 249
Bulgar pilaf with vegetables, 127
Couscous with cashew nuts, 257
Cucumber ribbon bowl with onions & egg, 153
Millet side dish, 190
Pearl barley risotto, 125
Pearl barley soup, 167
Sweet porridge with berries, 267
Vegetarian paella with quinoa, 119
Char sui with pak choi, 208
cheese dumplings, Curd, 271
Cherry clafoutis, 278
Chestnut soup with Camembert quenelles, 163
chestnuts, caramelized, 243
chestnuts, Shoulder of venison with glazed, 242–243
chicken. *see* **also poultry and game**
cooking times, 296
Asian chicken soup, 172
Chicken and vegetable curry, 224
Classic Paella, 118
Farmhouse terrine with mâche & caramelized apples, 205
Indian butter chicken, 226–227
Mafé de poulet with eggplant, 190
Red Thai curry soup, 174
Spicy rice salad with chicken, 144–145
Spinach with pasta and chicken (baby food), 263
Spiralized zucchini with chicken, 115
Teriyaki chicken with brown rice, 284
Tom kha gai, 174
Vietnamese noodle soup with chicken and seafood, 183
Chickpea & stockfish salad, 139
chickpea stew with beef, Etli nohut -, 231

chili-seasoned. *see also* **curries**
Asian chicken soup, 172
Asian salad with succulent pork fillet & shrimp, 147
Beef fajitas, 214
Chili sin carne, 133
Chinese beef salad, 147
Five-bean chili with ground beef, 133
Korean Gochujang, 177
Mackerel in chili sauce, 121
Pho bo with rice noodles, 183
Pulled pork carnitas, 214
Spicy rice salad with chicken, 144–145
Thai sweet chili pork bowl, 155
Tom kha gai, 174
Vietnamese noodle soup with chicken and seafood, 183
Chinese beef salad, 147
chocolate
Chocolate cheesecake with a biscuit base, 276
Chocolate pudding, 272
Glazed brownies, 281
Mocha pudding, 272
cinnamon, Red cabbage with, 259
citrus
Asian pears in white wine & orange syrup, 268
Carrot soup with orange, 161
Cauliflower salad (with orange), 141
Lemon cake with hazelnuts, 281
Classic hummus, 149
Classic Paella, 118
Coconut & lentil curry with vegetables, 223
coconut soup, Vegan green pea and, 112
Cod with ginger, 121
coleslaw, Brisket with, 217
Colorful vegetable mash with salmon (baby food), 263
Colorful vegetable rice (baby food), 263

Cooked-potato dumplings, 250
couscous, Braised butternut squash with date, 231
Couscous with cashew nuts, 257
cranberry pears, Venison stew with, 290
Creamy herb soup with poached egg, 158
Creamy mashed potato, 261
Creamy potato soup, 168
Crème brûlée, 275
Crème caramel, 275
crème fraîche
Carrot soup with orange, 161
Chestnut soup with Camembert quenelles, 163
Creamy potato soup, 168
Cucumber ribbon bowl with onions & egg, 153
Squash soup with ginger, 161
Cucumber ribbon bowl with onions & egg, 153
Curd cheese dumplings, 271
curries. *see also* **chili-seasoned**
Chicken and vegetable curry, 224
Coconut & lentil curry with vegetables, 223
Curried lentils with lamb, 130
Green cabbage curry with potatoes, 223
Ground lamb curry, 224
Indian butter chicken, 226–227
Pork vindaloo, 228
Thai green vegetable curry, 220
tofu variations, 224

D

date couscous, Braised butternut squash with, 231
Delicate and aromatic mussel pilaf, 126
desserts. *see* **sweets and desserts**
dim sum
Fish dim sum, 253
Vegetable dim sum, 253

dips and spreads
- Baba ganoush, 149
- Beet hummus, 149
- Classic hummus, 149
- Greek fáva, 149
- Pepper hummus, 149

dressings
- Garlic ginger dressing, 200
- White balsamic dressing, 136

duck legs with fried potatoes, Braised, 206–207

dumplings
- cooking times, 301
- Apricot dumplings with potato dough, 270
- Bacon dumplings, 247
- Beef baozi, 254
- Beet dumplings, 247
- Bread dumplings, 247
- Buckwheat dumplings, 249
- Cooked-potato dumplings, 250
- Curd cheese dumplings, 271
- Half-and-half potato dumplings, 250
- Pretzel dumplings, 249
- Spinach dumplings, 247
- Stuffed mushroom dumplings, 247
- Vegetarian gyoza, 254
- Venison goulash, 236
- Yeast dumplings, 271

E

egg, Creamy herb soup with poached, 158

egg, Cucumber ribbon bowl with onions &, 153

eggplant
- Baba ganoush, 149
- Biryani rice with eggplant, 256
- Mafé de poulet with eggplant, 190
- Veal paupiettes with ratatouille, 287

enoki (mushroom), Tonkotsu ramen with broccolini and, 181

Etli nohut - chickpea stew with beef, 231

F

Farmhouse terrine with mâche & caramelized apples, 205

feta, Warm bean salad with olives and, 136

fish. *see also* **seafood**
- cooking times, 296
- Chickpea & stockfish salad, 139
- Cod with ginger, 121
- Colorful vegetable mash with salmon (baby food), 263
- Fish dim sum, 253
- Fish stock, 293
- Greek potato salad, 117
- Lima bean & tuna salad, 139
- Mackerel in chili sauce, 121
- Nigiri sushi, 150–151
- Nori maki, 150–151
- Quick fish soup with saffron and vegetables, 170–171

Five-bean chili with ground beef, 133

G

Galician octopus, 185

game and poultry. *see also* **chicken**
- cooking times, 295–296
- Braised duck legs with fried potatoes, 206–207
- Farmhouse terrine with mâche & caramelized apples, 205
- Game stock, 293
- Glazed brownies, 281
- Glazed carrots, 258

grains. *see* **cereals**

Greek fáva, 149

Greek potato salad, 117

Green beans with tomatoes, 258

Green cabbage curry with potatoes, 223

Ground lamb curry, 224

H

Half-and-half potato dumplings, 250

hazelnuts, Lemon cake with, 281

I

Indian butter chicken, 226–227

K

Käsespätzle with fried onions, 186

kasha (Buckwheat) dumplings, 249

Korean Gochujang, 177

Korean octopus salad, 142

L

lamb
- cooking times, 295
- Braised lamb shanks, 232
- Curried lentils with lamb, 130
- Etli nohut - chickpea stew with beef (variation), 231
- Ground lamb curry, 224
- Lamb stock, 293

leek, Ribollita with, 164

legumes and pulses
- cooking times, 297
- Baked beans with bacon, 257
- Bean stew with sucuk, 194
- Beet hummus, 149
- Beluga lentil & pomegranate salad, 139
- Black-eyed pea salad with cherry tomatoes, 139
- Chickpea & stockfish salad, 139
- Chili sin carne, 133
- Classic hummus, 149
- Coconut & lentil curry with vegetables, 223
- Curried lentils with lamb, 130
- Etli nohut - chickpea stew with beef, 231
- Five-bean chili with ground beef, 133
- Greek fáva, 149
- Lima bean & tuna salad, 139
- Minestrone with pancetta, 164
- Pepper hummus, 149
- Red lentil soup, 112
- Ribollita with leek, 164
- Spicy bean purée, 261

Stuffed mushrooms with lentils and broccoli, 200
Warm bean salad with olives and feta, 136
Lemon cake with hazelnuts, 281
Lima bean & tuna salad, 139

M

Mac 'n' cheese with cheddar, 186
Mackerel in chili sauce, 121
Mafé de poulet with eggplant, 190
mango, Sticky rice with, 267
marinades. *see* **sauces and marinades**
meats. *see* **individual meats**
Minestrone with pancetta, 164
Mocha pudding, 272
Moroccan carrot salad, 141
multi-level cooking
    Ossobuco with gremolata and risotto Milanese, 288–289
    Teriyaki chicken with brown rice, 284
    Veal paupiettes with ratatouille, 287
    Venison stew with cranberry pears, 290
mushrooms
    Braised beef with radish & shiitake, 235
    Mushroom risotto, 123
    Porcini mushroom soup with fried bacon, 163
    Stuffed mushroom dumplings, 247
    Stuffed mushrooms with lentils and broccoli, 200
    Tonkotsu ramen with broccolini and enoki, 181

N

Nigiri sushi, 150–151
noodles. *see* **pasta and noodles**
Nori maki, 150–151
nuts
    Chestnut soup with Camembert quenelles, 163
    Couscous with cashew nuts, 257

Lemon cake with hazelnuts, 281
Shoulder of venison with glazed chestnuts, 242–243

O

octopus
    Galician octopus, 185
    Korean octopus salad, 142
    Octopus pasta, 185
    Portuguese-style octopus salad, 142
olives, Beef roulades with, 241
olives and feta, Warm bean salad with, 136
onions & egg, Cucumber ribbon bowl with, 153
Ossobuco with gremolata and risotto Milanese, 288–289

P

paella
    Classic Paella, 118
    Seafood paella with mild chile peppers, 119
    Vegetarian paella with quinoa, 119
pak choi (bok choy), Char sui with, 208
pancetta, Minestrone with, 164
pasta and noodles
    Asian chicken soup, 172
    Asparagus ramen with udon noodles, 181
    Bolognese sauce with beef, 128
    Käsespätzle with fried onions, 186
    Mac 'n' cheese with cheddar, 186
    Octopus pasta, 185
    Pasta and polpette in tomato sauce, 189
    Pho bo with rice noodles, 183
    Rigatoni with pepper and tomato sauce, 189
    Spinach with pasta and chicken (baby food), 263
    Tonkotsu ramen with broccolini and enoki (mushroom), 181
    Vegan bolognese, 128

Vietnamese noodle soup with chicken and seafood, 183
pea and coconut soup, Vegan green, 112
Pea risotto, 124
Pearl barley risotto, 125
Pearl barley soup, 167
pears
    Asian pears in white wine & orange syrup, 268
    Pears poached in red wine, 268
    Venison stew with cranberry pears, 290
peppers
    Pepper hummus, 149
    Potato and pepper purée, 261
    Rigatoni with pepper and tomato sauce, 189
    Stuffed peppers, 130
Pho bo with rice noodles, 183
pilaf
    Bulgar pilaf with vegetables, 127
    Delicate and aromatic mussel pilaf, 126
    Pilaf with tomatoes, 127
pomegranate salad, Beluga lentil &, 139
Porcini mushroom soup with fried bacon, 163
pork
    cooking times, 295
    Asian salad with succulent pork fillet & shrimp, 147
    Asian-style spare ribs, 213
    BBQ-style spare ribs, 213
    Char sui with pak choi, 208
    Farmhouse terrine with mâche & caramelized apples, 205
    Pasta and polpette in tomato sauce, 189
    Pork belly braised in rice wine, 208
    Pork vindaloo, 228
    Pulled pork carnitas, 214
    Swabian potato salad with meatloaf, 205
    Thai sweet chili pork bowl, 155
    Vietnamese noodle soup with chicken and seafood, 183

Portuguese-style octopus salad, 142

potatoes
  cooking times, 301
  Apricot dumplings with potato dough, 270
  Asian beef stew with soy potatoes, 194
  Beef goulash with potatoes and sour cream, 192–193
  Braised duck legs with fried potatoes, 206–207
  Calamari ripieni (stuffed squid), 202–203
  Caldo verde, 167
  Carrot and potato mash with beef (baby food), 263
  Cooked-potato dumplings, 250
  Creamy herb soup with poached egg, 158
  Creamy mashed potato, 261
  Creamy potato soup, 168
  Galician octopus, 185
  Greek potato salad, 117
  Green cabbage curry with potatoes, 223
  Half-and-half potato dumplings, 250
  Mafé de poulet with eggplant, 190
  Pearl barley soup, 167
  Potato and cream cabbage, 243
  Potato and pepper purée, 261
  Potato goulash, 236
  Potato salad with stock, 117
  Shoulder of venison with glazed chestnuts, 242–243
  Stuffed mushrooms with lentils and broccoli, 200
  Styrian potato salad, 117
  Swabian potato salad with meatloaf, 205
  Sweet potato dashi, 168
  Turkish kofta & potato stew, 196
  Vegan potato salad, 117

poultry and game. *see also* **chicken**
  cooking times, 296
  Braised duck legs with fried potatoes, 206–207
  Farmhouse terrine with mâche &
  caramelized apples, 205
  Game stock, 293
  pressure cooking times charts, 294–301
  Pretzel dumplings, 249
  Pulled pork carnitas, 214

pulses. *see* **legumes and pulses**
Pumpkin purée with amaretti, 261

Q

Quick fish soup with saffron and vegetables, 170–171

R

Rabbit stifado, 232
radish & shiitake, Braised beef with, 235
ratatouille, Veal paupiettes with, 287
Red cabbage with cinnamon, 259
Red lentil soup, 112
Red Thai curry soup, 174
red wine, Pears poached in, 268
Ribollita with leek, 164

rice. *see also* **cereals; paella; pilaf; risotto**
  cooking times, 301
  Biryani rice with eggplant, 256
  Caramel rice pudding, 266
  Colorful vegetable rice (baby food), 263
  Ground lamb curry, 224
  Nigiri sushi, 150–151
  Nori maki, 150–151
  Pho bo with rice noodles, 183
  Rice pudding with blueberries, 266
  Spicy rice salad with chicken, 144–145
  Sticky rice with mango, 267
  Teriyaki chicken with brown rice, 284
  Thai Buddha Bowl with tofu, 153
  Thai sweet chili pork bowl, 155
  Rice pudding with blueberries, 266
  Rigatoni with pepper and tomato sauce, 189

risotto
  Mushroom risotto, 123
  Ossobuco with gremolata and risotto Milanese, 288–289
  Pea risotto, 124
  Pearl barley risotto, 125
  Risotto with green asparagus, 125
  Squash risotto, 124

S

saffron and vegetables, Quick fish soup with, 170–171

salads
  Asian salad with succulent pork fillet & shrimp, 147
  Asian-style (Brussels) sprout salad, 140
  Beluga lentil & pomegranate salad, 139
  Black-eyed pea salad with cherry tomatoes, 139
  Cauliflower salad, 141
  Chickpea & stockfish salad, 139
  Chinese beef salad, 147
  Greek potato salad, 117
  Korean octopus salad, 142
  Lima bean & tuna salad, 139
  Moroccan carrot salad, 141
  Portuguese-style octopus salad, 142
  Potato salad with stock, 117
  Spicy rice salad with chicken, 144–145
  Styrian potato salad, 117
  Veal roast with beet salad, 210
  Vegan potato salad, 117
  Warm bean salad with olives and feta, 136

sauces and marinades
  BBQ rub, 217
  Bolognese sauce with beef, 128
  Coriander spice paste, 228
  Curry paste, 220
  Egg, onion and garlic marinade, 145
  Ginger and garlic marinade, 227
  Gremolata, 289
  Orange syrup, 268
  Red chili spice paste, 172
  Salsa, 215

Tomato mushroom marinade, 239
Vegan bolognese, 128
sausage
   Bean stew with sucuk, 194
   Caldo verde, 167
   Solyanka with debrecener, 177
   Veal paupiettes with ratatouille, 287
seafood. *see also* **fish**
   cooking times, 296
   Asian salad with succulent pork fillet & shrimp, 147
   Calamari ripieni (stuffed squid), 202–203
   Classic Paella, 118
   Delicate and aromatic mussel pilaf, 126
   Galician octopus, 185
   Korean octopus salad, 142
   Nigiri sushi, 150–151
   Nori maki, 150–151
   Octopus pasta, 185
   Portuguese-style octopus salad, 142
   Seafood paella with mild chile peppers, 119
   Vietnamese noodle soup with chicken and seafood, 183
shiitake, Braised beef with radish &, 235
Short ribs with carrots, 235
Shoulder of venison with glazed chestnuts, 242–243
side dish pressure cooking times, 301
Solyanka with debrecener, 177
soups. *see also* **stews; stocks**
   cooking times, 300
   Asian chicken soup, 172
   Asparagus ramen with udon noodles, 181
   Caldo verde, 167
   Carrot soup with orange, 161
   Chestnut soup with Camembert quenelles, 163
   Creamy herb soup with poached egg, 158
   Creamy potato soup, 168
   Korean Gochujang, 177
   Minestrone with pancetta, 164
   Pearl barley soup, 167
   Pho bo with rice noodles, 183
   Porcini mushroom soup with fried bacon, 163
   Quick chicken soup variation, 172
   Quick fish soup with saffron and vegetables, 170–171
   Red lentil soup, 112
   Red Thai curry soup, 175
   Ribollita with leek, 164
   Solyanka with debrecener, 177
   Squash soup with ginger, 161
   Sweet potato dashi, 168
   Thick oxtail soup, 178
   Tom kha gai, 175
   Tonkotsu ramen with broccolini and enoki (mushroom), 181
   Vegan green pea and coconut soup, 112
   Vietnamese noodle soup with chicken and seafood, 183
Spicy bean purée, 261
Spicy rice salad with chicken, 144–145
Spinach dumplings, 247
Spinach with pasta and chicken (baby food), 263
Spiralized zucchini with chicken, 115
spreads. *see* **dips and spreads**
sprout salad, Asian-style (Brussels), 140
squash
   Asian squash stew, 115
   Braised butternut squash with date couscous, 231
   Pumpkin purée with amaretti, 261
   Squash risotto, 124
   Squash soup with ginger, 161
   squid, stuffed (Calamari ripieni), 202–203
stews. *see also* **soups; stocks**
   cooking times, 300
   Asian beef stew with soy potatoes, 194
   Asian squash stew, 115
   Bean stew with sucuk, 194
   Beef goulash with potatoes and sour cream, 192–193
   Chili sin carne, 133
   Five-bean chili with ground beef, 133
   Turkish kofta & potato stew, 196
   Venison stew with cranberry pears, 290
Sticky rice with mango, 267
stocks
   Chinese chicken stock, 172
   Fish stock, 293
   Game stock, 293
   Lamb stock, 293
   Veal stock, 293
   Vegetable stock, 158
Stuffed mushroom dumplings, 247
Stuffed mushrooms with lentils and broccoli, 200
Stuffed peppers, 130
Styrian potato salad, 117
sushi
   Nigiri sushi, 150–151
   Nori maki, 150–151
Swabian potato salad with meatloaf, 205
Sweet porridge with berries, 267
Sweet potato dashi, 168
sweets and desserts
   cooking times, 301
   Apricot dumplings with potato dough, 270
   Asian pears in white wine & orange syrup, 268
   Berry cheesecake, 278
   Biscuit cake base, 276
   Caramel rice pudding, 266
   Cherry clafoutis, 278
   Chocolate cheesecake with a biscuit base, 276
   Chocolate pudding, 272
   Crème brûlée, 275
   Crème caramel, 275
   Curd cheese dumplings, 271
   Glazed brownies, 281
   Lemon cake with hazelnuts, 281

Mocha pudding, 272
Pears poached in red wine, 268
Rice pudding with blueberries, 266
Sticky rice with mango, 267
Sweet porridge with berries, 267
Yeast dumplings, 271

T

Teriyaki chicken with brown rice, 284
Tex-mex tortillas and tacos
　Beef fajitas, 214
　Pulled pork carnitas, 214
Thai Buddha Bowl with tofu, 153
Thai green vegetable curry, 220
Thai sweet chili pork bowl, 155
Thick oxtail soup, 178
times charts, pressure cooking, 294–301
tofu
　curry variations, 224
　Sweet potato dashi, 168
　Thai Buddha Bowl with tofu, 153
Tom kha gai, 174
tomatoes
　Bean stew with sucuk, 194
　Black-eyed pea salad with cherry tomatoes, 139
　Calamari ripieni (stuffed squid), 202–203
　Etli nohut - chickpea stew with beef, 231
　Green beans with tomatoes, 258
　Indian butter chicken, 226–227
　Mafé de poulet with eggplant, 190
　Pasta and polpette in tomato sauce, 189
　Pilaf with tomatoes, 127
　Pork vindaloo, 228
　Potato goulash, 236
　Rabbit stifado, 232
　Rigatoni with pepper and tomato sauce, 189
　Turkish kofta & potato stew, 196
Tonkotsu ramen with broccolini and enoki (mushroom), 181
Turkish kofta & potato stew, 196

V

veal
　cooking times, 294
　Ossobuco with gremolata and risotto Milanese, 288–289
　Pasta and polpette in tomato sauce, 189
　Swabian potato salad with meatloaf, 205
　Veal paupiettes with ratatouille, 287
　Veal roast with beet salad, 210
　Veal stock, 293
vegan
　Asian-style (Brussels) sprout salad, 140
　Asparagus ramen with udon noodles, 181
　Baba ganoush, 149
　Bavarian cabbage, 259
　Beluga lentil & pomegranate salad, 139
　Cauliflower salad, 141
　Chili sin carne, 133
　Coconut & lentil curry with vegetables, 223
　Colorful vegetable rice (baby food), 263
　Glazed carrots, 258
　Green beans with tomatoes, 258
　hummus variations, 149
　Moroccan carrot salad, 141
　Thai Buddha Bowl with tofu, 153
　Vegan bolognese, 128
　Vegan green pea and coconut soup, 112
　Vegan potato salad, 117
　Vegetable dim sum, 253
vegetables. *see also* **salads**
　cooking times, 298–299
　Bulgar pilaf with vegetables, 127
　Caldo verde, 167
　Char sui with pak choi, 208
　Chicken and vegetable curry, 224
　Chili sin carne, 133
　Coconut & lentil curry with vegetables, 223
　Colorful vegetable mash with salmon (baby food), 263
　Colorful vegetable rice (baby food), 263
　Creamy herb soup with poached egg, 158
　Minestrone with pancetta, 164
　Quick fish soup with saffron and vegetables, 170–171
　Thai green vegetable curry, 220
　Veal paupiettes with ratatouille, 287
vegetarian
　Black-eyed pea salad with cherry tomatoes, 139
　Cucumber ribbon bowl with onions & egg, 153
　Green cabbage curry with potatoes, 223
　Käsespätzle with fried onions, 186
　Mac 'n' cheese with cheddar, 186
　Pea risotto, 124
　Pearl barley risotto, 125
　Potato goulash, 236
　Red lentil soup, 112
　Rigatoni with pepper and tomato sauce, 189
　Risotto with green asparagus, 125
　Squash risotto, 124
　Vegetable dim sum, 253
　Vegetarian cabbage roulades, 241
　Vegetarian gyoza, 254
　Vegetarian paella with quinoa, 119
venison
　Shoulder of venison with glazed chestnuts, 242–243
　Venison goulash, 236
　Venison stew with cranberry pears, 290
Vietnamese noodle soup with chicken and seafood, 183

W

Warm bean salad with olives and feta, 136

Y

Yeast dumplings, 271

Z

zucchini with chicken, Spiralized, 115

You can find more information in the following videos:

 Fissler Vitavit® Premium Quick Guide – Made in Germany

 How a Fissler Pressure Cooker Works

 Fissler Vitavit® Premium Pressure Cooker

Publishing information

Published under the title Fissler®. The World of Pressure Cooking, ISBN 78-3-8338-9408-4, © 2024 by GRÄFE UND UNZER VERLAG GmbH, Munchen
© 2025 by Robert Rose Inc.

No part of this publication may be reproduced, stored in a retrieval system or transmitted, in any form or by any means, without the prior written consent of the publisher or a licence from the Canadian Copyright Licensing Agency (Access Copyright). For an Access Copyright licence, visit www.accesscopyright.ca or call toll-free: 1-800-893-5777.

Library and Archives Canada Cataloguing in Publication
ROBERT ROSE EDITION
Title: The world of pressure cooking : the healthy cooker®.
Other titles: Welt des schnellkochens. English | Fissler
Names: Fissler®, issuing body.
Description: Translation of: Die welt des schnellkochens. | Includes index.
Identifiers: Canadiana 20240520254 | ISBN 9780778807292 (hardcover)
Subjects: LCSH: Pressure cooking. | LCGFT: Cookbooks.
Classification: LCC TX840.P7 W4513 2025 | DDC 641.5/87—dc23

FISSLER EDITION
Title: The world of pressure cooking : the healthy cooker®.
Other titles: Welt des schnellkochens. English | Fissler
Names: Fissler®, issuing body.
Description: Translation of: Die welt des schnellkochens. | Includes index.
Identifiers: Canadiana 20240520262 | ISBN 9780778807322 (hardcover)
Subjects: LCSH: Pressure cooking. | LCGFT: Cookbooks.
Classification: LCC TX840.P7 W4513 2025b | DDC 641.5/87—dc23

Published by Robert Rose Inc.
120 Eglinton Avenue East, Suite 800, Toronto, Ontario, Canada M4P 1E2
Tel: (416) 322-6552 Fax: (416) 322-6936
www.robertrose.ca

Printed and bound in China

1 2 3 4 5 6 7 8 9   ESP   33 32 31 30 29 28 27 26 25

Project managers: Dr Maria Haumaier (GU), Claire Rauber (Fissler), Sebastian Hahn (Fissler)
Design: Dr Maria Haumaier, Katrin Wittmann
Writing and editing: Katrin Wittmann
Proofreading: Andrea Lazarovici
Recipes: Fissler, Martina Kittler, Andreas Neubauer, Inga Pfannebecker, TEUBNER, Manuel Weyer, Katrin Wittmann, Marianne Zunner
Photos: Mathias Neubauer, see also photo credits
Food styling: Andreas Neubauer, Manuel Weyer
Illustrations: Marion Feldmann
Cover: Mathias Neubauer
Cover design: Eva Stadler, Marion Feldmann
Interior layout & typesetting: Marion Feldmann
Production: Petra Roth
Repro: Longo AG, Bozen

ROBERT ROSE CREDITS
Production: PageWave Graphics Inc.
Project Editor: Amy Treadwell
Editing and Measurement Conversions: Jennifer MacKenzie
Proofreading: Kelly Jones
Index: Lora Marchand

Photo credits:
Alamy Stock Photo: p. 20-1 (Penta Springs Limited); p. 20-2 (Science History Images); p. 21-1 (Tony Claxton); p. 21-2 (Andreas von Einsiedel)
Fissler: pp. 22-1, 22-2, 22-3, 22-4; 23-1, 23-2, 23-3, 23-4; 23-5; 24-1, 24-2, 24-3, 24-4, 24-5, 24-6; 25-1; 25-2, 25-3, 25-4; 26-1, 26-2, 26-3, 26-4, 26-5, 26-6, 26-7, 26-8, 26-9, 26-10; 27-1, 27-2; 34-1, 34-2, 34-3, 34-4; 35-1, 35-2, 35-3, 35-4, 35-6; 36-2, 36-4; 47-1, 47-2; 54-1, 54-2; Illustration U4